Two Witnesses' Testimony
Long Lost Manuscripts from 1938
Vienna – Dachau – Buchenwald

to Stewart +
Kara –
June 14, 2015
Mike

Studies in Austrian Literature, Culture and Thought

General Editor

Jorun B. Johns

Maximilian and Emilie Reich

Two Witnesses' Testimony
Long Lost Manuscripts from 1938
Vienna – Dachau – Buchenwald

Edited by
Henriette Mandl

With an Essay
by Wolfgang Neugebauer:
Maximilian Reich and the First Transport of Austrians
to the Concentration Camp at Dachau in 1938

Translated by
Francis Michael Sharp

Ariadne Press
Riverside, California

Ariadne Press would like to express its appreciation to the Bundesministerium für Unterricht, Kunst und Kultur for assistance in publishing this book.

Translated from the German.
Zweier Zeugen Mund.
Verschollene Manuskripte aus 1938. Wien – Dachau – Buchenwald

Library of Congress Cataloging-in-Publication Data

Reich, Maximilian, 1882-1952, author.
[Zweier Zeugen Mund. English]
Two witnesses' testimony : long lost manuscripts from 1938, Vienna-Dachau-Buchenwald / Maximillian and Emilie Reich ; edited by Henriette Mandl ; with an essay by Wolfgang Neugebauer ; translated by Francis Michael Sharp.
p. cm. -- (Studies in Austrian literature, culture and thought)
Includes bibliographical references.
ISBN 978-1-57241-183-8
1. Reich, Maximilian, 1882-1952. 2. Jews--Austria--Vienna--Biography. 3. Reich, Emilie Mautzi, 1887-1959. 4. Holocaust, Jewish (1939-1945)--Austria--Personal narratives. 5. Dachau (Concentration camp) 6. Buchenwald (Concentration camp) 7. Austria--Ethnic relations. I. Reich, Emilie Mautzi, 1887-1959, author. II. Mandl, Henriette, editor. III. Sharp, Francis Michael, translator. IV. Title.
DS135.A93R45 2012
940.53'180922--dc23 2012033511

Cover:
Art Director: George McGinnis
Designer: Kerwin Siméus

270 Goins Court
Riverside, CA 92507

Printed in the United States of America.
ISBN 978-1-57241-183-8

We really dislike talking about our experiences: to those who were in camps, we need not explain anything. And to those who were not, we will never be able to make it clear how things were for us – and how they still are.

A former concentration camp prisoner
(Viktor E. Frankl, *Man's Search for Meaning*)

Contents

INTRODUCTION

Henriette Mandl

My father, Maximilian Reich, was deported to Dachau in the so-called "Transport of the Prominent" (*Prominententransport*) on April 1, 1938. He spent six months there and after that, a short time in Buchenwald. He was released in October and emigrated to England at the beginning of November 1938. It was there that he wrote a report about his experiences in the concentration camps and intended to publish it as quickly as possible. But none of the publishing houses to which he sent the manuscript were willing to accept it. The grounds for their refusal: they considered it atrocity propaganda and reasoned that such things could not happen in a civilized Europe.

We, my sister and I, knew nothing of the existence of this manuscript since my father had never spoken with us about it. He died in 1952 without ever having mentioned it. My mother also felt committed to this silence until her death in 1959.

In 1962, while I was preparing for a year at a university in the United States and intended to sublet my apartment, I was forced to clean out various boxes, and in doing so discovered the manuscript. I gave it along with other documents to my sister for safekeeping. Although it ended up in my hands again after my return, it remained unread in a box.

And then the year 1988 arrived, that lamentable "Year of Remembrance." A spurious willingness to break through the silence about the past became apparent already in the run-up to the celebrations. But about this time something unexpected happened. I no longer remember on what occasion I mentioned to my physician that my father had made a record of his stay in the concentration camps. In any case he asked for my permission to read it. I was amazed and touched. Then when I had the manuscript in my hands, I thought to myself, "you really ought to read it again yourself." Yes, "again" since I was convinced I had already read it once years before. Later I realized that I had only glanced though it, at best.

I had known so little about my father, and about his family, absolutely nothing. He never spoke about himself – even after the concentration camp. Now it seemed to me that after reading his words – postponed for much too long – I had a much closer connection to him.

My mother's contribution depicts a facet of the *Shoah* that until now has gotten little or no attention. That is, how did the wives in mixed marriages fare while their husbands were in camps?

During the "Year of Remembrance" in 1988 there was another attempt to publish the manuscript. Only this time, the reasons for rejecting it were astonishingly different ones than those given much earlier in England. Now the manuscript was found to be too "innocuous"; it would only strengthen the view of those who liked to deny the atrocities and wanted to believe that things had not really been so bad at all!

After this recurrent failure and the silence that gradually spread once again following the "Year of Remembrance," the manuscript would probably have fallen, once and for all, into oblivion. But that was not to be.

In 2003, the Exile Library of the *Literaturhaus* in Vienna was planning an exhibition about exiles and their descendants called "Divided Memory." After my sister and I were asked to participate, I sought out photographs of my parents as well as all other extant documents that had to do with their arrest and emigration. It was at that point that my father's manuscript emerged anew. Apart from the typewritten record there were as well many handwritten notebooks and notepads. I had never looked that carefully at these sources since I had been convinced that they were drafts for a book that he had intended to publish in England. At one point I probably had glanced at them, determined that his writing was a strange mix of the old German and Latin script and simply let the matter drop.

The success of the exhibition persuaded me to publish these papers.

The problem that now arose was feeding these handwritten texts into the computer. To my surprise and contrary to my expectations, I found that I could easily read my father's script. But how could someone else deal with the German script who had not learned to write it in school like I had? So the next step was pretty much a given.

In the course of my work, wherever it was possible, I wanted to use the correct names of people who appeared in the text. When my father had tried to publish his notes in England in 1939, he had altered the names in order not to endanger those people remaining in Vienna or those in camps. With relatives it was simple to insert the correct names since they were familiar to me. On the other hand, I was not familiar with the names of his colleagues at the newspaper where he worked. I did, however, find a list in the first notebook that matched fictional names with the real ones although the list was not complete. So I began my research.

I must admit that the work on the manuscripts was stressful, but the Center for Psychosocial, Socially Therapeutic and Sociocultural Integration (ESRA) came to my aid. They provided me with a counselor. When the negative reactions of my friends and relatives upset me and doubts arose in my mind whether or not my parents would still have wanted a publication, my therapist told me: "If your father had not had even a glimmer of hope, he could have destroyed the manuscript himself . . ." This made sense to me since there was not only the carbon copy of the original but numerous handwritten notebooks as well. And I became convinced that it was up to me to procure a hearing for my father and mother, even though it was late. I hope it is not too late.

Maximilian Reich

School for Murderers

March 11, 1938

On the weekend it now and again happened that I found time to have lunch at home together with my family. March 11, 1938 was just such a festive day. Even better, the weekly that I ran[1] was already in press, so I had nothing to do in the editorial office until evening. I had hiked with my wife Mautzi[2] and my children Traudl and Etti from our home in Gersthof across the Schafberg to Pötzleinsdorf. And there we had strolled back and forth along the Sommerheidenweg.

We then walked along Julienstraße back to Pötzleinsdorf where our ways parted: Mautzi went home with the children while I climbed onto the trolley to go into the city.

The hike had been refreshing and the nippy air in the Vienna Woods had invigorated my lungs and calmed my mind. And now, scarcely half-an-hour's ride later, I had come out of a peaceful, sheltered realm into a chaos of strident sound and wildly agitated movement.

I stood on the corner across from the opera – on the so-called "Wuzerecke,"[3] the crossing between Kärtnerstraße and the Ring. Year in, year out, from morning until night, it was the customary meeting place of an endless parade of friends, the idle rich, and socialites. This procession of those looking and those wanting to

---

[1] *Das Frauenblatt*, Vorwärts-Verlag.

[2] In the circle of family and friends Emilie Reich was called "Mautzi."

[3] Typical Viennese term for the meeting place of those promenading ladies on Kärtnerstraße who ply a certain trade.

be seen was not as teeming today as usual.

Yet like always during the evening hours of the last few days, the roar of the Nazi youth demonstrations could again be heard coming from the inner city. You could see police running back and forth on Kärntner Street, as high ranking officers sprang from their cars, gave orders, and then sped away again.

I was still standing on the corner and looking down toward Stephansplatz in the direction of that ominous roar. And suddenly a flood of demonstrators, flanked on both sides by hundreds of police, surged into view, completely filling the street. The marchers were boys and girls, mostly between ten and sixteen, who were identifiable as Hitler Youth by their white stockings. They shouted out chants in their adolescent voices that cracked in the upheaval. Now and then some of the words became audible: "Schuschnigg to the gallows!" – "Death to the Jews!" – "Down with priests!" Incredible, that children had been taught such words!!

Although trying to scowl heroically, their efforts were in vain. The policemen walking to their right and left looked bored. Just what should they do, I thought? Scatter them in all directions with their nightsticks?

Right in front of me a little tyke screams: "Kill the traitor Schuschnigg!" I take a look at the little guy. He's nicely dressed and appears so upsettingly innocent! Does he have any inkling of the horrendous meaning of his words? My gaze moves from the little screamer to the policeman marching beside him. He looks nervously in the other direction, apparently trying to avoid hearing the words.

An older gentleman observing the scene expresses his indignation: "How can parents be so stupid and disrespectful to allow their children such naughtiness?" Then another one: "The Nazi murderers have brought us to the point that children now demand assassination!"

I watch this nonsense shaking my head. I feel sorry for the policemen. What are they supposed to do? While their duties have for months become increasingly stressful due to the Nazi terror, they are expected to ride herd on this bunch of squealing urchins. There were people, however, who viewed the situation in a more serious light. The merchants lowered the metal awnings in front of their windows as the crowd got bigger and bigger. Women and children fled in panic behind their front doors.

Someone shouted, "This is the vanguard of the bomb throwers!" This exclamation generates unbridled alarm. The crowd rushes to the opposite side of the Ringstraße in order to escape this caldron. The shouting grows increasingly strident, building to an almost unbearable pitch.

I have to use all my strength in order not to become wedged into the corner where I'm standing. I begin to wonder how I can free myself from this uncomfortable situation since it is time for me to go to the editorial office. Then I hear a deep bass voice above the shrieks of the children: "Hi, Max!"

Overjoyed, I call out: "Hiya, Willy!" By then this massive man who had called out my name had found his way to me. Willy's appearance had a certain soothing effect not only on me, but on everyone around me. Willy is a gigantic figure and his whole way of talking and moving radiates calmness. He is one of my oldest friends. "Camaraderie formed in sports lasts forever" is an old adage heard among athletes. And we got to know each other through sports. We were both "prominent" in our "branch" – I played soccer and Willy was a boxer. A decade ago Willy had been heavyweight champion and since that time an official in all kinds of sports associations. Every other person in Vienna knows him. So now people greet him from every direction: "Hello, Herr Kurtz!'—"Hi, Willy!"—"God bless you, champ!"

"What do you think of this adolescent extravaganza?" Willy laughed and asked bluntly in a loud voice. "The brats should be in bed, don't you think?" "I have to say," I responded, "that I'm appalled, above all else, at the irresponsibility of the adults who misuse children for their political aims."

"Who takes this kind of thing seriously?" Willy shot back with a laugh. "But it'll be different when the adults who arranged this teen spectacle come out of their hideouts – we'll give them a piece of our mind. You should have seen how the rascals ran when our Protection Corps showed up armed the first time. The mob was cleared out of the inner city in half an hour. Then today they send us these pint-sized demonstrators – neither we nor the police know what to do with them."

"Somehow we've got to keep this from happening again. You can see how businesses are stagnating. The restaurants and coffee bars have been empty for a week because people are scared to be on the streets after dark. The city is full of rumors. By the way, have you heard the most recent one that the Nazis are circulating?"

"They are quite imaginative liars – that can't be denied," Willy laughed. "What's their newest brilliant idea in this field?"

"German troops on the Tyrolean border are supposedly ready to march into Austria if Schuschnigg doesn't resign today."

"Nothing is too stupid for these guys!"

I looked at my watch. "I have to get to the editorial office. If you don't have anything better to do, come along with me. Incidentally, the Chancellor will be on the radio at seven and we'll hear how things really stand."

"Why not?" Willy agreed. "Anyway, I'm full of news I want to tell you on the way."

The procession of the diminutive demonstrators had begun to grow smaller since Kärntner Street in the direction of the Ring was blocked off by a strong cordon of guards. Now the crowd just stood there, not knowing how these masses that had become dangerous for the children could be dispersed. The youngsters seemed to feel somewhat intimidated as well – their shouting had become more and more infrequent.

"They're already tired or hoarse," Willy joked. He took me by the arm and dragged me directly into the mass of noisy little troublemakers. The gigantic man towered like a lighthouse above the surf. Could be that the children took him for one of their own just because he barged right in among them with such a naturally insistent gesture – or did such a powerful figure command their respect? Anyway, they opened a little corridor through which we reached the Naschmarkt on the opposite side of the Ring.

While we quickly hurried toward the building of the Sezession, we heard whistles and shouting for a while that was carried our way by the wind, but gradually it quieted down and we could chat in peace.

I began: "So, Willy, how do you feel about being a prospective husband? Your hours as a bachelor are numbered. I can hardly imagine how you'll come to terms with your new role. Especially when I think how you have lived to this point: busy with soccer on Sunday, meetings almost every weekday at one of the sports associations, boxing matches now and then until after midnight. Will you be able to do without all that?"

"Me, do without? I would never have paid *that* price for my marriage to Mia. And you know how much I love that girl! But for me to give up sports would be to rob my life of meaning. Mia has nothing against me continuing to live just as I like. There will surely be a middle way. She'll try to develop a taste for sports and I won't get in the way of her bridge parties or her evenings at concerts or in the theater. Your wife, after all, has to accept the fact that you lead a similar life due to your work schedule; you never get home for lunch, and never before eleven or twelve at night. Mia loves me in spite of my vices and quirks. She has absolutely no plan to put me on a leash. Besides that, she has immersed herself in the business with an unbelievable enthusiasm. You know that dealing in art takes for granted all kinds of skills besides the profit-making ones. I've spent a quarter of a century of study to get to the point I'm at now: a recognized expert in the arts as well as in the arts and crafts."

Willy straightened up to his full stature. He had great pride in his title, and it was one of his weaknesses to talk about it while others listened. I teased him a little: "What does commerce in art have to do with love?" – "Well, in this case, a whole lot. She'll never get bored. She's already completely wrapped up in the business. She sits for hours reading art history, marches from one gallery to the next, from one auction to another, and I'm often amazed at the knowledge she's accumulated in the one year that she's been my secretary."

"So, Wednesday is your big day, Willy? I think that your wedding will turn into a mass demonstration of Vienna's athletes."

In the Editorial Office

In the meantime we had reached the editorial office. As we came around the corner, Willy pointed to the entryway: "What's going on there?"

I glanced in that direction. Groups of policemen stood on both sides of the main gate. When we got closer, one of them came up to us: "Gentlemen, your identification, please!" The doorman came out: "Everything's fine, officer. These gentlemen belong here." After that they let us in.

Walking past the doorman, I asked: "What's going on?" I forced a smile although I felt puzzled. "Nothing of any consequence," the doorman answered. "We've just heard that the Nazis are planning to pay us a visit." Right at that point, the typesetter Krause went past.

"Let them come," he said, rolling up his sleeves. "We'll greet the chaps appropriately."

Himself a former athlete, Krause recognizes Willy: "Good to see you, Herr Kurtz! Now we don't need to rack our brains. The champ Kurtz is here. I hope you've brought some classy uppercuts along that you can present to the Brown Shirts if they show up." – Willy laughs: "Only too happy to oblige. I'm available for athletic jobs at any time, day or night."

Agitated movement filled the hallways. Men and women from all directions rushed toward the conference room. It just now occurred to me again that the Chancellor was supposed to speak today.

I had scarcely taken off my overcoat when the telephone rang. It was chief editor Dr. Leo Margitai who sounded noticeably worried: "Good day, Reich! Please be ready to support the local editorial staff. Why don't you come over and we can talk about the situation."

I immediately went to speak with Dr. Margitai. Even he had trouble hiding his inner concern as I stepped into the executive office. "What do you think the Chancellor is going to say?" was my first question. Margitai shook his head as if to say: The devil only knows!

"Up to just an hour ago," he said at last, thinking about every word, "I was very confident. There has not been a word from the Council of Ministers that is still in session. Finally, though, it has leaked out that the referendum slated for Sunday will be postponed. Just a few minutes ago, after trying again and again, I got through to the Chancellor's Office. Some totally anonymous bureaucrat put me off quite abruptly with the explanation that I would find out everything I need to know when the Chancellor spoke." – "So we don't need to rack our brains since the next thirty minutes will solve all the puzzles."

"By the way, Reich, how do things look in the city?" I tell him what I've seen and heard. While I'm talking, Dr. Margitai makes some notes on the manuscript paper spread out in front of him. Then he says: "If the Chancellor finally decides to speak bluntly with the Nazis in Austria, then I as chief editor will insist that we get rid of the Nazis and half-Nazis in the editorial office. The level of spying and intrigue has become intolerable."

Skipping from one thought to another, he suddenly asked: "How did the police react?" – "The police," I replied, "couldn't do much more than escort the parade of adolescents. What else could they have done with the small fry?"

Dr. Margitai bolted from his chair in a state of agitation: "The nefarious nature of the Nazi system lies precisely in this abuse of our youth. This is the school of the Hitler Youth! It extinguishes every spark of belief in the children's souls. That's just the way they need their robots: totally devoid of belief and piety. Would they otherwise allow themselves to be used in throwing bombs at the defenseless as well as committing robbery and murder? We failed to combat its dangers during its evolution. We failed to wipe out the Nazi specter in our schools. Now they have the young people totally in their grip. We've come to this point via that tolerance we've shown and which they interpret to our children as cowardice."

"If they now at least restore order with absolutely no compromises!"

"But how, for example, do you propose restoring order in our editorial office? Aren't obvious Nazi spies like Kirchner and Holfeld sitting there openly among us? When I've suggested to the court counselor that I'm ready to supply evidence that these two as well as Benze, Kmoch, and Lackenbucher are traitors, he covers his ears and says: 'But please, dear friend, let's not have any public scandals. Everyone seems to be a Nazi in your suspicious eyes.' You know, Reich, it's not easy for me as a Jew to convince the counselor that these characters – as I well know – counter every criticism by asserting: some Jew must have said that. It's not an easy situation for me. You know that Holfeld had the temerity to tell Kandler, his replacement – just before the counselor had placed him on temporary but compulsory furlough for two months: 'Be careful what you say in your articles because the time is coming when every word will be checked.' It was an obvious threat that Kandler should be wary of writing anything against the Nazis."

They heard steps coming toward the door. It was the editorial assistant Hlinek with the message: "Gentlemen, please come to the conference room. The Chancellor is speaking in two minutes."

We hurried over. The room was full. There was an excited murmur going through the crowd. Up front there were four rows of chairs. In the first row by the door, two places were reserved for Margitai and me. Right up front, directly in front of the radio, there was a bench. Sitting on the bench, strangely stiff and motionless, were Kirchner, the photographer Zwacek, the illustrator Kmoch and the young Lackenbucher, the Nazi foursome. Remarkable that they separated themselves here so publicly from the others! None of them said a word as the chief editor entered the room.

I now looked more closely at the four supermen. Each avoided my gaze. They seemed to be smiling ironically. In my excitement was I deceiving myself? Or did they know more than I did?

Sounds started to come from the loudspeaker. Then there was dead silence in the room. I heard my own heart beating.

THE SCHUSCHNIGG ADDRESS

And suddenly Chancellor Schuschnigg begins to speak:

> "Citizens of Austria! May God protect Austria in these ominous times!"

The hour of Austria's demise had arrived.

For a short time, a pall hung over the silent room. Then women's sobbing became audible. Dr. Margitai and I stood motionless, grown stiff like pillars. Tears ran down my cheeks – for the first time since the death of my child. My Austria, my beloved Austria had perished.

What happened now seemed to me like an apparition. I was

incapable of thinking or moving. The four Nazis seemed not to know what to do for a moment. Only partially awake, I felt an arm on my shoulder. It was Willy Kurtz who had also listened to Schuschnigg's speech. "Just look at these shameful scoundrels!" he shouted and pointed to Kirchner and his fellow Nazis who had slipped on swastika armbands and insignia. "You wretches," Willy bellowed with such thunder in his voice that the walls shook. He grabbed the incredibly heavy radio and threw it in the direction of the group of traitors. He then kicked the door off its hinges and, roaring unintelligible curses, he sprinted out of the building.

The four Nazi supermen had crawled under the table where they had taken refuge during Willy's rampage. Half the room's occupants had fled. At this point the four crept out of their hiding place, and when they saw that the unruly Willy was no longer there, they were gradually able to recover their external composure. The repulsive dwarf Kirchner with his coarse flaxen hair and squinting slit-eyes sprang onto a chair and, with his arms wildly flailing about, delivered a speech. It seemed to me both stupid and arrogant:

"Austria's new government has ordered me to take charge of the editorial office. Whoever declares loyalty to National Socialism, return immediately to your workplace and wait there for my further instructions. Jews and those of Jewish lineage as well as Schuschnigg troublemakers are to leave the building immediately. Heil Hitler!"

I was still unable to move from the spot. The typesetters had already left the room during the speech while the women still stood there, helpless. They debated whether they should go or stay. Remaining meant betrayal of Austria while going meant hardship and misery for them and their children.

Kirchner scared them out of their brooding with a voice that sounded comical in his attempt to give it a military tone. "You women, get to work! You'll hear tomorrow who stays and who goes."

I began to move as if in a dream. Like a blind man I groped my way to the door and out into the hall. Yet suddenly the thought of my wife and children flashed through my mind and I gained my self-control once more. I was a Jew and my dismissal from the editorial office was certain. Now it was a question of keeping my wits about me. To be without a job is not the greatest misfortune. I just can't lose my head! I had struggled through difficult times so often in my life. God will help me through this time as well. I just can't let myself become an object of ridicule by showing this rabble a sign of weakness! And I pulled myself together and had again found peace of mind when I walked into my office.

There around my desk stood my colleagues who during years of working together had become my dear friends: Prohaska, Lechner, the editorial photographer Blaha, and the secretary Emmy Tomberger. The courageous Prohaska assured me: "We're with you, come what may!" Lechner declared: "If you go, we go as well!" At the moment when my very existence seemed in peril, I now found myself shifted into the role of the one giving comfort. "Just no rash moves, dear friends! You have to promise me not to do anything without my approval. You aren't helping me if you lose your jobs as well. You know that I've always been your friend. Listen to me! Just stay on the job and keep up the good work. Don't let others reap the fruits whose seeds we have sown together over the years. You can only help me again when the time comes, if you now remain where you are. For the sake of our friendship, continue on."

Deeply moved, they gave me their promise. Then I left the building.

The Sisters

Looking for deserted streets on my way to our apartment, my temples throb from the tension. I debate whether I should take a taxi in my rush to reach Mautzi who will need my support. But first I have to restore my own composure and be strong so I can give her strength. After twenty-five years of marriage we have become so fused in our thinking and feeling that I can vividly imagine her frame of mind. Later I learned what happened at home after Schuschnigg's speech.

I find my way home as if in a dream. I hear Mautzi's footsteps. She opens the door and now stands silent and pale in front of me. We embrace without saying a word and enter into the room between our bedroom and our children's bedroom. There still hasn't been a single word between us.

Mautzi is the one who finally breaks the stony silence. She grasps my hands and says: "Was it hard to bear? How did your colleagues react?" I feel relieved since I see that Mautzi's curiosity has been roused and I tell her about the crying women, Willy's rage, and about the Nazi musketeers.

"And what now?" Hopelessness resonates in her voice. "What now?" I repeat. "I have no reason to think I've been fired. Kirchner, who ordered me to leave the office, had absolutely no authority to do so. Even if he should take over the reins of the editorial office – God protect our paper from this disaster! – he would not have the right to break the contract I have with management. Tomorrow, as always, I'll go to the editorial office, report to the board and request further assignments."

"That's right," Mautzi agreed. "You do have legal rights. Maybe management will let you go, but they can't dispute your claim to severance pay and your pension." – "No, of course not. But it's the children I'm worried about. If the Nuremberg Laws also come into effect in Austria, they would then be considered as genetically mixed. What will happen in school? The best thing to do would be to talk to Marie as a teacher. She could fill us in. If it's necessary, we'll send the children to my sister Thilde in Czechoslovakia. She's wealthy and crazy about both of them. They could wait there – maybe we could as well – to see how the situation develops."

"Marie? I don't think she will ever enter my house again after what just happened between us." For a moment I was speechless with surprise. What had happened? Had it come to a break in a relationship which I couldn't have imagined being any more intimate or affectionate?

"What happened? Did you quarrel? Believe me, Marie will suffer no less than we do from what's coming." – "No, it's finished between us," she exclaimed sadly, but with a steady voice and began to tell me what had happened:

The telephone had rung and Mautzi had rushed to answer it. It was Marie who asked if I were at home. "No, no!" Mautzi had screamed in frenzied anger. "Now you have exactly what you wished for. Your happiness is our death. Please, never cross my path again. I hate you as one of this blasphemous band. Please spare me your phone calls as well, now and in the future!"

Then she sat down in front of the fireplace. Her own words on the telephone echoed in her ears like an infernal scream: "Please spare me your phone calls as well, now and in the future!"

A relationship had been torn apart that is unusual between sisters. Although Mautzi was the older sister, a childhood illness had led to them being brought up as twins. They were in the same class and were university students together.

Both married at the beginning of the First World War. My brother-in-law and I were officers and came home safe and sound. We spent all the holidays and even summer vacations together. When the great tragedy in our lives occurred and we lost our ten-year-old son to a case of diphtheria that had been diagnosed too late, it was Marie who didn't withdraw from Mautzi's side and helped us bear the anguish.

A shadow had fallen upon this relationship in the last few months, however. Now and again Marie had made a comment that revealed a certain sympathy with the ideas of National Socialism. And her husband, a painter of established talent, also let slip into his remarks at times an expression of sympathy for the creation of "Greater Germany." They were on the best of terms with me – because of familial reasons – but with many other Jews as well. Their remarks were always articulated so as not to offend their Jewish friends. But in Mautzi's sensitive ears such words always had an unpleasant tone. She found them unkind and tactless.

I never took a political stance nor did I ever speak with my brother-in-law about politics. We talked about music, sports, and family affairs. But last summer while our wives looked on, a short political repartee developed between us because of a disturbing comment he had made. He finished with the words: "I'm certainly not a Nazi and do not agree with their terrorist methods, but the Schuschnigg clique and their Jesuit politics naturally force people like me who want to see signs of positive movement – from a purely oppositional standpoint – to sympathize with any counter-movement."

Our wives had directed the conversation toward less explosive topics, but from that day on, we both felt that the warmth of our friendship had perceptibly cooled.

Mautzi declares bitterly: "They are just as responsible for the misfortune now taking place in the world as Kirchner and Kmoch and the other fans of the political fervor who suddenly have discovered themselves to be of racially pure Germanic stock. She hasn't uttered a single word of contempt in recent months for the assassins hurling bombs or blowing up bridges! If she had only once said: 'I despise these murderous methods of political struggle!' She slipped away from me like an eel whenever I anticipated hearing a judgment coming from her mouth. No, no! I'm steering clear of anyone who has even one spark of sympathy for this godless riffraff! I don't want to hear anything more about her!"

I cringe as the doorbell rings. Were they already coming to pick me up? I look at Mautzi. She's as pale as the wall and clings to the back of the chair with trembling hands. I go to the door and open it. Marie stands in front of me.

She presses my hand warmly and kisses me. She obviously wants to show me that she still cares for me as before. Such greetings are not customary between us. I didn't like such a show of affection unless it came from Mautzi or the children.

I help Marie with her coat and take her into living room. It's empty. Mautzi has closed herself off in the next room. I go to her by way of the bathroom. I encourage her to greet Marie since she has shown by coming that we mean more to her than politics. "I can't look her in the eye again. She's partly at fault."

Marie has followed me and now suddenly stands between us: "Just think, Mautzi, about everything we've been through together. You are more precious to me than any wretched political development that was inevitable because Austria has been governed partly by incompetence and partly by scoundrels."

Mautzi is still pushing her away: "You shouldn't talk about the government that way. After all, in human terms, it still towers above that Nazi rabble!" – Marie replied with real sadness: "Well, in any case, the calamity *has* occurred." "In your eyes, is it really a calamity that the Nazis have broken into Austria?" Marie takes her sister's hand: "A terrible calamity has come down on us and we all have to be smart in order not to be destroyed by it. If we lose our heads, we've lost everything! We'll stand by you in every way. Your adversity is ours as well, and we will fight it together with you. And let's just wait and see how the publishing house treats Max. They surely won't treat him like some second-rate employee and kick him out just because he's Jewish – surely not!"

Marie had once again struck the right note to calm Mautzi down. She had always been a master at that and I'm happy that Mautzi hasn't lost this support.

"As far as the children are concerned, you needn't worry at all. Those with mixed parentage have the same rights in school as those whose parents are both Aryan. If it changes, I'll find a way to spare them anything painful or awkward. You can depend on me! At the very least Max will get his severance pay, and that will get you by for a few years. What happens then remains to be seen. Perhaps – and hopefully – everything in Austria will have gotten straightened out by then." – "God willing!" Mautzi and I spoke these words with one voice.

A Visit with my Brother-in-Law

During the evening I have to use all my strength to keep calm in order not to frighten Mautzi even more. The telephone rings again and again and it is always friends who apparently want to convince themselves that I am still at home. Some don't even dare say their names. And I learn more and more that shocks and scares me at the same time: Dr. Margitai has been arrested, as have been the illustrator Humpoletz and the writer Auernheimer. Colonel Wolf has committed suicide.

I can't stand it any longer at home. Since Traudi is still awake and studying and Marie declares that she, in any case, is staying overnight, I ask Mautzi, if she doesn't want to go with me to visit her brother Pepi. We have grown especially fond of him. The poor guy has such a wretched life! A passionate mountain climber in his youth, he had suffered a fractured spine in a fall, an injury that had finally led to paralysis of his legs. For three years now he has been confined to a wheelchair. Whenever I have a free evening, I feel compelled to visit him. And this time, more than ever before. As much as I try to shake off the thought, it returns again and again: Maybe this is farewell forever!

Mautzi, whose agitation has grown from minute to minute, agrees. Half an hour later we are standing in front of his house on Heumühlgasse. Just as we are about to go into the house, I hear my name being called from the street. Pepi's father-in-law, an old man bent over from age, is standing in front of me. He lost his wife just two years earlier; he visits her grave every day. In the evening only wine can keep him from seeing things in such a sad light as they really are. This time, too, he is coming from the wine bar next to the house – it is easy to see from his gait and behavior: "Greetings to you, my dear, dear friends," he says in a German that has a clear Czech undertone.

Just then a man rumbles around the corner in military stride. It's Viktor, the old man's son. He's wearing the uniform of the SA. "Hello Father!" Our presence seems as objectionable to him as his is to us. He stammers a few words, takes his father's arm and moves off with him.

Pepi had apparently thought of us, maybe even talked to his wife about us, because when we enter the room, he says with a sigh of relief: "Now, thank God, you're here!" I don't let any sentimentality arise and immediately strike the tone of mutually friendly and cheerful rowdiness that has been our habit for years. I joke about acquaintances in common and soon that gaiety, always present in our group and directed by him in such expert fashion, that conviviality is once again there. In the meantime, both his children, Trude and Hansi, have arrived home. Surprised to have found us in such good spirits, they can scarcely say a word. And I feel compelled to carry my gallows humor to the extreme and tell joke after joke.

In the middle of this seemingly spooky conversation, I am again seized by a terrible agitation. It has already gotten late and so we say goodbye. Pepi now seems to realize that perhaps we should have talked about more serious matters and calls after us through the door: "Please, please, do come again tomorrow for sure!"

Both children have stood up in order to take their leave from us. Hansi steps into the light of the lamp and I notice with horror: He too is wearing the brown shirt of the SA.

I take Mautzi's hand and, without a word and without turning around, we rush out of the building . . .

At home we find that Marie is still with the children. Willy's fiancée has called and asked to meet me tomorrow evening in the Café Bastei. She has important news for me from Willy. So, Willy had made it home safely!

I pick up the evening papers that already allude to the announcement soon of the Nuremberg Laws. Names of known and unknown detainees are listed. It's clear that the State Secret Police, the notorious Gestapo, has taken up operations in Vienna. It's reported that the Chancellor has been placed in custody in the Belvedere palace.

I turn on the radio. But with lightning speed, I turn it off again when the evening news is read by a Prussian sergeant with a grating voice. The Viennese can't even understand him!

The telephone rings until midnight. All kinds of people call us. They speak very carefully. We can hear that our conversations are being monitored by the Gestapo. Acquaintances call we haven't spoken with for weeks. They apparently are having a hard time sleeping and are trying to find out something that will calm their agitated nerves.

It's Prohaska on the phone. It seems that he is not alone and says nothing more than: "Tomorrow at nine, like always!" He means that we should meet at nine o'clock in the morning at the Café Dobner as we have for years. We have breakfast there every day – I've seldom eaten at home – read the newspapers and devise our work schedule. So tomorrow, just like always!

Marie stayed with us overnight. There wasn't any question of getting any sleep though. I searched my desk drawers for things I'd rather not let fall into the hands of the Nazis.

Then I sat down with the sisters. I sat and struggled with myself. Shouldn't I really talk about things that could take place in the next few hours? What would happen if I were arrested?

Yet I don't want to escalate Mautzi's uneasiness. So I describe to Marie our visit with Pepi, repeat his jokes, and finally we are laughing in spite of the threatening clouds that hover over our heads. What was it Marie had said? "If we lose our heads, we've lost everything!" And I suddenly say loudly: "If we lose our humor, we've lost everything."

My Departure from the Editorial Office

The following day I meet with Prohaska at nine o'clock at our usual table in the Café Dobner. It's as if nothing had happened! First, we read the papers and then discuss what we should write about this, that, and the other. While we're talking, Lechner and Emmy Tomberger show up and give us a report about everything that had occurred the night before in the editorial office. Emmy does this in words and gestures with such originality that several times I have to burst out laughing. She tells the story about our colleague Holfeld who, because of his treasonous actions against the state, was fired from the editorial office a few weeks before Hitler's troops marched in. Emmy puts out her best efforts in describing how Holfeld was let go. "I asked management why Holfeld was let go if he was truly an enemy of the state. Why didn't they lock him up? The Nazi rabble in Vienna toss bombs, steal, and murder. And then, when it's proven that a man in a government newspaper belongs to this gang, he's released! All our management colleagues could do was shrug their shoulders. "'Will this guy also get severance pay?' I ask the publisher. 'Absolutely,' he replies. 'Even if the Nazis don't have any regard for justice and the law, does that mean we're supposed to act the same way?' But now I understand everything. We see that most of the managers were themselves Nazis. Or at least of that sort who carry an ID of the illegal NSDAP in their vest pocket on the right, one from the Social Democrats on the left, and one from the Patriotic Front in their wallet. Those who were especially cautious could even prove that they were monarchists, if necessary."

She speaks so loudly and brashly that I have to ask her to speak somewhat softer since there are other guests in the café.

"Okay, just listen to this! After the Nazi invasion, Holfeld calmly strolls into the editorial office with a martyr's expression on his face and heads for the desk of the chief editor. But who's already sitting there? Kirchner! Kirchner doesn't give way to him, so Holfeld picks up a second chair and places it next to him. A grand chaos ensues when both issue orders, give reporters directions, etc. That was last night. The situation automatically straightened itself out this morning. An hour ago the new Nazi commissioner arrived with a gentleman – recognizably Aryan only because of his Swastika – whom the commissioner introduced as the new chief editor. It was such a pleasure for me to see the dumbfounded look on the faces of Kirchner and Holfeld!

"The new boss's voice was as grating as a Prussian sergeant's: 'Comrade Holfeld, you're to stay near me at all times and anticipate my orders!' And just imagine, Holfeld, the man we know as the epitome of an unmilitary wimp, clicks his heels together and, standing at attention, responds: 'Yes sir, boss!'"

Emmy quivers with laughter and the rest of us must laugh as well when we imagine this scene.

"But that's not all," Emmy continues. "When he's alone again, I walk in and ask Holfeld: 'What is it that's on your mind?' He first looks to see if Kirchner is somewhere nearby, listening. Then he says softly: 'Something unpleasant happened to me, Emmy.' 'What's the matter?' 'They've pensioned off my brother-in-law, the court counselor, because his wife's mother is Jewish. You know, I hadn't imagined National Socialism in practice to be so bad – I thought it would all stay theoretical.' 'You're the worst kind of idiot. You're going to get the shock of your life with your Nazis. By the way, Kirchner told me that your wife looks less than racially pure and that you should, at the earliest possible moment, check out her family tree.' Holfeld's wife has pitch-black hair and a hooked nose. I look at him from the side to see what kind of effect my words have on him. But I'm astonished as I see his face brightening up: 'If it should be the case that my wife isn't racially pure, then you know Emmy, that would be – as I think more about it – the only benefit that National Socialism would have for me!'"

I look at my watch: "Well, it's high time now. I'm going to the editorial office as well, but I don't want to be seen there together with you. So, go on ahead! Bye-bye for now and I'm really grateful that you came!" "So long until tomorrow," the others call out simultaneously.

A few minutes later I leave the café and also strike out in the direction of the editorial office. A new employee announces me to the new government commissioner. He lets me know that I should take a seat in the directorate's conference room. I don't have to wait there long. The government commissioner, the youngest of the former executives – a Herr Rubesch – appears in the presence of the man who has been secretary general up to now. He stands in front of me and, with a solemn look on his face, makes a short speech. In his speech he thanks me in the name of the management for the services I've performed for the company and, in the name of the new administration, he explains that all of my legal entitlements will be granted. Herr Rubesch is visibly touched and has tears in his eyes as he gives me a parting handshake: "Sir, in view of the circumstances, I am sorry to have to ask you to consider yourself suspended pending further administrative rulings."

Up to this point I have stood up straight and not uttered a word. Now, making a mute bow, I leave the room.

After such a leave-taking that demonstrates a certain humane attitude, my concern decreases appreciably. I see the possibility of keeping my family and myself afloat for a time in whatever direction fate might cast us. And then, only God can help us further.

I remember that I have another appointment near here. A friend of my nephew Hansi asked me to look in on him when passing by. It would be for me – as I heard – an urgent as well as interesting matter. The boy I was to visit had inherited a technical journal along with a small printing press after his father's death. He now seems to be overwhelmed by the task that he faces and so he probably wants some kind of technical advice from me about newspapers.

He welcomes me with great respect, shows me the press operations, and then, without further lead-in, he makes me the offer of taking over management of the journal. At first I thought it was a trap, but the boy had such a naïve, childlike face that I had to say to myself, he really is thinking about the possibility of such collaboration. "No one needs to know that you put out the journal. You can work at home, read the manuscripts there, get things organized. I'll send things to you every day in the mail, and outwardly I'll be the owner and manager of the journal. And I'll pay you enough so that you and your family can still lead the same respectable lives that you've lead up to this point."

I see that the boy has good intentions and don't want to offend him, so I reply in a friendly tone of voice: "Young man, it contradicts my notion of morality that I would be partly to blame for misleading someone to any deceitful action." I pointed at the Hitler image on the wall: "You are a National Socialist and I'm a Jew. If I did what you want me to, I wouldn't merely be a scoundrel, but also to blame that you turn into one as well. You haven't thought this through. Good bye and good luck!"

I left the boy standing, looking discouraged, and departed. While I was still at the door, however, the boy took me by the hand and asked trustingly: "But maybe you could think it over, Herr Reich!"

Dismissal of the Housemaid

I look at my watch. It's one o'clock. So I hurry over to the bus stop. I don't want to keep Mautzi waiting anxiously. With my head down – I can't stand the sight of the fluttering swastika flags – I walk from the bus stop to my house. Just as I'm about to walk through the gate, I am witness to a scene that sends shivers up my spine. Everything happens lightning fast. An automobile drives up and parks in front of the house across the street. Two SS-men with weapons jump out and run through the gate. I duck into the entry-way and peer through the glass panes. Only a few minutes go by and both Nazis appear again. They usher a pale-faced man between them whose tangled hair hangs in his face. He wears no coat or hat. They push him with the butts of their weapons and force him into the car. My heart is beating to the point of bursting because I recognize that the man being taken away is one of my colleagues. He has lived there for years and led a modest, quiet life and never in any way attracted any attention due to his politics. As the car is turning the corner, I again look across the street and see the unfortunate man's eighty-year-old mother standing at the window. So, him too! Who would be next?

Apparently Mautzi has not noticed the incident, since when I walk in, she is sitting with Marie by the corner window. I find her much more relaxed than in the morning and I was grateful to Marie for coming – as so often before in difficult hours – in order to help Marie tolerate her worries.

The telephone rings. It's Lechner. Extremely agitated, he informs me that all Jewish journalists had just been arrested. Only with great effort am I able to hide my alarm in front of Mautzi at hearing this bad news. I'm confused and unsteady. I jump up when an automobile stops in front of the house and flinch when the doorbell rings. But first, it's the baker, then the custodian, and finally the children arriving home from school.

Traudl, our older daughter will soon take her school-leaving examination and is very happy that her last year of school is causing her fewer difficulties than earlier ones. Her teachers are treating her, as she tells it, just as nicely as earlier and she doesn't notice any kind of impact from the changed political situation. We question Etti about all kinds of things to see if we can detect any change in her teacher's attitude. But everything seems to have remained the same. The children were still not being singled out.

Marie notices my agitation and keeps trying to put me at ease. As if she were able to read my thoughts, she says: "There's no indication that you can be affected, especially after the appreciative farewell you got from the new management. Most likely they'll continue to keep you busy. They left many Jews at their posts in the German Reich. And the commissioner definitely said: 'You're temporarily on leave.'" She continues her attempts to cheer me up: "Finally after years you've gotten a compulsory vacation that you never wanted to allow yourself. You'll finally get to enjoy getting paid without having to work. That's great, right?"

Mautzi is in the kitchen. Already that morning she had dismissed the housemaid – in spite of her insistent pleas to be allowed to remain – since, according to newspaper reports, it was now illegal for Aryan housemaids younger than forty-five to be employed in Jewish households. "But Ma'am," the girl had pleaded, "if I myself want to stay, nobody can prohibit me from doing so." – "My dear, that's where you're wrong. Everything will be different from now on. You have to obey and be quiet about it. And I don't even know if my husband will continue to get his salary – what am I supposed to pay you with?" The girl had replied with tears in her eyes: "Then I just wouldn't get paid. I've never had it as good as in your home. I've felt like a child here . . . " – "Maybe things will change, will you come back then?" And so Klara left.

While Mautzi is busy in the kitchen, Marie obstinately returns to the conversation that had been interrupted by the children returning home: "But Hitler will never allow Austrians retroactively to make amends for fulfilling their duty toward the state that was recognized by the whole world as an independent state."

She is herself obviously not completely convinced of the truth of the things that she is trying to lecture me about.

I'm only half listening and, in order to preserve a semblance of interest, I interject a word now and then without thinking. "May be," or "Let's hope." Mautzi comes into the room from time to time where her questioning stare meets my own. I notice the worrisome thoughts – just like in my head – also passing through hers.

Arrested

Toward evening on March 17 I'm sitting together with my wife and sister-in-law at our house.

The doorbell rings. I go to open it. Two men stand in the dark entryway. "Are you the editor Reich?" one of them asks. "Yes, I am," I respond. "How can I help you gentlemen?" Outwardly I was the picture of composure. Yet I felt that my heart had congealed into ice. A dying man may well feel this way. That was the end. "We've come by order of the state police. You're under arrest, so follow us."

My wife who followed me into the hallway has turned pale as a sheet. She says nothing, but hurries into the bedroom and brings a little bottle of tranquilizers, a medical prescription I've been taking for years.

One of them frisks me. Everything happens at lightning speed. I take a last look at Mautzi and hear her distressing cry: "Max, stay strong!" Then the door slams shut behind me. It's as if a coffin lid has closed down over my head.

Inside the official automobile that stood in front of the house I was the only passenger apart from the detectives and the policeman driving. I kept telling myself: "Stay calm, stay calm!" and peered through the window. I suddenly saw my little girl coming around the corner. I involuntarily called out her name. She heard my voice but, understandably, was unable to locate me. The automobile was quickly out of sight. The driver asked in a surly voice why I was shouting. I told him that my daughter had just walked by and I hadn't been able to say goodbye to her. The man murmured sympathetically: "That is sad." Was that the last spark of the "golden Viennese heart"?

We drove for hours through several of Vienna's districts and stopped in front of houses where journalists lived with whom I was acquainted. Besides me, however, only one other person was taken in. At one point the car had to wait for a particularly long time. Then a shot rang out. One of the two returning detectives said: "That guy just didn't want to come along. Now he can stay home." And both then laughed . . .

Most of those being sought after had apparently been smarter than we had and had found refuge in a timely manner. Had they really been the smarter ones? On our long hunting expedition through half of Vienna I had enough opportunity to reflect on this question. I came to the conclusion again and again, that I would not have fled abroad even if I had thought about the possibility of my arrest. I admit that this thought hadn't even occurred to me since I had never been politically active and my work and interest areas had essentially been in sports, while my hobbies were music and the theater. In my eyes, I thought at the time, running away would have amounted to the admission of some kind of guilt. I examined my conscience but found no accusation that anyone could legitimately bring against me. In my twenty-five-year career as a journalist, I had not done or written anything that I couldn't still vouch for. The only crime, of which I could now be accused, was that I had always felt myself to be an Austrian. I had been an officer during the war and had served Austria afterwards – not always in support of the governing powers – as well as I was able. In any case, I had done nothing more than to practice my profession dutifully and as long as law and order prevailed, there could be no punishment for that. At the time, it was not clear to me that this condition had ceased to exist with the Nazi assumption of power and that it was possible to be locked up and convicted without legal proceedings, to lose one's position and assets, to be torn from one's family – even if innocent of any crime. I had omitted one factor from my calculations that would be hammered with merciless cruelty into my head every minute for the next seven months: that is, Austria had ceased to be a state under the rule of law since it had become overnight a part of the Third Reich.

THE ELISABETH-PROMENADE

In the prison where they bring us I find a number of good friends – Willy Kurtz among them – who embrace me with gusto. Willy's eyes are bloodshot, his face swollen as if he had been in a challenging boxing match, but despite that he's in a good mood. He immediately pushes two straw mattresses together and lays our coats across them as a sign of occupancy.

The huge hall gets increasingly crowded as more and more prisoners are brought in. Gradually I regain my composure. A sorrow shared is a sorrow halved, and so an individual can scarcely feel a sorrow shared by thousands.

I recognize government secretaries, generals, the Viennese mayor, and many others. Finally, they all have to squeeze together with three on every two mattresses. Are the new masters of Vienna intent upon bringing half the city under lock and key?

One of the directors of my newspaper's publishing house, a Herr Fliegel by name, and a sweet old man known throughout the city because of his good-natured character, shares the two mattresses with Willy and myself as the third member of our group. We force ourselves to get some sleep in order to gather strength for the coming hours. We are not allowed to write to our families for three days. Nor do we receive any correspondence. Our morning, noon, and evening meals consist of soup and bread.

Everyone is convinced that our detention will not last more than a few days. Maybe hours! We pass the time talking, while some play chess with chess-pieces made out of pieces of bread. A man is brought in on the evening of the second day who has adhesive tape over his right eye. SS-troops had gouged out his eye in a café where he had refused to respond to them with the Hitler salute. He's about thirty, a great guy who hasn't lost his lusty Viennese humor. He entertains us all with his jokes: "Just don't let yourselves get soft, gentlemen!" he says over and over when he hears someone lamenting in desperation. "Just don't cave in – we've got to stay strong to get revenge on this pack of criminals!"

On the fourth day I receive a few lines on a postcard from Mautzi. She tries to cheer me up and says she hopes to see me again soon. Since prisoners are now allowed to write their families, composure and confidence return to our ranks.

"I will stay strong, come what may," I write. "I'm in control of my emotions, always thinking of you and the children."

I find a lot of opportunity to keep busy since I have two "children" to care for, Fliegel and Willy. The serenity that Willy had shown in our first meeting in detention had not lasted. "I should have gotten married yesterday," he lamented. "Instead, I'm celebrating my wedding day in prison." "Who knows who benefits from that," the one-eyed jokester responds and everyone laughs. Willy is the only one who doesn't perk up. It is indeed an eerie contrast between his former and present situations.

Trying to console him, I offer: "I got married on August 27, 1914, at one in the afternoon and at three I moved out into the field with my regiment. That lasted four years and you know that my marriage has been a happy one."

But Willy completely breaks down. He already sees himself condemned to death and in his thoughts takes leave, again and again, from his bride and the wonderful life without cares that he had led to this point. The meager diet undermines his strength more than anything else. Accustomed to good and plentiful nutrition, his body shrinks in an alarming manner. His shoulders fall and he scarcely has the strength to get up from the straw mattress. He often lies there for hours without moving.

I begin to seriously fear for Willy's sanity. Only when I start to talk about sports am I able to distract his attention for a short time from his fantasies.

My second "child," old Fliegel, is in his mid-sixties. At the moment he is again in good spirits but when he was brought here, I had my hands full. Fliegel had first been brought to an SS-guardhouse where the guards amused themselves by pulling the old gentleman's moustache hairs out of one side of his face. Due to this barbarous treatment, Fliegel had bloody shreds of flesh on his upper lip. With the nail clippers that I had been allowed to keep I cut off the other half of his moustache so that the poor man looked human again. In the quiet manner he was known for, Fliegel switched from his mistreatment back to the everyday agenda. Shaking his head, he simply remarked: "Those young guards didn't treat an old man very nicely." I help him get his bedding ready for the night, arrange the blanket, and help him again at reveille straighten out his bedclothes.

The confinement was not pleasant. Apart from sleeping in our clothes, the food was inadequate and poorly prepared. Soup and bread were all we got, morning, noon, and evening. And although we were allowed hardly any movement – we were led on a daily walk in the courtyard for half an hour – I lost more than ten kilograms during the fourteen days of our confinement in Vienna.

Viennese police were on duty in the police jailhouse. They treated us as prisoners but never as criminals. We could even dare to ask them questions that, in general, were answered in a friendly manner. We also made the momentary acquaintance of Viennese SS who were mostly intelligent looking young men making obvious efforts to deal with us as subhuman beings in accordance with their schooling and their orders. As we were later to learn the hard way, however, they had not completed the advanced course of study in Nazi brutality. They were, incidentally, soon relieved, apparently because they had not received sufficient weapons' training. Police officers returned to provide surveillance.

DISPATCH INTO THE INFERNO

On April 1 there is suddenly a call for certain prisoners, whose names are read out, to report immediately to the corridor with their clothes bags. Willy and I are among them. The general opinion is that those called are to be released from custody. Fliegel asks me, in the event I am set free, to notify his wife that he is healthy and in good spirits. Also, she should send him some warmer underwear.

We take our leave from those remaining behind and step out into the corridor. There were about one hundred fifty of us. "Will they really release us to go home?" – "No question! What can they do with us? Are we criminals? We've done nothing more than our duty as citizens, as officials, as officers!"

Everybody is extremely tense. We all careen between hope and fear. Who knows what is in store for us. Half an hour later a column of five military vehicles, fully loaded with prisoners, moves out along the Ringstraße.

I sit in one of them next to Willy. The giant is quivering with fear. I try to calm him down. The trucks then turn onto Mariahilfer Street toward the Westbahnhof.

For the moment a deathly silence hangs over the motionless, cowering figures in the trucks. Then suddenly someone cries out in a frenzied voice: "We're going to Dachau, to the concentration camp!" Another scream pierces our ears: "We're lost!" Here and there sobbing becomes audible. I hold my friend's hand in my own. "Willy, now's the time to be strong so we can survive in even worse conditions and still have our revenge!"

With screeching brakes the truck comes to a standstill. Our two police escorts whisper to us: "Glasses off, protect your eyes!" And now a diabolical dance begins with harrowing images. For the entire time I keep hold of my friend's hand. Everyone is driven into a circle surrounded by SS-troops. Only a narrow path is kept open to the rail cars of the train standing there. Everyone is forced to scramble through this "narrow pass."

Neither I nor anyone else is able to describe fully what now occurred. It happened much too quickly and each of us was so completely occupied in preventing any bodily injury that the compelling fear driving us generated only dismay and terror. It was at night. A throng of uniformed figures encircled us. Only a scant glimmer of light fell here and there into this spooky, dark circle. Volleys of boots kicked at us. Clubs, rifle butts, and fists rained down on us. If you fell, you were lost. An infernal noise filled the air. Our cries of pain mixed together with bellowed commands, and now and again a shot rang out. I was incapable of hearing myself think. We all thought we were finished. At times I saw a bayonet flash, a comrade fall – shoved back and forth, it was impossible to tell how and where to escape. There was no way out. We clustered closer and closer together like sheep in a storm, and like sheep, we waited submissively for our end. I still remember how a command drowned out the chaos: "Close your windows! Or we'll fire at you people up there!"

This command was apparently aimed at those spectators watching this SS-orgy from their windows opposite the switchyard of the Westbahnhof.

Maybe it was for us Viennese their foreign word "*funken*" ("to fire") that buried itself unconsciously in my memory. In any case it's the only thing that I can clearly recall. This hour of horror had its own tempo. Probably it lasted for only twenty to thirty minutes but for us it was an unbearably long period of the wildest mistreatment, aggravated even more by the prevailing darkness.

The black devils struck at the huddle of innocent human beings with the butts of their weapons and stabbed at them with their bayonets. Many collapsed and some never stood up again. The sounds of sobbing and moaning filled the air. The SS shouted orders that no one understood. Everyone surged toward the railcar doors in a scramble for safety.

I finally found myself inside a car, but how I got there I'll never know.

We were jammed into narrow compartments. Twelve people sat on each of the two wooden benches that were intended for eight. "Sitting" is really an incorrect term – we were positioned more on top of each other than next to one another, but we had escaped the black circle, even though each man bore scars from the experience. There were already a few badly injured individuals to whom no one paid any attention – except us, of course.

The car we are now sitting in is brightly lit, yet the windows are opaquely draped. It gradually fills up with our comrades. Some are bloody and sink onto their seats while others have been disfigured beyond recognition by the abusive treatment. At the sound of its whistle, the train begins to move.

What were we supposed to do? The shades were drawn and, until the train left, the SS with their steel helmets patrolled the corridor. Scarcely had the train's wheels begun to turn when an SS-guard appeared in every compartment, issuing instructions for our conduct during the trip.

The prescribed posture was: hands on the knees, eyes directed toward the lamp! So we sat during the entire journey, a journey that lasted from eight in the evening until ten the next morning. Straining to sit quietly and staring into the light neither calmed nor cheered any one of us.

Since lunch – soup and bread – we had had nothing to eat and now it was late in the evening. To make a long story short, we had our next meal on the following evening in Dachau – soup and bread. And what all transpired between these two bowls of soup! And what all we had to endure in those thirty hours!

The Games Begin

The prelude at the Westbahnhof continued on the rolling stage. It was unfortunate for anyone whose eyes fell closed from exhaustion. A punch to the face would immediately follow. From time to time an SS-guard came into the compartment in order – as he put it – to give us "some exercise." We were forced to slap each other's face and the smacks often resonated for many minutes. We were so battered that we couldn't recognize each other. A guard appeared again and again, just for his amusement, in order to plant his fist between the eyes of one or the other of us. Our faces were covered with blood. We could hear moaning and groaning from every direction.

At one point in time when I had clearly regained consciousness, I experienced the apotheosis of this performance by the sadistic ensemble from hell: a woman with a cigarette hanging from lips grotesquely smeared with lipstick went from compartment to compartment gloating over the bloodstained victims of these SS-bestialities. This phenomenon seemed to me to be so far beyond possible reality that I was uncertain whether I had really seen it or whether it was merely a nightmare with roots in the horrific events of the night. Later in camp, several of my companions confirmed for me the appearance of this "evil fairy." She had, indeed, been real, and not a monstrous fabrication. How could even the most feverish imagination have conceived of such a thing? There is no such thing in a dream, only in the reality of Nazi Germany.

After a few more punches to the face – I lost one tooth – I was so stunned that I could no longer consciously follow what was happening. I can still see some of the images in my mind's eye from this night of terror: guards who jabbed with their bayonets and others who hit the faces of their defenseless victims with their fists, often directly in the eyes. Many sank to the ground. Right in front of my eyes, one of my fellow prisoners ran straight into one of the guard's bayonets. It was an obvious suicide.

Dazed by the battering, the compulsory position, and the noise, I must have fallen into a coma. I was convinced that I was in hell. For the first time in my life I saw young and powerful men slamming their fists into the faces of old and defenseless men, kicking and otherwise brutalizing them . . . This could not be the earth which God had created for human beings.

The command "Up and out!" brought me once again to consciousness. The thunderous roaring of the black-shirted SS-guards tore at my harried nerves: Shouts of "Exit right!," "Exit left!," "Exit right!" mixed together chaotically. In between, shots rang out, bayonets were thrust at us, and volleys of blows and punches poured down on us. It was only much later that I learned that even these contradictory commands were part of a system that had been contrived to the last detail. The confusing "Exit right . . . left" commands were used to bring the prisoners into a state of indecisive movement back and forth so that those who moved a few steps too far could be shot down as flight risks and, for everyone without exception, to facilitate an even more vicious beating.

Incapable of reasoning, I was only able to move as if by instinct and came to my senses again only as we sat in the trucks that brought us from the Dachau train station to the camp.

Our Reception at the Camp

Anyone who believes that we were granted a reprieve after such a trip – all of us exhausted from the mental and physical harassment, some gravely injured, and tormented by hunger and thirst – that person does not know the depravity of the SS-apparatus. The first act after the confinement took place on a square between the garrison buildings of the Dachau concentration camp.

On one side stood all the off-duty SS-troops. From our perspective they seemed to be on a kind of podium that was about half a meter higher than we were. The camp commander and senior SS-officers had taken their positions on the other side. The prisoners stood in two ranks in a long row, and each had to step forward individually when his name was read out by the senior leader.

Each individual summons by the senior leader was accompanied by a few introductory words that were followed by appreciative laughter from the "gallery." This SS-audience, however, lacked even the slightest knowledge of political particulars. Every official as well as every employee in the public sphere in Austria was forced to belong to an organization called the "Patriotic Front." It was supposed to reconcile the parties and to encompass all Austrians. Naturally, many members of this organization had retained their former political convictions and, consequently, there were clerics and socialists, Nazis, and members of the Rural Federation and, above all, partisans of Dollfuß and Schuschnigg in the "Patriotic Front." In the SS-school, however, it was portrayed as a communist organization. And of course, it was not taught that membership in the "Patriotic Front" was a prerequisite for every public position. The speaker's remark – "member of the Patriotic Front" – following individual names triggered invectives and ironic applause. Later I was often able to observe that membership in this organization of Austrian patriotism was viewed by the SS as involvement in a sinister plot and considered particularly annoying.

I was personally acquainted with the prominent figures. Most were honorable men who, even up to the last moment, had fulfilled their duty to Austria. There were eminent diplomats, politicians, leading industrialists, scientists, journalists, and economists. Yet they formed only a small minority in the great mass of unknown soldiers of labor who had been lifted out of their modest life circumstances. They were, if anything, even more respectable than most of the important men. Everyone responded when they were summoned by name. As far as their strength and physical condition permitted, they stepped forward with pride in their bearing and put up with the obligatory mockery. During these hours almost all of the men seemed to have undergone a remarkable transformation. The scene of the spectacle stood in such contrast to the experiences during the horrific train ride the preceding night that one's own returning pride joined with the contempt that we felt toward this mob. It became clear to us what noble human beings the privates and corporals of the old Austrian army had been, compared to these unmilitary robots of ruthless destruction. In view of this deliberate demonstration of cowardice and the precise opposite of chivalrous behavior, the conviction permeated my thoughts almost palpably that this Third Reich must be headed for an appalling downfall if any human beings still remained on earth.

The effect on the prisoners of this theatrical performance was without doubt a different one than the one intended. Even the weakest among us pulled himself together to demonstrate our composure. The magical word "Austria" – a dirty word in the mouths of our tormentors – restored pride and even the will to live to these scarred, humiliated, and tormented human beings while facing this mob.

There was no physical abuse during this welcoming ceremony. We were merely spat at when we marched by the "platform."

New Wardrobe and First Harassment

It only became clear to me later, when I again thought about what had happened, how confounded we had been. For us, the entire initial ceremony had been a short period of rest, especially since it had, at least, not been accompanied by any new mistreatment; that is, in a physical sense. We realized how necessary it had been for us, a realization that immediately proved to be true. The path through the jeering cordon of SS-guards – who were spitting at us as we passed – led to the bathroom where we were supplied with prison garb. We received a pair of heavy shoes, socks, a shirt and undershorts, plus pajamas with bluish-gray stripes made from some kind of surrogate fabric, as well as Russian military caps that were apparently left over from the World War. Our heads were shaved and any beards were clipped off. The whole prisoner "kit" was grotesque and, in some cases, deliberately and absurdly "customized." They tried to make us into caricatures of human beings. But we quickly got used to it. The intended effect, to make us appear ridiculous to one another, did not succeed since we were always together.

The attempt at playing with our minds began anew as we were allowed out of the bathroom one by one. No one knew where to line up and we were not given instructions. This was, once again, one of the many tricks of this contrived system. When one of us attempted to find a spot, he was chased away by the SS with kicks and punches. We fled from our pursuers like a flock of agitated hens until they became worn down by the physical exertion of their blows and let us line up. After that our block leaders took over and led us to our barracks. We still had to stuff our straw mattresses.

We then finally were given our first meal after more than thirty hours – soup and bread. Our comrades, moving toward us as discreetly as possible from the barracks, slipped one of us a piece of sausage, another some cheese, butter or marmalade – each gave what he still had in his locker. The camp fellowship had admitted us.

The path to our dormitory was cleared. I was again able to arrange it so that my straw mattress lay next to Willy's. This gigantic man fell into a leaden sleep immediately after he had thrown himself down on his pallet.

In spite of debilitating fatigue I scrutinized in my mind the pernicious events of the last twenty-four hours. One thing became clear: whatever might come now could not be more traumatic than what we had just experienced. So, why fear what the future holds? I had survived four years of the World War and God would help me escape this hell as well.

I am unable to think through any one of the thoughts that feverishly race through my brain. Except for one: what drives these people to martyr God's defenseless creatures whom fate has delivered into their hands with such demonic cruelty? It's the spirit that has haunted the brains of those eternal scoundrels for decades, those fully bearded faces beneath students' caps. The seeds that were sown bore bloody fruit: the heroes of the dueling grounds and the mighty deeds of the beer guzzlers. The dictatorship of scoundrels had dawned![4] A man with a flowing beard, a ribbon looped around his breast, swung a broad sword over my head . . .[5]

I sat down on the edge of my pallet to ponder the situation, but through the conscious effort to hold myself up, my entire store of stamina failed me. I must have simply fallen on my back and into a dreamless slumber.

The Work Day

The sound of a siren awakens us at three-thirty in the morning. The senior barracks resident bellows: "Up and out of bed!" Some jump up refreshed from their straw mattresses while others have to be shaken so that they recollect where they are. Three have already been released from all worry about what's coming. One of them hangs with his belt around his neck in the lavatory, while two have been liberated from their suffering by heart failures.

By now the "food servers" had been sent for breakfast. Black coffee was served in each room in two large and heavy buckets. Already at this point we had to force down the bread, marmalade and hot coffee in all haste, because even now the room cleaning had begun. This was indicated, like everything else in Dachau, by routine yelling. The various cleanup squads were deployed. Some had the task of tidying up the day room while others swept the bedroom while a third group had the task of cleaning the toilets and washroom. Half of the room occupants had a week on the room-cleaning squad; at the same time, the other half was forced outside immediately after breakfast in all weather conditions. It was here that a great deal of the communication among the prisoners took place. We met with each other, rapidly exchanged a few words until twenty minutes after five when we had to form up for roll call.

My comrades took courage since for the time being, no SS-

---

[4] The term "dictatorship of scoundrels" comes from a Scandinavian diplomat who coined it based on his long years of experience with the leading lights of the Third Reich.

[5] Jahn, the father of gymnastics is meant here.

guard showed up, and the senior room member – himself a prisoner and very friendly – was in charge. Dawn had arrived in the East when we reported for work. We looked at each other in amusement and made jokes about our appearances. Willy was a particularly funny sight to behold. They had not been able to find any of the vertically striped, bluish-gray pajamas for a man of his height. His pants reached down to the midpoint of his calves. The shirt was buttoned only at the top while the gap toward the bottom became wider and wider. A cap without a visor sat atop everyone's head – everybody was dressed alike. There were a few among us over seventy years old.

Roll Call

In every camp there is a large square where roll call takes place. In Dachau this square is situated right in front of the Jourhaus – the entrance building to the camp. The roll call takes place twice a day there, at five twenty in the morning and at six in the evening. At these assemblies the condition of the prisoners is reviewed, and all detainees – with the exception of those in the infirmary or those who had been assigned to the room-cleaning detail – are required to be present. The various blocks take up their positions.

I don't know if there was a Goya among us or even among the robotic guards, but I hoped for one. It isn't right that the world be spared all the horror that was suffered in this Germany and even the crassest Goya could only approximately depict the images in the scene that was officially called the roll call.

The man in charge of the reports now figures out the number present. He walks along the front of every block and receives the reporting books of the block seniors from which he ascertains the number of inmates from each block. We hear the command "Caps off!" and know that the camp commandant has appeared. "Eyes right!" rings out, as the man in charge of the roll call gives his report. A conversation ensues between him and the camp commandant while we are forced to remain standing at attention. Rain, snow, or thunderstorm – we might be standing in water up to our ankles – what difference does it make? When the camp commandant comes thirty minutes or even a whole hour late or, when he purposely lets us wait, the entire procedure stretches out that much longer. Standing at attention is strenuous even for less exhausted men. After hard, forced labor, every fifteen minutes seems twice that long, and some of us had old and no longer completely sound bone structures. The SS-guards, in warm and rainproof gear, are less uncomfortable and are not forced to stand at attention. We stand as still as mice in our all-purpose pajamas.

The silence is now and again interrupted by a strange sound. It's hard to put into words. It's a quiet scraping that sounds at first like a few grains of sand had been thrown on the ground, a noise that grows into a kind of scratching. Then a thud becomes audible. But the latter, only if you're near the man who has toppled over. This scratching – familiar to thousands of attentive ears – always signifies that someone can no longer endure the situation and will collapse into a heap. He was no longer able to control his limbs, rouse his feet, and: plop! The rest of us were not allowed to move. Those who pass out – and at every long roll call, there were several – remained on the ground until the ceremony had ended. Their comrades then brought them back to the barracks and everyone was required to be in place the next day before work.

It happens at times that the number of those reported present is not correct. Someone is missing! The SS disperse in search of the missing person. Sometimes he is found dead in the barracks. He had chosen to respond to the final roll call at the throne of God. It often happened that the report of a death was simply forgotten and, now and again, those responsible for reporting just counted wrong. In any case, the prisoners remain standing at attention or lie unconscious on the ground until the number on the paper matches the living numbers. A miscount by the commandant often costs us an hour of unnecessary standing at attention.

After the roll call, the work details formed up, and at six in the morning, we marched off to our work areas.

There were days and evenings, however, when everything ran like clockwork and roll call proceeded without a hitch. At those times the automobile that was to drive the camp commandant to Munich for some pleasurable entertainment stood in front of the Jourhaus. And, unlike in the case of the prisoners, it was never made to wait. Even when there was a bowling party going on in the SS apartment building, there were no delays because of trifles during roll call. Already during the counting, the call for "pin-setters!" could be heard and those prisoners granted this privilege marched off to the bowling alley. They even received beer and sometimes gratuities for this work after the night-duty shift. The rest of us enjoyed these bowling evenings as well, since we finally could be sure that no SS-guard would concern himself with us.

"In Lockstep, Maaarch!"

For roll call we had to be lined up in rows of four, and then came the command: "In lockstep, maaarch!"

Just imagine the group of individuals in such a prisoner block! There are men from twenty to seventy years old, large and small, feeble and robust, athletic and effete, healthy and ailing. There are cripples, some missing a limb, some limping – many have never served in the military nor participated in sports.

In the military I trained young, strong recruits, recruits chosen by specialists and physicians and I, like every training officer, needed weeks to achieve that simultaneity of movement of everyone in the detachment which the drill required. Here in camp the same quick tempo in carrying out commands was demanded of the old and emotionally demoralized – even cripples – as from the very youngest troops of the superbly drilled SS. And it wasn't just a matter of demanding it. Whoever became conspicuous for any reason while marching was taunted and punished. Our hearts bled when we had to witness how old, sick men – doing their best not to arouse the displeasure of their tormentors – were maltreated for no reason other than that the bodies of these poor devils were simply not able to do what was demanded of them.

"In lockstep, maaarch!" was, without doubt, the least onerous of unreasonable demands placed on us in Dachau, yet for many – and even for some of the more proficient in this skill – it was sometimes too difficult. Being out of step would invite a volley of blows upon the offender from the right and left. Then suddenly the order came: "Change step!" At times, even a skilled youngster is unsuccessful in managing this little trick the way he intends. Here in Dachau, sixty-, even seventy-year-olds, were supposed to pull this off and then were battered in any case.

As soon as a work detail left the camp, the crew was to begin a song. This directive was apparently issued in order to deceive the rural population in the vicinity into believing that we prisoners were happy and in good spirits as we passed by. Here too there was no difference between the old and young, the musical and unmusical. Ultimately, however, even the worst orgy of discordant notes played no role if the texts that we sang are taken into account. We bellowed this partially rhymed rubbish to old, often wonderful melodies that were almost always distorted beyond recognition. Those not singing had to be careful!

The guards on our flanks insisted that each one of us contribute his portion of noise to the collective song. Gradually, however, I developed a technique of soundless singing that stood the test of time. By the movements of my mouth I pretended to give voice to the words, yet with one single exception, I always refrained from singing along. The tune "Esterwegen" was named after a concentration camp that no longer existed. The words of this song won the solid approval of all prisoners and in this regard, it was entirely unique. All of us, myself included, performed it as loudly as we could and with the most unambiguous enthusiasm we could muster, especially the last stanza. The words were:

> And there will come the time for us as well,
> Hurray, hurray!
> When we are freed from arrest,
> Hurray, hurray!
> Then we will happily, happily
> Strike out for home, for home
> Never mind if it's snowing, or if roses are in bloom.

At this point our chorus rose to hurricane force. To be sure it was a flood of dissonant tones, but for us it was almost the music of the spheres. What passion lay in those words – or, at least, what passion we projected into them. No Chaliapin can ever have sung with more feeling. We "sang" to the furthest possible extremes of what our lungs and vocal cords could produce. It must have sounded provocative, but fortunately, the SS had no ear for timbre. It was as if we wanted to scream into their ears until their eardrums reverberated: "We will in time go home and *you'll* still be *here*! – You mechanical torture instruments of a bestial system that will soon have had its day."

We were less enthusiastic about the other texts, something anyone can understand who gets to know them. There was, for example, the song "Maruschka" – named after the Polish girl who absolutely refused to be kissed, who however gave her dancing partner a kiss under "the starry firmament" already in the second stanza. The marching song "Tyrol" was a special favorite among the Bavarian SS. The title aroused melancholy memories in our minds. The song, however, quickly cured us of our melancholy and demonstrated to us the intellectual power of the new masters in the land of Andreas Hofer:

> Tyrol, Tyrol, Tyrol, my native land
> Where the French horn is heard over hill and dale.
> The clouds disperse in the distance but gather again
> above us,
> Man lives but once and then no more.
>
> My parents are gone, already with the Lord,
> No longer a brother or sister – all have departed.
> Tyrol, Tyrol, Tyrol, my native land
> Where the French horn is heard over hill and dale.

But this "distinctive and comforting" song was eclipsed in the minds of our guards by yet another one, "High Over the Waves," a song they recommended to us again and again. It is a ballad with such poignant content that a short summary seems worthwhile. Ultimately, it is a good measure of the cultural horizon of the average SS-man. A mariner travels across the ocean. "Over there the shore divides, the land opens up . . ." The mariner remembers his wife and child whom he had earlier had to leave behind, but suddenly Louisa stands on the seashore, her hands folded, her gaze toward the heavens, and her mind focused on the Canary Islands.

The rest of the story is neither my invention nor a joke: it's there that her husband languishes, unable for some incomprehensible reason to return home. Suddenly Louisa sees the mariner. But instead of him heading for shore, Louisa walks toward his boat. The tragic consequences take their expected final turn. He has just time enough to sing: "I'm not a mariner, I'm your husband . . . ," when the waves crash over them both.

I am unable to present the entire sample collection of substandard quality tearjerkers here whose tones and texts caused SS-hearts to beat faster, but I think this selection suffices. The poets who wrote these sentimental songs were anonymous, just like the poet today is, who wrote about the Loreley. Based on the works mentioned above, art aficionados or psychologists will perhaps be able to draw inferences about the intellectual disposition and the predilections of those entrusted with life-or-death decisions over the prisoners in concentration camps. The camp administration attached great importance to the cultivation of the German song, particularly by the Jews. This was once made strikingly obvious to us when the camp commandant forced an entire labor crew to practice two hours extra because it had not sung loudly enough.

There were various jobs, but mainly ones working with the soil. A shovel was the most important tool, while the pickax came in second. The wheelbarrow was used to transport earth, bricks, stones, rubble, and sand – although there were also trucks that ran on tracks – but small machines were also employed, sometimes moved by human exertion alone.

Some of us toiled inside, some outside the camp. Each section had a capo, and each – according to its size – had one or more vice-capos.

The work was hard and could be managed only by powerful men. Our hours were daily from six to eleven in the morning and afternoons from one to six. It must be kept in mind that even cripples and critically ill men were considered healthy in Dachau and that the same job performance was expected from everyone. Many staggered toward the barracks in an incomprehensible state both at noon and in the evening. At the command of the block seniors who constantly bellowed "in lockstep" at the top of their lungs, they were forced to march or suffer the blows that rained down on them. Those who had fallen behind, who quite literally could no longer lift their legs, were goaded on with kicks and whacks.

As hard as the work was, it was by no means the worst part of our life. Many whose urns were shipped to their relatives, might have left camp alive if the SS had not "spiced up" the forced labor of these unfortunate inmates with specific bestialities.

Before we left camp, Hans, our senior resident, had prepared us for horrible things that could happen to us depending on the whims of the block leader in charge. But reality far exceeded our imagination. There was shoveling, digging, and moving heavy loads, all accompanied by the hellish roar of our guards and supervisors along with orgies of abuse. Four men died on that first day from the blows of raging SS-guards.

Hans calmed the desperate comrades when they returned from work: "This rage only lasts a few days whenever there is a new shipment. Then things become quieter. Remember, I've been here five years. Why? I was a Social Democrat and because of some slanderous accusation, I was indicted for high treason. I was never tried, but I've been here since 1933. In any case, it's rumored that you Austrians will soon be released." – "That's a comfort for those of us still alive," lamented one man, "but what about the women, mothers, and children of our poor comrades who in the past few days have been tormented to death?"

Terrible days followed. Days of the hardest slave labor, scorn, ridicule, and beatings. The number of Austrians dwindled. Some were not able to survive the work and the accompanying kicks and beatings. Everyday – swinging a pickax or pushing a shovel into the earth – someone collapsed and never got up again. There were suicides every day. Everyone, without exception, showed signs of the unfamiliar labor during the first weeks. Almost everyone developed festering sores on their hands. They trembled as they filed toward the barracks.

I, to my own great surprise, quickly became accustomed to the work and, by the end of the first week, my arms and legs were no longer exhausted, while the gigantic Willy began to completely buckle under the stress. He was the largest man among the prisoners and the SS-heroes fell on him with special ferocity. It apparently appealed to them in a perverse way to let off steam on this colossal man. Wasn't the poor guy defenseless just like everyone else? He often got back to camp in terrible shape. I really had to give it my all in order to console this friend who radiated such wretchedness. Willy's cheeks were sunken, his shoulders hung down crookedly. His massive back was bent. The burlesque-comical uniform added its own effect.

The excesses of the camp SS finally began to slacken and the numbers of the dead on the weekly reports decreased. Of paramount importance for all of us detainees in "protective custody," however, was the arrival of the first letters from home.

Mail Call

From then on, we were allowed to receive and send mail once a week. Whoever has spent time in a battle zone or far away from home will perhaps be able to imagine what a letter from loved ones at home meant for us. And that is naturally the case, almost even more so, the other way around. Even if the detainees' families are fortunately in the dark about the situation of their loved ones in camp, they know enough so that they have no tranquil moments and spend their days and nights waiting for some sign of life. When the family members or friends finally have the letter in hand – even if the letter can't really say anything, just like in times of war – it does however deliver the essential message: that is, that the sender is more or less well and, above all, still among the living. Conversely, mail was for the prisoners the most important factor in camp life. For six days and nights all of our thinking and hopes, our entire emotional life was focused on the impending postal delivery. When we had the letter in our hands, all of our misery was forgotten and every word in that familiar handwriting gave us strength for continued perseverance.

The call "Line up for mail call!" raised the tension level to a fever pitch among the prisoners but reading letters in front of the barracks was forbidden. We had to wait for the command "Dismissed." Then everyone hurriedly rushed into the barracks.

Very often, however, our impatience had to be restrained further. When we had arrived back from work on rainy days, then we had to clean our shoes and clothes before we were allowed in the room. Finally, the festive moment arrived when the letter could be opened. We sat in the corners of the room, squatting down on the benches. You could hear a pin drop. Here and there, the only sound might be a sigh of relief, but often a sobbing. Every pair of eyes stared at the lines that meant their very life to them.

Mail distribution mostly took place on Fridays and no one needed much psychological insight to know which of our comrades had gotten good or bad news or – perhaps worst of all – no news. One look sufficed. If the diagnosis fell into one of the two last-mentioned categories, then we tried to console, to explain – as we all knew – that the stupid censorship often delayed letters and that we ourselves had received good news that applied to all of us. That was particularly important since we had been cut off from the outside world – the German newspapers could be considered news sources only to a very limited degree. We knew nothing, especially with regard to our own fate, and read rays of hope into the letters from our wives, children, mothers and fathers, which for the most part had no concrete source.

It was particularly unfortunate for those whom the block senior told during mail distribution that they had in fact gotten mail but it could not be given to them. Certain things were not quite clear, and the mail would be handed out on the next day in the Jourhaus. The concerned prisoner would then still not get the letter, but instead perhaps the callous news that his mother was dying and had requested of the camp management that he be granted a short leave so that the dying woman could see him one last time. He was driven away with scornful laughter and the words: "Do you want to ruin your mother's dying moments with your hideous looks?"

Women asked their husbands what they should do. They had been summoned to the Gestapo and advised to divorce their Jewish spouses immediately or they would otherwise starve along with their children.

The camp censor always let through letters without delay that contained unpleasant news for prisoners. But there were also some letters that amused us and made the rounds through the entire camp. The young wife of a factory worker in our room wrote him that she was expecting a child. In view of this she asked him not to be unfaithful to her.

Another wife told her husband she was sending a package with sportswear – and equipment – since he would without doubt want to make excursions into Dachau's beautiful countryside. The people at home created such strange images of life in a concentration camp!

We ourselves could write on Sundays, and we mentally composed these letters during the entire week. Since we were neither allowed nor did we want to write the truth, these letters naturally congealed into set phrases. Yet they were a sign of life and the only solace for the family. I often woke up at night with a start because it suddenly occurred to me that I had forgotten to tell my wife something extremely important, for example, the name of a man who might be able to help or an agency to which she might turn. We would engrave these names in our brains so that they would not be lost. Then Sunday and the letter-writing hour arrived when we gathered all of the notes from our pockets, our wallets – all of the slips of paper where important notes had been scratched. We sat down to write – and wrote about something completely different. Some who had decided during the week to intimate to their wives the real bleakness of their situation suddenly changed their minds and described it in such exaggeratedly bright and rosy terms that the responses from home sometimes took on truly grotesque forms. Our tragedies did not lack an element of the ridiculous. One wife, for example, asked if her spouse had found a nice bridge partner. Many wives wrote of sending items that were to make their husbands' lives more interesting and comfortable, items that naturally never reached their destination. At times, letters were handed over with the friendly commentary of the block senior: "Quit writing your wives such doting letters, you dirty Jewish swine! If I read 'honey' or 'sweetheart' one more time, I'm tearing up the letter and you get twenty-five lashes so that your skin will be on fire. You idiots are acting like lovers. You can bet that your wives are cheating on you."

One prisoner received twenty-five blows with a cane because

his stepfather – an Aryan – closed his letter with "Heil Hitler." It was especially interesting in this case that the stepfather's name was Brausewetter, just like the man who got twenty-five blows. The stepson of the Mr. Brausewetter who wrote "Heil Hitler" was, however, a certain Mr. Schmiedeisen. The punishment was really intended for him, while the Mr. Brausewetter who was beaten had nothing in common with the letter writer except the name. When it was realized that a mistake had been made, the prisoner Brausewetter suffered ridicule in addition to the beating.

In his next letter Schmiedeisen implored his stepfather – in view of the sensitive backside of his Jewish stepson – to avoid any hint of a political belief . . .

The stepfather had naturally thought that the Hitler greeting would have won the special good favor of the camp management for his stepson.

Except when letters were held back as a punishment, something that fortunately did not occur that often, the mail functioned on a regular basis so that at least we were spared the terror of uncertainty. Mautzi wrote in detail and always so cleverly that her letters were always handed over and never shortened. Many prisoners went without mail for weeks. It would be held back or passed out after being severely trimmed with scissors due to suspicious appearing expressions. A few got only a fraction of a letter from home, a narrow strip of paper with the words: "Greetings from your wife."

From the end of our first month in camp, we had Sunday afternoons free. The prisoners were allowed to walk along the broad camp avenue. There, for a few hours, a flood of human beings moved back and forth. On the one side of the street were the Jewish barracks, on the other, the Aryan housing blocks. But in the middle, the inhabitants walked in pairs, arm in arm, and spoke from their hearts to each other about their pain. Most of the conversations revolved around letters from home. Although anything much more than "I'm healthy and doing well" could only be hinted at, it was possible to read things in some letters that gave an impression of the atmosphere in Austria.

Naturally, a circle of those seeking comfort formed around the prisoners whose letters passed through the censorship in spite of explicit hints. When Mautzi wrote that she had absolutely certain assurances that we would see each other at the end of May, everyone clung to this date, a date that spread with lightning speed as the day of liberation. No one bothered to ask: "Why at the end of May?" Although May had just begun, cheery faces were everywhere. The men almost delighted in their work and put up with the kicks and blows with equanimity. For the few days left, we'll survive.

I twice fell into the hands of guards eager for a little conversation and both times they left me alone only after I was lying unconscious on the ground. They thought I had had enough. But I got up again after a short while and continued with my work.

Gradually a group of men gathered around me whose slogan was "Hold out at all costs." I was finally able to win over Willy Kurtz for this motto. I egged on Willy's athletic determination and convinced him of the efficacy of a peculiar method of working in a kind of sportsmanlike rhythm and adopting the correct breathing technique. That gave meaning to the work. Willy recovered slowly, especially now that the food had also gotten better. We were now able to purchase extra items in the canteen with the money we received from home.

We could hardly wait for Sundays when we could exchange the contents of our letters and analyze and interpret every sentence. In this respect I sometimes took on a certain culpability by consciously making false statements, yet by doing so, I imparted strength and motivation to my comrades and prevented some from taking that last desperate step. In the final analysis we needed hope more than anything else, literally even more than nourishment. When I saw what a tremendously calming effect Mautzi's letters had on all my comrades, I finally began to distort their content by reading things aloud that weren't even in them. The end justifies the means. In fact, these "Reich-letters" gained a certain renown in the camp. When mail call had passed, delegates from every barracks came to my room. "What does your wife write?"

Mautzi's letters were themselves full of hope that made me strong and confident. I, however, became ever bolder in elaborating them with my own fantasy's images. And I read these additions to the comrades around me with such aplomb that no one doubted their authenticity. "Hans met personally with Gauleiter Bürckel who told him verbatim: 'They'll all be home in the summer.'"

May had already turned into summer but they were satisfied when I explained that political events were delaying the examination of the prisoners' documents. Anyway, what difference did it make if it were two weeks earlier or later?

At the end of July we were notified that from now on letter writing would only be permitted every two weeks. The announcement almost triggered a panic. That had apparently been intended. In any case we were unable to detect any other reason for this blow, a blow that seemed to come down on us out of a clear blue sky. As with everything else, we simply had to come to terms with it and hoped even more fervently that this new torment would also soon come to an end.

"ARYANS" AND JEWS

This is not the place to analyze the concept of "Aryan," that concept used by authoritative scientists of all nations as a racial category. We know, and everyone in the world knows by now, how Hitler and his henchmen understand the term. This understanding is law, even though race researchers are able to prove categorically that an Aryan race neither exists in fact nor as a possibility.

In the Viennese jail, the separation of Aryan and Jewish prisoners was a foreshadowing of what was to come. One evening at the beginning of our internment in Dachau, when we were still together, the Jews and Aryans had laid down to rest when a prisoner, the former police chief Dr. Paul, called for the Aryans to separate themselves from the Jews. A few, very few responded to his call, while most – in robust phrases – made it clear that they attached no value whatsoever to his advice. The popular Viennese whistle-like sounds signifying "Ziag o"[6] were loudly audible as well. The separation was put into effect on the next day on orders from a higher source. There was, however, no segregation at meals or for sleeping arrangements. We still were fed in common, without racial

---

[6] Viennese for "beat it!"

or confessional distinctions, in "Liesl."[7]

Jews and Aryans were separated from one another in their own blocks in Dachau and Buchenwald. At first in Dachau they were left together in work detachments, although gradually, as less and less work was available, the full workload was reserved for the Jews alone. On some days entire block crews were sent back to their barracks. Later, during the very last weeks before the move to Buchenwald, the Jews with no work assignment were allowed to exercise until noon. Most of the Aryans, at least as far as the political prisoners were concerned, worked indoors in the workshops and on the camp grounds. Many were allocated to small work details as capos and vice-capos and didn't work at all.

At the outset, some of the prominent figures, especially among the Austrian Aryans, suffered as much as the Jews at the hands of the block leaders and guards. Most notable in this group were: Dr. Schmitz, the former mayor of Vienna; Baron Stillfried, the commander of the Austrian concentration camp in Wöllersdorf near Wiener Neustadt; Dr. Osio, the Chief Public Prosecutor. The dukes of Hohenberg – sons of the murdered heir to the throne, Franz Ferdinand d'Este – can also tell a tale or two about SS harassment. The murder of Franz Ferdinand had been the trigger setting off the World War. Since the archduke had married beneath his station, his children were not accepted in Austria as members of the archducal family, but acquired only the title of duke. As residents of Vienna or their estates, they were loyal supporters of Otto, pretender to the throne, and peaceful citizens. In Dachau they were almost exclusively employed in the most menial jobs available. These included cleaning the sewers and servicing the latrine carts. As far as I could observe they never gave up their masculine dignity, reacted calmly and with dignity, and always retained their composure.

I also am aware of several Aryans who stayed under the fists and boots of the SS; for example, the Viennese executioner Lang, who in the course of his duties had to execute the murderer of Chancellor Dollfuß. He was tortured with all inmates looking on until he collapsed and died. His aide was killed as well while we

---

[7] In the vernacular, the name for the police jail on Elisabeth-Promenade.

watched, broken on the wheel, even though in modern form; that is, by using the wheels of the small camp train. The attempts to put another Aryan to death by clubbing seem to have fizzled out. The man in question was the above-mentioned Dr. Osio, who in the course of his official duties appeared as the prosecutor in several trials of National Socialists. In my estimation, scarcely a dozen other prisoners combined received as many beatings as he did personally. I never heard him utter so much as one cry of pain. One day he asked the capo who was so maliciously harassing him just why he had it in for him in particular. The capo answered that he had the order to silence him. Several times Dr. Osio lay apparently dead on the ground, but as if by some miracle, he again rose to his feet. It finally seemed to the merciless tormentor just stupid to concentrate exclusively on him and up to the departure for Buchenwald he was left in relative peace. There, however, he fell into martyrdom.

In general, the relationships between Jews and Aryans were no worse than the internal relationships within each group. During free time on Saturday afternoons and Sundays there was a lively parade along the main camp avenue. Aryans and Jews, exchanging thoughts, walked harmoniously side by side.

The Jews were forbidden to go to the Aryan blocks, yet the Aryans could come to the Jews for visits. There existed many friendships from earlier times between the two "camps." With all necessary caution even the political situation was discussed. From the sum of what we read between the lines in many letters we were sometimes able to develop a view of things that, if anything, reflected a truer picture of reality than the depictions in the German newspapers that we were allowed to read. Regular small-talk areas took shape, but I prefer not to mention their focus. It's only natural that old acquaintances and friends banded together and used the opportunity to converse. There was no separation of Jew and Aryan. Everyone had one wish in common: liberation from the dictatorship of the scoundrels!

It was often interesting to observe who all was counted as Jews. We had half-, quarter- and eighth-Jews. Many of these learned themselves for the first time of their Jewish ancestry through the yellow patch they were forced to wear.

Among these were politicians, officers, and scientists. Most exhibited more official characteristics of the "Aryan" race than Goebbels, Hitler, and Ley put together. Even a well-known leader of the Home Guard, one who had belonged to the most radical anti-Semitic wing of the Home Guard, suddenly found himself as a Jew among Jews.

INSIGNIA AND NUMBERS

The groups of prisoners wore various insignia. The so-called "political prisoners in protective custody" to which we belonged wore a red triangle on the left side of the chest with its vertex pointed downward.

The sign of a career criminal was green, while the "175er" or male homosexuals wore pink, and those interned because of sexual relations with a non-Aryan wore a black-rimmed triangle.

Jehovah's Witnesses who were tortured because of the loyalty to their beliefs displayed a purple triangle.

In all the groups except for the last one, there were Jews who always stood out by dint of a yellow triangle as a racial insignia in addition to their group insignia. It was stitched on so that together with the red emblem it formed a Star of David.

Those labeled "anti-social" formed a unit of their own and bore the mark of a completely black triangle. This group consisted of prisoners who had been punished before their internment for asocial behavior such as abuse of apprentices, drunkenness, non-payment of alimony or the like. However, the real reason for their imprisonment was, in most cases, simply "political unreliability."

Later the insignia had to be worn on the right side of our trousers. That was apparently mandated because we often took off our shirts when working in the blazing summer heat. The SS could then not tell the difference between Jewish and Aryan inmates and were somewhat impeded in their activities since they were far more diligent in mistreating the Jews than the Aryans. It turned out, in spite of all racial instruction, that the difference between Jews and Aryans in most cases could only be determined with the help of the insignia. Since the Jew was beaten and tormented because he was

Jewish, it happened that many Aryan prisoners were "innocent" victims when the insignia were not in view. For that reason and in order to avoid misunderstandings, the insignia were sewn on the pants as well.

It was not possible to learn who undertook the division of the prisoners into the various groups with distinct insignia. From a few examples I could only ascertain that it was carried out incorrectly. I had a very good friend who had been disciplined under the Dollfuß government for membership in a leftist political organization but was otherwise entirely respectable. He wore the green insignia of career criminals in Dachau! I met an acquaintance among the members of the asocial group, a former federal official, who had been retired for years. He was classified in Dachau as . . . unwilling to work.

These few examples from my personal contacts do not in themselves represent any kind of proof, but many of the more than ten thousand prisoners must certainly have experienced something similar happening within the circle of their acquaintances. It was considered established fact in Dachau that the camp management did not take the division of the inmates into groups all too seriously. Consequently, the prisoners considered the insignia in no way reliable as a measure of the moral qualities of those who wore them.

Himmler in Person

One day we again heard: "Austrians, form up!" The gate sentry roared the order and everyone in camp who heard it was duty-bound to pass it on by repeating it at the top of his lungs. The prisoners were seated at the noon meal. We were chased out onto the square where roll call was held just as we were, with shoes only partially tied and open shirts. It was only after we got there that we could complete the process of making ourselves presentable. After we had stood there for an hour, a group of about fifty uniformed men moved out from the command center. We prisoners stood motionless. A large gaunt man led the way. As he came nearer we recognized him from his pictures: the Gestapo chief, Reichsführer

Himmler, Hitler's bloodiest executioner, had come to inspect the camp. This was still before the arrival of the very large consignments that brought thousands of new prisoners captured on the streets of Vienna and other cities. At the time we Aryans and Jews together totaled about one hundred fifty Austrians. He seemed cheerful and it visibly amused him and his companions – all high-ranking SS officers – to see the pillars of the Schuschnigg government, as he later called them, "in such splendid formal attire."

At the midpoint along the front line of the ranks of the persecuted – who cringed in terror as they stared into the face of this pale, compassionless, and cynical man – Himmler stopped. He began his speech in his cackling voice, striking the pose of a self-satisfied man: "Austrians, you must realize that from now on you are in protective custody; that is, I intend to provide you with my own special protection." He paused in order to give his followers the opportunity for an ironic laugh. Then he continued: "I make a distinction between four groups of prisoners. First, there are the career criminals who are the most sympathetic. They have committed a murder, a break-in or some other kind of crime, served their sentence, and are here really only as a kind of follow-up cure in order to be 'retrained' for civic life. Most of you belong to the group of political criminals, a category less innocuous. You will experience our protection to a lesser degree. The third group will be the focus of our very special attention. This group consists of individuals regarded as the very scum of humanity and those are the Jews among you. If I now tell you that there is a fourth group which stands below all others, then I may just spare myself any further designation of this riffraff. You will be able to guess that it is the Communists who make up this group."

Accompanied by a detail of SS-leaders he then inspected our ranks. Each one of us was expected to give our name and profession in a loud voice. Himmler acknowledged every report with a scornful remark. He had one prisoner who had not spoken in a loud enough voice tied to a tree. His retinue underscored every comment that was thought witty with raucous laughter. This imposing figure questioned an industrialist why he was in Dachau and got the answer that most of us would truthfully have had to give: "I don't know."

At just this instant Himmler's passionately sadistic facial expression gave perfect expression to the satanic nature of the entire system. For me it literally mirrored the face of Nazi Germany's ruling clique. Shaking with laughter, the German Torquemada screamed: "He doesn't know why he's here! Put him in solitary confinement at once so that he can think about it."

The bigwigs on all sides of him doubled over with laughter. This colossally powerful man had indeed cracked a good one! Cold chills ran down our backs. In our thoughts we took leave of the comrade who had drawn the unlucky card that could well have fallen to any of us. Fortunately, the man in question was a particularly hardy human being who survived four weeks in the hole. Sometimes we even said with bitter gallows humor: "The choice between the hole and camp labor was a difficult one," because after any kind of torture, the victim had to report the next morning for the forced labor detail – if he weren't so mortally injured that he had already been brought to sickbay.

When we came back to the barracks half an hour later, we had just enough time to gulp down the cold lentils before we had to start work again. No one spoke a word. Everybody who had looked into the eyes of that beast was still shaking with terror. Then it was Willy who in his lusty manner found the words that produced a liberating laugh. The old athlete declared: "I predict that this Himmler will easily eclipse that unbroken record of depravity held for centuries by Kaiser Nero."

Free Time

From the day that we arrived in Dachau, the second day of April, until the beginning of June, there was not a single day off. At the end of May new consignments arrived which were then followed by others in June. At the end of June we were given Sundays and Saturday afternoons off. We now even got breaks on major holidays. There was always plenty to keep us occupied during free time, which however bore no comparison with the forced labor. We cleaned our so-called clothes, washed our cloth rags and handkerchiefs, scrubbed the cupboards. We wrote letters and read the German newspapers that were allowed. We thoroughly scrubbed ourselves, something we couldn't do every day.

We were able to go to the canteen, drink a cup of coffee and get a piece of cake with it for 15 cents. When it was raining, we sat in the barracks during free time. Smokers stood in the doorway because smoking was forbidden inside the room.

On Sunday afternoons the most famous Austrian cabaret artists – Fritz Grünbaum, Paul Morgan, and Hermann Leopoldi – would perform. The Berlin dancer Kurt Fuß also took part. Just like in better days or on New Year's Eve, they went from one tavern to the next with their sketches and gay recitations – that is, in this case, from barracks to barracks. The performances weren't really permitted, but neither were they forbidden. That too was entirely consistent with the Dachau method. Neither the performers nor the audience could ever abandon themselves to the pleasure of these fifteen-minute sessions since they always had to be prepared for disruptions by the SS. At first, these shows only took place in the Jewish quarters since the artists – all Jews – were not allowed to enter the Aryan blocks. It required the lengthy and friendly persuasion of several block seniors before the four bards of "German" humor dared display their art in the Aryan block and cheer up their tormented comrades there as well. It did come to the attention of the SS, however – such treachery did happen – and one Sunday, a narration in progress by the comical Grünbaum was brusquely brought to an end by the sudden appearance of block leaders. All of the Aryans in attendance were written up and reported. Fritz Grünbaum seemed as pale as a sheet – his face even turning a shade of green in our barracks – but apart from the momentary fright he suffered no further repercussions.

There were also Sundays when we were not able to enjoy our free time because the hour of roll call had been very cleverly left unclear. It was suddenly announced – sometimes for 2 PM, sometimes for 3 or even 5. All of a sudden, the announcement came: "Roll call, line up!" We then had to quickly pull on our clothes and shoes and rush to our spots. This uncertainty was particularly unpleasant for those who wanted to use their free afternoon for a nap. The bed was off limits during the day, but with a rolled-up shirt under the napper's head, it was possible to arrive in the land of dreams in spite of the confusion that reigned in the rest of the room.

Block and Room Seniors

The camp consisted of large barracks that were consistently called "blocks." Every block included four "rooms" or living quarters – two of these rooms shared a washroom and toilet. The room itself was subdivided into a day room and a sleeping area. Each day room had six tables. Inmates took their meals here, wrote letters in their free time, or played checkers or chess with pieces they had made themselves. All card games were forbidden. In the day room or dining area there were lockers or small containers where – according to a precisely mandated arrangement – the hand towels and dishcloths were to be stored as well as bowls, plates, knives, forks and spoons, drinking glasses, toothbrushes, clothes and shoe brushes; and, at night, our clothes as well. We also stored there the small items we were able to buy in the canteen like bread, sausages, and such things. There were 50 to 54 narrow beds in the sleeping area of each room. Every inmate had his own bed, together with a thin mattress, a pillow, and two blankets.

A block senior, also called sergeant, supervised the barracks. The four room seniors were called corporals. All five were Aryan inmates, even those in Jewish blocks. Before my time, Jewish prisoners also supposedly served as corporals and sergeants. The block and room seniors were responsible for the order in their area and, since every infringement was severely punished and those in charge fared badly as well, they were extremely careful that the inmates kept scrupulous order.

As far as their lives in the barracks, the fate of the inmates was largely dependent on the character of the room and block seniors. In every block, a member of the SS – the block leader – was in charge of these "non-commissioned officers" who had been recruited from the inmate population. In his own squad he had the rank of a mere private, but here he was lord and master over life and death situations. I'm not sure if it was a plus for his career if he mistreated prisoners or even killed them, but it certainly didn't do him any harm. There were block leaders who inspected their barracks daily and always found something to criticize. Sometimes it was a bit of toothpaste on the toothbrush that no one else could see with the naked eye, sometimes a speck of dust on the locker that even the most careful room senior completely overlooked. It was just like during forced labor that when the block leader had his eye on someone, even if he were among the most diligent and orderly inmates, he was ultimately unable to escape one of the most feared camp punishments.

The sergeants and privates, all political inmates, were basically decent human beings and good comrades. But there were also some among them who carried on just as terribly as the SS. That can be explained. Some simply behaved in insane fear of the block leader's brutality that naturally was aimed at them at times. Others, who had been imprisoned for years under the threat of bestial punishments, had themselves – with the many horrific role models – become beasts and found pleasure in sadistic cruelty. During the six months that I was in Dachau, there were, as far as I know, five inmate deaths due to mistreatments handed out by room or block seniors. The guilty parties were arrested and removed from Dachau. We never found out where they ended up, perhaps in other camps. As I was to find out, however, Dachau was – in comparison with Buchenwald – almost a paradise. Yet at the time we still didn't know that and so we took it to be hell on earth.

The Capo

After roll call the work units were formed up. Some toiled away inside, some outside the camp. Every unit had a capo and, depending on its size, one or more vice-capos. If a capo had a reputation for dealing halfway humanely with the prisoners in his group, then being assigned to him was naturally in great demand. On the other hand, the greatest of fears was to be under a capo who was known to mistreat one's comrades like the highest level of supervisory SS-officers did. In camp the block leaders were the direct superiors of the capo. Outside of camp we were guarded by

SS-sentries with weapons ready to fire. Bayonets were, of course, already affixed to the rifles. Besides, the work parties both within and outside the camp worked in areas that could be sprayed with machine gun fire from the guard towers.

Each in accord with his own character, the various capos treated inmates quite differently, although they all had exactly the same tasks; that is, to keep us working at the most arduous and rigorous pace possible, to allow us no breaks, and to prevent any communication between inmates during these hours of labor. They were themselves obliged to impose the most severe punishments on offenders; report them, for example. At least for newcomers, it was a matter of luck if you were assigned to a good or a vicious capo. In time you realized, this luck might be corrected, if you had the means. The assignments usually took place in the morning after roll call. Because deaths or sickness took a constant toll on the make-up of units, their numbers had to be augmented daily. It was natural that many tried to curry favor with those capos who lived like normal prisoners outside work hours in one of the Aryan blocks. Those who were particularly fortunate found someone on good terms with their assigned capo and who was able to act as an advocate when they were in danger of being reported.

I have met all types of capos and learned the hard way about them. When I came to Dachau, there were already 2500 inmates, some Aryan and some Jews. The transport I arrived with brought about 100 Aryans and 50 Jews from Austria. The barracks were finished, but within the excavations for the camp, there was still much work to be done on the paths, roads, and garden sites indicated in the building plan. The concrete buildings were demolished and the concrete slabs piled up in a mound. On the south side of the camp there was another mound. It consisted of topsoil that had allegedly been brought here from Romania during the World War. I had no opportunity to check this claim. At first our work consisted of using pickaxes to take out the concrete from the old buildings being torn down, loading the blocks on wheelbarrows that were then wheeled several hundred meters further by other comrades. It was hard work that demanded a lot of strength, but because of the continuous bullying by the capo and block leaders, it also put a tremendous strain on our nerves. We only gradually got used to the constant noise during the hours we worked. With the full power of their voices chaotically intermingling, block leaders as well as capos bellowed almost without interruption. That was apparently in order to show the devotion with which they carried out their duties to the higher-ranking SS-guards who suddenly appeared on the scene. At times the ongoing verbal abuse was accompanied by physical abuse. In this respect there was the greatest variety imaginable. Mostly when SS-guards or block leaders were nearby, the capo would burden a prisoner with such a load that he was incapable of lifting the pushcart, let alone moving it from the spot. "Filthy Jewish pig! So you're trying to get comfy!" – That or something similar was the lead-in to punches or kicks. One time when I vainly exerted my not-insignificant powers to budge a pushcart from the spot that was loaded with 150 kilograms of concrete blocks, I got a blow to the neck that knocked me senseless for a few seconds. When I came to, I felt a pain in my jaw – I was missing a molar, and another one is still quite loose today.

As already mentioned, there were decent as well as mean capos. As soon as SS-guards came into the area, they began to roar with all their might—"Get to work! Don't loaf! Cheer up! Cheer up!" – out of fear that they themselves might be collared. That was not at all meant to encourage us to display good spirits but in camp dialect, simply: "Quickly, quickly." It took a while to get used to the hellish noise that gradually faded as the SS-troops moved out of earshot. Apparently some capos had had very bad experiences and no longer took any chances. They seemed to suffer permanent hysterical seizures as they bellowed unremittingly the craziest absurdities over our heads and into the world at large. Some of them, who were basically good-natured, felt the need to explain their lack of comradely behavior. Once, after he had bloodied me with blows on the approach of a block leader, a capo said to me: "My friend, I only wanted to draw your attention to the fact that that bastard was sneaking up on you." He perhaps could have managed that in a more delicate manner, but that the punch turned out worse than intended didn't make me any angrier with him.

Individual block leaders attacked the capos just as viciously as the prisoners. They kicked and beat them until the poor devils – in order to save their own necks – finally lapsed into such bestialities as those employed by their commanders.

There were also capos who misused their status by extracting payment in return for gentler treatment. There were even set fees cleverly levied that often gobbled up a great deal of the money sent from home to prisoners intended to enhance their simple diet. The common preamble to such an attempt at extortion – the block leaders had very similar methods – was a command from the capo to a comrade just about to collapse: "March, march – double time!" Only very few athletically trained young men were up to this unreasonable demand. The others could do nothing more after indescribable suffering than literally to pay the ransom. The capo never ran this miserable business by himself. A go-between would appear one evening at the bunk of the mentally and physically despondent victim, collected the fee, and the "unfriendliness" of the capo ceased just as long as the fee was promptly paid. It was often the case that the capo himself profited little from this toll since he had to pay off the senior capo who had entangled the entire camp in a network of corruption. The capo's reward consisted simply in being allowed – by the grace of the senior capo – to function as a capo. The following case proved to me that the channels of corruption reached up into even higher levels:

One day I had been so knocked around on the work detail that I fell unconscious that evening at roll call. That same evening a capo in the barracks found me and, as a humane act, he said he wanted to help me. The next morning during the formation of the work units I was simply to attach myself to his group; he would take care of everything else. In other words, he would put things in order in my old unit. No sooner said than done. My new unit was assigned a light outdoor job. For me, however, it was one of the worst days in camp. The "boss," a low-ranking member of the SS, personally took over my introduction to the new job. He ordered me to move a heavily loaded wheelbarrow at double time and with his whip lashed my pus-filled fingers still festering from an earlier injury. The infected wounds burst open. The wheelbarrow slipped from my hands. The "boss" lunged at me, drew his pistol, and roared that I was refusing to work.

I had already become completely apathetic and was slumped

over. A kick in the head left me unconscious. When I woke up, the capo stood in front of me, wrapped me in his woolen vest and promised to rescue me from the hands of the "good-natured but somewhat temperamental 'boss.'" From then on I paid a weekly contribution to the capo and had my peace and quiet.

What especially gave me pause about the situation was the following episode: I didn't quite know how and where I should make my first weekly payoff installment. We were all under constant surveillance, and long-term comrades maintained that the place was crawling with spies. The capo said he would arrange the desired opportunity. In point of fact, he called me over to the toolbox in the afternoon and whispered that I should let the money drop into it. Since I had seen how the "boss" had hurried after us and observed all of our movements, I didn't dare follow the capo's instructions. I later found an opportunity to slip him the money undisturbed. He asked me: "Why didn't you give it to me in the workshop?" Quite truthfully I said: "The 'boss' was watching us the whole time." – "Oh well, he . . . ," he let slip, "you still could have given it to me."

My suspicions were given further validation on the day the camp commander summoned us all and asked if the SS-storm trooper Theuringer – this was the "boss" – had demanded either money or cigarettes from us. Quite naturally, no one responded and the "boss" remained in office, his dignity unscathed.

At the end of May and the beginning of June when the transports of Jews rounded up during raids began to arrive, corruption took on virtually grotesque forms. I can only imagine how it must have looked after the days of the pogroms in November! At the time in the early summer of 1938 a kind of market developed which offered the assignment to the various labor gangs at fixed prices. I don't know how far up this organization reached. I only know that one day nine capos with heads hanging down were led to the place of execution behind the brig where they were given 25 lashes for bribery. Somewhat later even the senior capo was removed when 200 Marks were found in his locker.

The Most Malicious Beast

We were all accustomed to the magnitude of inhumanity and sadism in the behavior of the capos and SS, but one man easily eclipsed all the rest. Sterzer, a gray-haired, fifty-year-old man, was Herculean in build, radiated an imposing vitality, and represented the pinnacle of depraved bestiality. He had served a sentence of several years for incest. The humorists among us guessed that he had come to Dachau for a follow-up cure. The camp leadership believed he was capable of anything and was the choice to carry out the most horrible and bloody sentences. He performed these with gusto and enthusiasm. For him a simple murder was not sufficient to slake his thirst for blood. Just like the buzzard thrusts its talons into the body of the field mouse and revels in its helpless distress, so Sterzer liked to dispatch his victims into the beyond by stages. For this he needed no other torture instruments than his own murderous hands. He used only his own steely hands to crush the bones of those unfortunate ones whose murder he was assigned. Once in Sterzer's talons, the chances to escape with bones intact were not great.

He was the capo for the work unit "gravel pit." Those sent to Sterzer were mostly those whom the Gestapo had "unofficially" given a death sentence. Although many died in there, Sterzer was never called to account. He was master over the life or death of all those condemned to the gravel pit by the block leaders' direct superior, the report leader. This gravel pit was a sandy basin and its only use was as a trench where murders could be carried out. The worst thing that could happen to a prisoner was to be assigned to Sterzer. If we can even talk about conscience when talking about this beast, then it must be said that he had many dozens of human lives on his conscience. Most of the suicides in camp occurred in connection with the assignment to the "Sterzer gravel pit." The scoundrel's daily output was a mosaic of cruelties. The inmates he attacked left the workplace, if at all, as cripples. When the report leader made the labor assignments and pulled out a prisoner from the special task force – the designation for the prisoners not assigned to a permanent work unit – he pronounced sentence – "the gravel pit" – with a kick for good measure. As the unfortunate victim walked off, the sympathetic eyes of all his comrades followed him.

Sterzer was unusually creative in coming up with heartless acts that afterwards couldn't be verified. For example, once while whinnying like a horse, he tripped a comrade in the process of pushing a heavily loaded wheelbarrow and sent him together with his burden careening several meters into a ditch. He would often give a prisoner a violent shove, throwing them against a sharp strut or the frame of a cart. Officially, the episodes were labeled "on-the-job accidents." When the number of accidents in the gravel pit grew too large, the rumor went around in camp that an investigation had been initiated against Sterzer. Once we even heard that he had been taken to the "tree." But, in fact, everything remained the same and Sterzer continued to command the "gravel pit." He was simply an indispensable requisite in the camp's torture chamber. It was also occasionally rumored that communist Aryans wanted to pay back Sterzer's crimes in kind by burying him alive in the gravel pit, but that remained a rumor, unfulfilled in reality, notwithstanding its laudable intent . . .

Alongside Sterzer's unmatched bloodthirstiness, at least two other vicious capos deserve mention. Their names were Zock, from Hamburg, and Bertl, from Bavaria. Either directly or indirectly, the deaths of many prisoners fall on the shoulders of this shameful trio.

Confinement Hysteria

But in critical times many capos proved to be great support for the prisoners under their supervision. My capo was a wonderful human being, a good comrade. From time to time, however, with no hint of change, he would terrify us. In a near frenzy he began bellowing loudly and, in doing so, adopting the impoverished vocabulary of the SS, sometimes committing violent excesses. These excesses arose like fits of aggression, subsided quickly; afterwards he took great pains to make us forget by displaying a special affability.

A well-known Viennese psychiatrist who belonged to our

room contingent explained to me this kind remarkable mental transformation as a kind of hysteria brought about by the extended restriction of the sexual drive. Our capo was a strong, healthy man, not over forty who had been in camp for four years! My comrade with the expertise further explained that these fits of confinement psychosis and hysteria were relatively seldom occurrences due to the systematic addition to the camp food of certain chemicals that helped diminish the sexual drive.

I remember that Major Segrave, the holder of the world speed record, defined the art of race car drivers in his book *The Lure of Speed* in the following way: to utilize 99.9% of the motor, but never to go beyond that last fraction of a percent since that meant death. Camp inmates were also forced to control this balance on the scarcely perceived breadth of a fraction. They were poised between life and death. It was a tightrope walk of tautly strained nerves because it was the nerves that decided in most cases. Whatever situation you encountered, you had to keep your nerves in check if you wanted any chance of emerging with your life or without crippling injuries. How few were able to fulfill these requirements!

A murderous scoundrel might suddenly appear at a group work site. Those with weak nerves forgot their firm resolve, lost their heads, and lowered their guard. Stored-up knowledge acquired through thousands of bloody experiences was forgotten. It was not unusual for a man collapsing under excessive work demands to implore the guard to go easy on him. Mortal fear came gushing out of him: "Think about your own father. I have a wife and children at home and have committed no crime – why are you torturing me to death?"

How often I have witnessed this right next to me. The "result" was, without exception, always the same.

"Aren't you dead yet, you filthy bastard. Trying to get comfy, are you? Don't want to work, do you, you parasite? Get up, you dog!" And then the kick that perhaps took the last spark of the slumping man's will to live; the kick brought this "conversation" to its end and was often a precipitous death sentence.

I often thought about what this country would become, a country in which the young grow up being schooled for "life" in this way. For six years the youth has been raised to regard Jews as mortal enemies and to show them absolutely no mercy. But "Jews" is only a code word and anyone, even an entire people, can be declared Jews or communists. The same hatred, the same murderous lust then applies to them.

The world may well believe that Nazi hatred is only toward the Jews. But the Jewish blocks in the concentration camps are by no means the only areas where aspiring murderers train. That's one of many Nazi lies. Non-Jews or so-called Aryans, make up an immense majority inside as well as outside the concentration camps. I'll never forget my first impression as a new arrival in Buchenwald as the thousands of seemingly Aryan walking corpses passed by me.

WILLY'S BRIDE

Several weeks had passed. My friendship with Willy had become even closer. Everyone was as familiar with the stories of each other's life and loves as he was with his own. If he ever again won his freedom, Willy had vowed willingly to be fettered by the bonds of marriage. He had made my philosophy his own by not agonizing over how he would earn a living, how he would construct a new life in a foreign country. The main thing was to stay strong and healthy and everything else would take care of itself. And he asked me again and again, if I believed – based on Mia's letters – that she was the woman he could make happy. I knew the story about how they became acquainted.

Mia Petersen was a foreigner and, at the time she met Willy, a language teacher. He liked to be seen with this elegant woman and it wasn't long before he hired her as secretary of his art gallery office.

I have to admit that I always had an aversion to Mia. She always seemed calculating to me. It flattered her to be seen in the company of this man who was conspicuous because of his massive build, a man moreover who wasn't stingy with his father's money and darted from one amusement to the next.

I put some distance in our relationship and met with Willy only at meetings of the sports association on whose board we both served.

Fate had now brought us back together again and mended our broken friendship . . .

Mia's letters glowed with such warmth that I apologized to her in my thoughts ever to have doubted her feelings for Willy. And she turned out to be a woman of incredible competency in business matters. With the help of Willy's aides and with documents that Willy's attorney obtained by intervening with the camp administration, she was able to rescue the valuable art gallery from expropriation as well as get Willy's house and its sumptuously furnished living areas signed over to her name. With passionate vows of undying love she suggested to him in her letters that he need not have any worries about the future.

One day Willy was called to the camp administration where he met for a short time with a lawyer who had just arrived from Vienna. This impressive woman had even been able to manage this. Willy was allowed to speak only a few words with the lawyer but he learned that Mia – with the help of an SS officer – had secured the entirety of his significant fortune and had safeguarded their future together.

Willy quieted down, recuperated both emotionally and physically until he finally took camp life as a transitory experience – like I did myself – an experience from which we would emerge prepared by this adventure and made even more sensitive for the joys of life by the suffering we endured.

One thing that led to an ever-closer friendship with Willy was that we both belonged to those few in camp whose inmost nature stayed basically unchanged during the long imprisonment. The suffering that weighed on every wretched one of us here induced a tension that heightened sensitivities. But we all functioned from the core attitude of showing mutual consideration for each other by smoothing over everything that might lead to anxiety.

The Execution

One day during lunch we all heard: "All Austrians, line up!" We had just shoveled the first spoonfuls of our favorite food, baked peas, into our grumbling bellies. And now we had to abandon everything and line up. "Everybody line up, just the way you are!" someone bellows in from the door. The room senior shrieks: "Get out, get out!" The barracks is empty in a flash and now we are standing in front in two long rows. "Nobody move!" One prisoner's shirt hangs out of his pants, another has only one shoe, a third is barefoot. I had pushed a piece of bread into my pants pocket that I was now secretly crumbling to pieces with my fingers and sticking into my mouth. I glance around and see in the movement of others' jaws that I'm not the only one whom hunger has driven to the point of risking twenty-five lashes.

Terrified faces, trembling figures everywhere. What's up this time? Will there be punishment exercises for all Jews or mandatory standing naked outdoors with arms raised? Or maybe something even worse? The block senior will know for sure. Somebody dares to ask him. He clears his throat, then declares momentously: "We have to attend an execution." – The word "execution" is whispered from ear to ear. "What's that?" someone asks. "The end for somebody," someone else calls out louder than he had intended. Those standing a bit further away heard only the word "end" forced out in a horrified murmur. A cold sweat breaks out on the ashen brows. We're still standing here. The command to move out hasn't yet been given. Since there's no block leader in sight the men begin to exchange opinions.

"Maybe they'll shoot every tenth one of us!" somebody calls out. Now there's a sudden back and forth in the ranks. Everybody tries to figure out if he is the tenth man. "What's going on you idiots? Stay in your positions!" In spite of that, Grießer leaps two spots away from his position. But at this point the others won't allow him in the row. A scuffle arises. In the meantime there is a new announcement: "Four men are to be flogged and we have to observe." And then a moment of silence. "Ranks, right face! In lockstep, March!"

Agitation again arises in the ranks on the way to the square for roll call. Everybody tries to figure out which row will be in front on the square. The worst thing would be to stand in this row where you'd be forced to have the horror happen right before your eyes without being able to turn away or hide behind the man in front of you! Now we've arrived at the square. There's no longer any moving from your row, come what may.

Our detachment stops and faces the entry building. About fifty SS-troops stand across from us, motionless in full battle-ready uniform: steel helmet, submachine gun, ammunition belt, and knapsack. They stand stock-still like tin soldiers. There is dead silence on the square. Suddenly we hear the sound of military footsteps. A group emerges through the gate of the entry building: two men in front with fixed bayonets and two behind. Between them are the four wrongdoers. Four poor human beings upon whose backsides the bullwhip of the hangman's assistant will rain down in the next quarter of an hour.

I envy those who are standing in the second row where the view of these sadists' disgraceful acts is obstructed. My gaze is directed straight ahead and I nod off into a semi-somnolent state and convince myself that I will be able to look without seeing. The group with the "poor troublemakers" now stops between us and the fifty SS-troops move into place. The old Katzenstein who is standing next to me prays: "God keep you from feeling the pain!" The *Sturmführer* opposite us had either heard the words or the loud "shh!" that followed them and peers over at us. At the same moment, however, a signal reverberates from the tower of the Jourhaus. The camp commander Kögl appears to witness the flogging personally.

He stands in front of us and addresses those present: "These four pigs are guilty of a criminal violation of public order and therefore are ordered onto the trestle. Each one gets twenty-five lashes on the backside. If he screams he gets ten more. And, let me add that every one of you who looks away or moves the least bit will be pulled from the row and brought up onto the trestle as well."

Now in plain sight of men who had experienced four years of war's miseries and atrocities a quarter of a century earlier, the most appalling things take place that their eyes had ever seen, their ears had ever heard. Four trestles are set up. They are similar to those pieces of equipment off which we vaulted in school gymnastics. On each of the four trestles one of the victims is strapped down, his tautly stretched backside turned upward.

At this point the block senior Lüdtgemeier picks up the bullwhip. The first flogging begins. The other poor devils have to wait right beside the first for their turn where they can hear the moans of their tormented comrade.

I pray to God that He blocks my senses of seeing and hearing and numbs the sense of feeling in the victims. I believe that the thousands who were ordered here to witness this disgraceful event have only one fervent plea: "God, punish those who have committed such sins against you!"

Lüdtgemeier raises the whip for the first blow. Deep inside, I feel as if my heart wants to stop beating. My cheeks get moist. I berate myself: "Don't let yourself get weak! Every lash has to become a call for revenge."

And now the first stroke comes slashing down. Motionless, I glance at *Hauptsturmführer* Kögl, the gallant Hitler officer who stands in front and to one side of me not twenty steps away. His grimacing face reveals boredom as well as lust. A sound reaches my ear that sets my teeth on edge. I understand for the first time in my life what the expression "set my teeth on edge" really means.

The cries of pain that the agonized victim ejects are like those of a dying animal. The sound resembles neither a moaning nor wailing, but rather a lament sent to heaven for the gates to open . . .

Blow follows upon blow, endlessly! God has heard my prayer. I stand like I had been turned to stone – I neither see nor hear anything. My fixed gaze remains on Kögl who stands there with a ghastly-contorted face, letting his clenched right hand swing in rhythm with the whip. I allow my gaze to wander. I see the young men in the SS unit behind the trestles. I search in vain for a spark of compassion in the eyes of a single one of them.

The nightmare finally comes to an end. The humiliated sufferers are cut loose from the trestles. No, but not yet! Something is happening on the trestles that we can't immediately comprehend. We are incorrigibles who still believed that a spark of humanity existed in the breasts of these beasts! Kögl devises yet another apotheosis of this pagan festival: "Pants down!" he commands. And the *Hauptsturmführer* convinces himself with his own eyes, as he goes from backside to backside, that his executioner Lüdtgemeier has performed proper German work. The pathetic rear ends of the tormented victims are bloody shreds of flesh. He shares a few pithy words with his troops, then gives the appropriate military commands, and with a dashing "Heil Hitler!" the festival comes to an end.

We report back to the barracks. There is still a quarter of an hour before our afternoon work detail. For many of us hunger numbs every other feeling. Some lunge at the peas that have congealed to a cold mush and cram the stuff down. Most of us have lost our appetites, empty our mess kits into the garbage can and scrape our containers clean with wooden scrapers. No one says a word. Language doesn't suffice to express what five thousand detainees in protective custody have just witnessed . . .

Then Willy breaks the silence. "The whole thing reminds me of the words of the painter Liebermann who in 1936 answered someone who asked how things really were in Hitler Germany." Several called out at the same time: "What did Liebermann say?" "He said: 'No decent human being in the Third Reich can eat as much as he would like to throw up.'"

Physical and Emotional Suffering

The almost total inability to exert any influence on our own fate, the impotence in every situation, was the most dreadful evil of this confinement. Added to this was the searing pain of uncertainty, a pain that never abated, about the duration of the imprisonment. On top of this were the ignorance of the political situation and the uncertainty about our families at home, who – like the prisoners themselves – dared hint at feelings and facts only with extreme caution.

Those of us who had not brought inhibitions of tradition and culture with us from our home lives had an easier time of it here. Easier, that is, than those who were ashamed of responding to nature's calls and other personal necessities, things normally considered private matters, as showpieces performed in plain view of others. It was for many quite simply an agony to use the latrines where they felt stripped of all human dignity. On such occasions there were even some who would tie a cloth around their eyes in order not to see that they were being watched.

The censorship of mail was no less a difficult trial for the nerves. Letters had to be written so that the uneducated SS-censor found no reason to make deletions – at least not of anything of any consequence – but, at the same time, so that loved ones might infer what the prisoner was feeling and seeing.

Subject to all this, an inmate could lose his equilibrium. And there were only very few who, despite these influences, could remain essentially unchanged. Among those in my immediate surroundings who were imperturbably decent fellows, I counted Willy as well as Leo and Otto. There were many others of this type with whom I seldom came in contact, however. During dangerous moments while working or on other occasions when it depended on a word or a gesture to get off the hook on someone else's initiative, they demonstrated their solidarity as comrades.

How pleasant the difference was between men like these and scoundrels like Tischreiter, once a political leader, but here in this setting practiced a mean-spirited petty thievery against his comrades. As buyer for the canteen he trimmed off portions of the purchases in order to procure a kind of buyer's commission for himself. The famous Dr. Withalm is an example of another more lethal scoundrel who for months spied for the camp administration and had the death of dozens of our comrades on his conscience.

There were groups formed in which like-minded types joined forces. They sat together at tables for meals and knew how to arrange it so that they were deployed in the same work parties. In this kind of circle each had knowledge of the others' entire life story. Each in his own way would narrate quite objectively certain stories from their married lives. Only very few knew how to restrain themselves and keep from burdening the others – who had their own worries and anxieties – with their own concerns.

All of us lived in constant fear of death for ourselves as well as our loved ones at home and each, according to his character, was distrustful, irritable, or pretentious. Many collapsed under the pressure on nerves and emotions. The cases of men going mad or committing suicide multiplied.

Among the most horrible occurrences in camp life were, as we called them, the cases of "miniature delusions of grandeur." All prisoners were in charge, by turns, of room supervision. On his appointed day, each was responsible for the cleanliness of the room. This unimpressive and transient rise in rank had a curious effect on some prisoners: they imagined themselves elevated over the others, roared at them without reason – as if they had suddenly become SS-thugs themselves – merely to show, "I'm in charge now!" It was this kind of prison madness which often had the worst consequences. Because, if this yelling reached the ears of a block leader or an unpleasant block senior, he would naturally want to know what was going on. And at that moment the disaster had already occurred since the little Napoleon who had caused the ruckus – wielding his broom like a field marshal's baton – was now on the spot and had to explain the reason for his loud display of outrage. And he was unable to reverse himself even though he had become aware of his despicable act at the last moment and reported sheepishly that X or Y had not straightened up his space adequately.

Then the punishment followed, twenty-five lashes or a forced march with full equipment or standing outside for half an hour with scant clothing and arms raised, always at the whim of the camp leader. And each of these punishments could lead to infirmity or death. Sometimes, while the detainees were in the room, someone would call out: "Watch out!" A block leader had appeared. It was a matter of course that he would glance into this or that locker. The fright made the timorous shake all over. In this situation I often saw horrid things take place. I often saw how, with lightning speed, one man would reach into an adjoining locker and exchange his own dirty mess tin for the brightly polished one of his neighbor or how an edible leftover saved from lunch – always forbidden – would be stuffed into the pocket of a comrade's shirt hanging by the window. What a cowardly scoundrel who, by such wretched means, saved himself from peril by placing his comrade in exactly the same danger.

An Examination of Conscience

Whenever I was by myself and had soberly reviewed my situation, it became clear that I had to face the fact that I probably would not leave the camp alive. The murderous desires of the SS young men who in general were not yet eighteen years old demanded new victims daily. For one of them to decide that he would get rid of one or the other of the prisoners was tantamount to a death sentence. He could then only be saved by accident. No one could count on clemency! How often was I a witness! Wolfstein, for example, an old man over seventy was afflicted so severely with gout that his shovel fell out of his hands. "What's going on?" the guard had yelled at him. "Are you rebelling, you old criminal?" "Have a bit of compassion. I'm over seventy and have grandchildren as old as you, officer. God will reward you." A blow with the rifle butt was the boy's answer and the old man, a pleasant, helpful comrade, had suffered for the last time.

"When will it be your turn?" That was the question everyone asked himself when this happened. I asked myself as well when I witnessed such shockingly nefarious acts. Often the murderer had not yet reached manhood. What would such a world be like in which such acts went unpunished? "Is this what the future holds?" I asked myself.

But such despondent moments passed quickly. Could I allow myself to become weak when I was the mainstay of so many others? No, such godlessness could not stay unpunished. The day had to come when the people would realize that they served a crazy man, that they had sworn an allegiance to the devil against God. Only God could save the world from dehumanization!

I didn't dare pray. I hadn't prayed since I was a child. Yet, I was religious. My prayer had been my joy and jubilation in passing through God's glorious natural wonders. And now? Was I supposed to pray that God allow human beings to become human beings again? What crimes must they have committed that such a penance was imposed on them? What strength and faith it took to persevere and not to leap into the camp graveyard. One burst of fire from the machine gun tower and it was over.

But somehow I was able to sustain my hope and that of my comrades. I devoted every free moment to this project. But it was difficult to infuse these exasperated and devitalized men with the courage to face life. How were they to bear this kind of life any longer, especially the old and sick?

Over and over I agonized over the question concerning the wrongdoing I must be guilty of that I had to undergo such things. I examined my life. Was I made to walk upon this path to that Calvary of abuse and debasement?

What evil had I committed for which I now had to suffer and atone for? I searched through the stages of my life. I had married against the wishes of my parents and those of my wife's parents. Mine learned only at the end of the War that we had gotten married at its beginning. The reconciliation, however, came at this point. My parents accepted Mautzi as a daughter, and her mother lived with us after the death of her husband. If I'm being made to suffer for this, then I must bear it without being remorseful. If fate again placed me at that point where I met Mautzi, I would choose no other path.

Two latrines were put up at one end of camp. When we sat tightly squeezed next to one another, there was room enough for fifty of us. And there were ten thousand who at daybreak all had to do their business within a quarter of an hour. The punishments were horrific when someone, driven by the desperate urgency of his needs, responded to nature's call at another location. A place at the latrine was fought for with fists. At times it happened that someone fell into the human waste and drowned.

That was the day's start. Then it was the labor with all its horrors that originated in the mood of the SS-guards and their notion of work. Then, the camp punishments, the meager nourishment, the lack of water for cleaning and drinking.

When a prisoner got bad news from home, was it any wonder that he made a quick end of it? For what reason should he still hold out when a loved one at home died, someone for whom he had born all previous abominations?

In the Nursery

At the end of May the Austrians were put to work for the first time outside the boundary fence of the camp. Willy and I were lucky. We worked as gardeners planting medicinal herbs. Marching there was like a dream. For the first time in months I saw people at liberty walking on paths, peasant men and women in the fields, and children playing. Bushes were in bloom and flowers grew on the edge of the meadows.

On the "plantation" our job was to pull weeds from the beds by hand. In long human chains and equipped with rakes we were then instructed to turn the soil. The air was delightfully aromatic. One of my tasks was to take all the uprooted weeds on a cart and unload them between the hedges. The guard paid no attention to me. Escape was out of the question since a threefold cordon of guards surrounded the plantation.

My companions sought me out not only during free time but also during work hours. They seemed comfortable with me. They strengthened their own resolve through the example of my confidence. And I became stronger knowing that I had their trust. Yet when I was alone, I often lost hope for liberation. I frequently brooded about things that brought me to the limits of reason. I plunged from the expanses of belief into those convoluted regions of superstition. It tormented me that I was unable to transform my meditations into words. I believed that I myself was not capable of finding the path to God's ear and called upon the deceased to serve as my intercessors. When I was alone at work or lay awake at night in spite of a leaden weariness, I felt closer to the dead than the living.

I tortured myself by trying to project the images of Mautzi and the children onto the dark recesses of my imagination. I was never successful. I perceived only blurry likenesses that misted over ever more quickly the harder I tried to capture them.

In contrast, those I loved and who were already gone – my father, mother, and my son Heinzi – appeared on my inner eye in idyllic, yet eerie clarity. The apparitions were often of such vibrancy that I forgot my surroundings while I stood there holding a shovel. The tool fell out of my hands and, to the horror of my comrades, I rested with folded hands, my gaze pointed heavenward, in a kind of ecstasy. These were moments of enormous danger. If an SS-guard had seen me! But that never happened, and so I believed more and more that I stood under God's protection.

Amazingly, I was gradually able to establish contact with the deceased. They became so clearly and consciously visible to me that I had conversations with them. I set them around a table in a room in our old residence where they had felt so much at home, and I let them enjoy themselves at their games listening to the jokes our father laughingly told while holding his pipe in his mouth. And Heinzi sat on my lap and laughed and laughed . . .

Whatever my comrades might have thought of me when they saw me in my trance-like state, one thing was certain: I was capable of shifting my consciousness to a point which allowed me to tolerate the martyrdom and debasement with composure. I stood at the gate between this life and the afterlife.

Labor as Food Servers

Willy and I have jobs as food servers. That means that we have to be finished with washing up and making our beds by 4 a.m. and be standing ready at the corner of the barracks with the large eating buckets until we hear the command: "Food servers, front and center." Then it's double-time to barracks 1, the staging area for the food servers. Willy and I carry one bucket, Tschatschan and Leo the other one. An icy wind blows across the square that we have to cross, the square where roll call is held. While crossing we can cast a glance at the only clock in camp, a clock gleaming from above the gate to the Jourhaus. It's ten minutes after four. It's getting brighter in the eastern sky. In front of the stairs to the kitchen we are ordered to stop. There's a nervousness hovering over the column of food servers, an anxiety triggered by the proximity of an SS-guard. We can hear the cooks yelling from the kitchen. The roar is transmitted to those in charge of overseeing the column of food servers. They're yelling as well. Thoughtlessly. They're screaming something that even they don't understand. It's true. A block leader appears. He hears the attendants yelling and goes on by. If they had been quiet, he surely would have stopped us.

I stand absorbed, watching the rising sun. I scarcely sense the kick of the guard who advises me that I have missed the command to resume the march.

There is an earsplitting mix of chaotic noises in the kitchen, mostly the loud rattling of the eating buckets and the roaring of the cooks. It is intended to demonstrate to the block leaders on duty that even picking up the food is no pleasure for the prisoners. They spill hot coffee over the fingers of the food servers, let the heavy buckets fall on their toes, kick them in the backside with their heels, and with diabolic shrieking, they strike at them with the ladles when coffee spills. Willy and I look at each other knowingly but without saying a word: even this they can turn into an excruciating experience! We're happy when at last we are on the camp road with the full coffee urns.

Our escorts are yelling again. A full urn weighs about 110 pounds. It's no easy task lugging it 300 paces at a march tempo as was demanded of us. Here and there someone's strength gives out. Tschatschan suddenly loses his grip on the urn because the sloshing coffee is scalding his hand. A stream of the precious liquid pours out onto the ground. A passing block leader lunges at the poor man and hits him in the face. Willy, Leo, and I now carry both urns. As the strongest of the three, Willy marches in the middle, helping carry both urns, one with the left hand, the other with the right. Tschatschan walks alongside, bloodied and whimpering with pain.

In the barracks the coffee is portioned out, again accompanied by shouting and yelling. The food servers take the empty urns and, in double time, head for the kitchen. Again we are forced through a cordon of kicks and a tirade of obscenities. Then back to the barracks at an even faster tempo. Those picking up the food don't have the opportunity to take even a mouthful from the rations container before moving out. The drink can only arouse melancholy memories of the breakfast coffee at home. But it's warm and you have something in your belly.

Instead of drinking the swill in camp I often chose a cup of cold water to go with my morning snack. "At least then I know what demands I've put on my belly," I used to say when Leo wanted to force me to drink something warm, "whatever it might be."

"What is that, actually, that they call coffee here?" Willy once asked. That set off a lively exchange of opinion. Lebak, who had already been in camp for five years and was considered an expert in these things, declared: "You all know that even in normal times everyone joked about German coffee. It was called 'floret coffee' and was made by pouring hot water over a coffee bean hanging on a thread. And in Austria, where Viennese coffee enjoyed an international reputation because of its quality, no one could comprehend why a German housewife was not capable of serving guests the same good drink. Now here at least we get a halfway enjoyable white coffee on Sunday, right?" His joke sparked a booming laughter.

"Don't forget one thing," Lebak continued, "whatever we call our beverages here, you must certainly notice the taste they all share. That comes from the addition of bromine given us to settle our nerves – or, more precisely, to suppress our sexual drives."

Willy interjected: "One of our comrades told me what happened last Sunday in barracks four. They also were given a similarly nondescript swill to drink for breakfast. And when they had tasted it, the guessing game began. 'This milk coffee is not bad,' one of them said. Another one replied: 'Don't talk such ridiculous nonsense, that's tea!' A third one: 'Have you lost your mind? This cocoa is not bad at all!' Hearing that, the server found an answer to the puzzle by roaring out into the room: 'Who wants another serving of soup?'"

This technical discussion about the chemical makeup of what was served here under various names (yet always found lacking in the quality of its taste) threatened to buoy up the room's mood to the point of joviality. But with a single command everyone again became conscious of the melancholy present, when they heard the voice booming though the camp street: "Fall in for roll call!"

Harassment

In the Austrian army there existed a class of so-called "replacement reservists" who did only eight weeks of service and were therefore treated contemptuously by the regular military troops who had at least three years training. When the "replacement reservists" were issued uniforms, it sometimes happened that the sergeant would push a cap down to a soldier's ears. The inductee was only then able to exchange parts of his uniform that didn't fit when the racket and fuss of the outfitting process was over. That wasn't the case in Dachau.

The complicated mechanism of oppressing the detainees also took into account their clothing and laundry. In general we received a shirt, handkerchief, and five pairs of socks on Thursdays – we got a pair of underpants every second week. But it often happened, especially on hot summer days when a change was most important, that the laundry didn't get there on Thursday. In that case we received a change a week, sometimes two weeks later.

It might occur to someone that such a detail isn't worth mentioning since, after all, what meaning can a change of clothes have in Hell? But I'm writing from the point of view of the prisoner who feared torture, yet who was not so worn down by it as by the perpetual, unrelenting torment of the harassment during every moment of his day. This ordeal was targeted at fraying our nerves, removing the last spark of our will to live, filling us with apathy, transforming us into victims of the apparatus or to suicide.

Even the day of the laundry exchange had been cleverly chosen. After a hard workday we were naturally happy to sink down onto our stools and eat a meal that could barely be called modest. Then we heard: "Shirt exchange!" So we had to get up again, take our shirts off, fold them in the prescribed way, and hand them over. The same thing happened with the socks. Then we got a laundered shirt. Most of the shirts were too small – they were boys' shirts. There was no point in protesting, a response that could at best lead to unpleasantness. How we came to terms with this ingenious idea was up to us. Some had to slit the back of their shirt just to be able to slip into it, while others kept their old dirty shirts that they had fitted to their bodies by an arduous combination of patching and string. Whoever got a shirt that more or less fit was a winner, since the next night he need not worry about the small but not insignificant problem of turning a boy's shirt into a man's. It needs to be said that besides this shirt we had only a thin tunic protecting us from the weather – we had wind and rain in abundance. The shirt naturally served as our nightshirt. Since there were frequent laundry inspections, this shirt had to be washed continually and dried at night. This caused many excruciating hours, especially in Dachau's cold spring and autumn nights – I was no longer there during the frosty winter. The poor quality of the shirt material was often so flimsy that it fell apart in the laundry and all attempts to repair it with thread and needle were in vain. It was finally possible to patch up the shirt's holes, at least it seemed so. But then one of us would try to crawl into the garment and it would fall apart again. Only those who have experienced it themselves can understand how unsettling and nerve-racking this desperate battle against the perversity of an object can be – which was of course the perversity of our tormentors. Punishment threatened the offender if he wasn't able to sew up the rips, but what could be done after all attempts had been for naught? I often saw men collapse mentally or physically in making such efforts, men who had previously stood up heroically to the most painful ordeals and the most profound degradations.

After a man had practically worked himself to death and still wasn't successful, he finally gave up and left it to fate to determine if he were to remain unchallenged or not until the next laundry exchange or if he would have the good fortune to get hold of a shirt that fit tolerably well. He would climb into bed still trembling with tension and exhaustion.

For most, the unfamiliar hard labor with shovel and pickax led to the formation of blisters and, since we weren't able to spare our skin, to painful suppurations. The most serious inflammations occurred on the arms and legs in places where the shirt or pants rubbed against them. Profuse and acute swelling developed. We found an explanation for this in that our clothes were made out of synthetic material that elicited infections oozing pus. In sickbay these swellings were treated with alcohol baths and, in many cases, surgical procedures. Amputations were not unusual. For example, it happened to two of my friends, the Viennese journalist Felsenburg and the art dealer Kende: one lost his right arm, the other his left. Less extreme interventions were carried out in sickbay. The patient was slightly anesthetized and, after the operation, pushed out the door. Some were still so dazed, almost unconscious, that they fell over and had to be carried back to the barracks by their comrades. This is the reason why a man would think twice, even if he had serious suppurations, before asking for help in sickbay. Mostly, we preferred to leave it to God and nature and it turned out that this method was more successful than that of the incision-happy Dr. Eisenberg in sickbay. Many of my comrades in Dachau lost an eye through maltreatment or physical injury while others had either a hand or foot crippled in an on-the-job accident. Even if they were to attain their freedom again, they would remain a Dachau cripple their entire lives.

"REPORT FOR INTERROGATION!"

The block clerks were detainees, Aryans whose task it was to keep records of the number and names of the prisoners in their blocks, to deal with those inmates who had been ordered – i.e., authorized – to see a doctor, to implement expenditures, to expedite the mail, to ensure that those convicted were punished and the like. The instructions of the camp administration to individual detainees went through the block clerks. They were free of labor on the campgrounds or in the rooms. They made their announcements after reveille at 3:30 a.m. or at the first assembly at 5. The notifications were always tersely expressed: "Detainees X, Y, Z, report to sickbay; detainees A, B, C, report for interrogation." A guessing game immediately began among those who were to report for interrogation: "But why?" It often happened that they were ordered to hearings regarding punishments without any forewarning about what they might have done. They learned about the accusations against them only from the camp commanders. In most cases it was a matter of a claim made by the block leader in which he had determined during an early morning inspection that: a blanket had not been folded completely according to regulation; there was a spot on a pillowcase; or the rations container hadn't been sufficiently polished; or whatever else had occurred to him. Once he found a tiny bit of toothpaste on a toothbrush although the owner of the toothbrush hadn't used toothpaste for weeks. Anyway, what difference did it make? The "offense" was secondary. The punishment was the important thing. Even today I do not understand the psychological process that invariably drove these vermin to cover up their addiction to sadistic torture with a flimsy wrapping of "legal" reasoning. They were driven to find fault, even though they were able to punish whomever and however they wanted without this fine distinction. Often during these notifications there were name mix-ups that made it clear that it was all a matter of formality. In this procedure, names were of no importance at all. There was not the slightest possibility of attempting a rectification. After all, it was always assumed: one Jew is no different than the other, and they were all culpable. Thus it really didn't make any difference – except for those concerned, of course – if Maier or Meyer suffered. For the SS-masters it mattered not in the slightest as long as someone was punished. In this courtroom there was no difference between guilty and not guilty. This so-called hearing had no purpose other than bringing a bit of diversion into the monotony of daily torment of their prisoners.

Those ordered to appear formed up in front of the Jourhaus and God forbid that they dare move a muscle. Suddenly an SS-guard appeared and with great emphasis blared out superfluous instructions. Finally the presentation to the camp commander began, often after hours of standing at attention.

When his turn came, each prisoner took leave in his thoughts from his loved ones, because he knew – as we all knew – that at this point anything could happen. One might be informed, cynically and without any trace of compassion, that his wife had died. Another, sentenced to twenty-five lashes, would return to the barracks, deathly pale and shaking his head. He had no inkling what crime he had committed. Still another man returned with a smile on his face, since he had merely been asked to sign some document and he now nurtured the hope of soon being set free. Some who had been written up days ago at work brought with them the sentence: "One hour bound to the stake." They bore it calmly because they had been prepared for it since their notification, and only a miracle could have saved them. Your life and health hung in the balance when you had been ordered to such a hearing.

A personal experience illustrates what else could take place at a hearing: I, too, was called up and stood one evening, ninth in the lineup in front of the Jourhaus. It was pouring down rain, so it's easy to imagine how I looked when I was summoned after six hours of waiting.

"Are you the Jew Reich?"

"Yes sir, *Herr Hauptsturmführer*."

"There's a registered letter for you from Vienna, family matter."

"Yes sir, *Herr Hauptsturmführer*."

"The matter is of a very personal nature."

A cold sweat had broken out on my forehead. I knew that just a few days ago how, with serene barbarity, one of my comrades had been told of his mother's death.

"You wretch, if you ever get another such letter, you'll do disciplinary drilling until you bust a gut. Dismissed!"

By giving him a look that expressed my complete wretchedness, I tried to move the brute at least to one further remark but just this short second of faltering after the command "Dismissed!" had sufficed to spur the block leader posted at the door into action. He dispatched me out of the door with a frightful kick in the back. The doorkeeper, a prisoner, stood at the foot of the stairs. He assumed my further dispatch outside through the main house door with a further kick.

This is the way that the "hearings" were conducted.

To this day I have no idea whether a letter for me had really arrived, whether it was, in fact, a registered letter, let alone what its content might have been. In any case, I wrote home that no one should send me registered letters.

WÖLLERSDORF AND DACHAU

When the theme of the concentration camp is up for discussion, the highest leaders of Nazi-Germany love to point out that the English invented this institution during the Boer War when they let women and children go hungry in such camps and thereby forced the Boers into capitulation. This lie also gives them the opportunity to underscore their own chivalry since there are only men in German concentration camps.[8] Let me interject that in my experience this includes males from the age of 14 to 84. The

---

[8] This was still 1938.

Nazis also point out that there was a concentration camp in Austria under Schuschnigg, in Wöllersdorf near Vienna – geographically more correct – near the Viennese suburb Neustadt, about 50 kilometers from the city proper. The National Socialists based a lot of their propaganda on the sufferings of those interned in Wöllersdorf who were sympathetic to National Socialism. Everyone held there was adorned with the aura of a martyr.

But there were not only Nazi prisoners interned in Wöllersdorf. Austria's leftist parties also contributed a large contingent to its population. It so happened that there were many former Wöllersdorf internees in Dachau, Social Democrats and Communists who had already suffered under the earlier regime in Austria for their convictions. They had become acquainted with that actual Wöllersdorf – depicted by the Nazis as an inhuman hell – where people had been starved and tortured. I have had long discussions with those prisoners held in both camps. I emphasize that these former Wöllersdorf internees had no reason to remember the past tinted with rosy colors. They had been opponents of the former regime, just as they opposed the present one. They had been imprisoned by the former government just as they were by the present one. They can surely be regarded as reliable witnesses. Their feelings towards the earlier regime were understandably not of a charitable nature.

Every one of them agreed that the inmates in Wöllersdorf were seen and treated as political prisoners. None of the numerous and, to some extent, prominent Social Democrats had ever been maltreated in Wöllersdorf. With very few exceptions, meat was on the table every day, and vegetables and soup were there in abundant amounts. There was no forced labor at all in Wöllersdorf. The inmates were responsible only for keeping clean those bedrooms, living areas, and courtyards that they used. In contrast, the labor in Dachau belonged to the worst example in all the history of slave labor – quite apart from the abuse. Those incarcerated in Wöllersdorf knew none of the cruel camp punishments that claimed so many lives in Dachau. There was no physical punishment in Wöllersdorf at all.

From time to time the Wöllersdorf prisoners were able to have visitors from home, and the mail exchange was unlimited. At this point the Nazis would probably make the objection: "Of course, that's the way the leftists were treated in Wöllersdorf, but we were truly martyrs. We were constantly abused." The assertions, however, of those who served detention time together with the Nazis in Wöllersdorf custody are at variance with this view. They unanimously substantiate the standpoint that even the Nazis were never mistreated and never used for hard labor. During the entire time that the Wöllersdorf camp existed, not one single fatality occurred as a result of abuse.

That, of course, had no effect on the fact that the Dachau-SS had received instructions to take "revenge for Wöllersdorf." It is easy to imagine what martyrdom Baron Stillfried, the former commander of Wöllersdorf, suffered. For a time we were forced, shoulder-to-shoulder, to tow in quick time the heaviest laden carts imaginable. I was thus witness to much of the abuse he suffered, as well the dignified and stoic manner of his heroic response.

To our amazement – and certainly even more to his own – these added abuses suddenly stopped one day as if on command. From the end of June until our departure from Dachau, Baron Stillfried was spared any further excessive brutalities.

Tantalus à la Nazi

There is a certain group of prisoners in camp who, at least emotionally, are better off than all the others. These lucky ones are aware of their release date. The rest of us are here for an indeterminate time. The legal underpinning for sending this group to a concentration camp is contained in the Reich's forced labor policy. The alleged reason is asocial behavior, but for everyone here it's crystal clear that we have been incarcerated for political reasons. With only a few exceptions, the forced labor policy prisoners are Aryans. I've spoken with many of them to learn about the reasons for their internment. Most of them point to a public denunciation. It is often the case that a rejected girl friend was at least able to vent her unrequited feelings and get revenge on his "arrogance" by betraying him to a friend in the SS or SA. And how! She would be proud of herself if she only knew. But maybe she does know because the terror of the concentration camp paralyzes all of Germany with fear and prevents what otherwise would have long ago set off an uprising of decent human beings. In today's Germany anyone can get anyone else hauled off to a concentration camp if one only knows how to go about it. And not just a few do know how.

As a rule, the "Reich's forced laborer" – Ye shall know them by their words! – is sentenced to one year of concentration camp. He is even notified formally of this in writing before his internment. But this more or less exhausts any advantage that he has over a normal detainee since the length of detention is only partially binding – the Nazis often ignore it. The way the camp commander increases the length of the sentence is again characteristic of the diabolical nature of the entire Nazi system.

During my confinement I worked together several times with forced laborers whose discharge was imminent. They were naturally elated, indescribably happy in their expectation to be free once more, since compared with camp life, the conditions under which the rest of the German population were forced to live could almost be called freedom. On the day prior to their discharge we all took leave of those being released. Our verbal gesture on this and similar occasions was: "Take care, comrade!" And we all knew what should and had to be taken care of. Powerful handshakes accompanied the pious wishes. If the detainee about to be released was a poor devil, we took up a collection and pooled our pennies so that – at least for the first few days – the long desired freedom would not be spoiled by the growling of an empty stomach. It was often the case, however, that we saw a comrade – his face etched with stony despondency – report for work duty the next day, the very one whom we had taken leave of the day before. Instead of handing him his certificate of discharge, he had been told that he would have to remain for another six months in camp since his "behavior as a detainee had been less than exemplary."

This heinous act could occur in an even more refined form. Instead of the prisoner himself being informed, a letter was sent to his family members who naturally were anticipating his discharge with as much trepidation as the prisoner himself. In this letter the camp administration informed the family that the prisoner's behavior had been so terrible during his confinement that he had been sentenced to another six months. The prisoner was never told until the day of discharge that he would have to remain in camp. He then learned of his "offenses" from his loved ones at home. In reality the people had, almost without exception, conducted themselves perfectly well, even in the face of the arbitrariness of the camp's "administration of justice" which reflected absolutely no sense of decency. It expressed the hidden agenda of some powerful authority or perhaps simply someone's wish to slam the door to freedom, a door already ajar, in the poor devil's face.

Gradually the word about this methodology got out, and one can imagine how it affected the mental state of the prisoners. We had envied them so; their plight seemed so much better than our own, but now they too waited with great foreboding for their release – mentally already at home with wife and children and preparing themselves for their homecoming when suddenly – all hope collapsed for what had seemed certain. This is the demonic nature of Nazism.

Rauneke's Suicide

It was one of those unusual, quiet evenings. We had eaten our soup, washed ourselves in icy water, and now we were sitting around the tables feeling like human beings for a few minutes. Ludwig declared: "Today was a peaceful day." But then he realized that a block leader might by chance walk by. He knocked on the table and said: "Knock on wood."

Rauneke, a fish merchant from Hamburg, sighed: "Tomorrow it will be five years that I've been detained. They dragged me away from my business like a criminal and didn't even allow me to take leave of my wife and child. If I'm not called to the gate early tomorrow morning and let go, then I'm going to end this miserable life." I tried to calm him down: "You mustn't speak that way, comrade. In time everyone will be set free and your hour will surely come soon. You just told me recently that in the past few months everyone who arrived here at the time you came – except for you – has been set free. Isn't it obvious that your turn is coming soon?"

Everybody agreed with me. Willy chimed in: "I wish that my release date was as near as yours. You have without a doubt been in this living hell for a long time, but you're still healthy and, at forty, still have half your life in front of you. As an old athlete, I can only advise you to exert all your energy and don't collapse short of your goal."

"You mean well," Rauneke says, "but I think they've totally forgotten about me. Either my file has been lost or some Nazi scoundrel has his reasons for keeping me locked up. God only knows!"

Until now the room senior had listened calmly. At this point he too tried to contribute something to the efforts to reassure Rauneke who was staring at the ground in front of him in a wretchedly gloomy way. "Look, I've also been here for four years, and I too have a wife and two children at home in Regensburg. But I haven't a thought about laying a hand on myself. That would be too convenient for our masters if we'd all do away with ourselves – after all, we are the ones destined to take revenge for all the offenses they've committed against our comrades." With a laugh he concluded: "And that would be pure stupidity if I killed myself today and I were called to the gate tomorrow." The entire room joined in the laughing – which, however, didn't sound so convincing.

Willy put his arm around Rauneke's shoulders and shoved one of the bonbons into his mouth that he had gotten hold of in the canteen. Finally, Rauneke also started to smile. The evening signal sounded a few minutes later from the machine-gun towers. Everyone stormed into the sleeping quarters that soon were in total darkness. The room senior called out: "Good night to all of you!" "Good night!" we all shouted back together. "Schema Jisroel adonai elauhenu, adonai echod." ("*Hear, O Israel: the Lord is our God, the Lord is one.*") This was the seventy-eight-year-old Jakob Katzenstein from Frankfurt who every evening begins his nightly prayer with loud singing, then fading into a whimper that clutches at your heart strings . . . Someone in one part of the room calls out "Amen" which is then echoed by someone else, then all is quiet.

Around midnight a cry of horror rouses the exhausted men from their deep sleep. The exclamation had come from Tschatschan. What's going on? The lights suddenly come on.

Tschatschan, an unfortunate crippled and feeble-minded idiot is standing at the door, white as a sheet and trembling as he struggles for words. Sobbing, his body shaking, he blurts out: "Rauneke hanging, our comrade Rauneke dead!"

We all immediately scramble from our beds. Willy is the first one who storms out. Rauneke's body is hanging near the window in the lavatory. Willy lifts him up, then with incredible strength, rips the rope apart. He carries Rauneke like a child in to the mess hall and lays him on a table. Rauneke's body is pale and rigid. As the others stand around in a circle trembling and sobbing, Willy tries to do artificial respiration.

Suddenly, a call from the door: "Heads up! The block leader." The glow of the lights had attracted him. Ranting and raving, the SS-guard walks through the door. "What's going on, you bastards?" The room senior reports that a prisoner has committed suicide.

"Everybody back into bed, you pigs. Don't you know that it's strictly forbidden to help somebody who is trying to kill himself? Tomorrow after work everybody will report for punishment drill."

The mess hall is immediately deserted. We're all once again lying on our bunks. Outside the "homicide squad" takes over. Jakob Katzenstein sings: "May God receive him in peace." And in response, "For eternity, amen."

Fifty comrades lie on their straw sacks unable to sleep. They think about the deceased. He was a good man who kept his suffering to himself, who spoke little, yet was always ready to help whenever he could. A cold wind blows through the window. Here and there a sigh is heard, resembling a fading prayer for the dead. Who would be the next one?

No one was allowed in the lavatory. They had hung the body at the window again.

We lie there for hours between waking and sleeping.

At wake-up call everyone springs up out of bed. And the bed making begins with the normal zeal. The straw sacks are shaken, the blankets rolled up and smoothed out. Even with all the great care taken, there's a sense of rush behind the effort. Everyone's thoughts are racing ahead of their legs. They sneak through the mess hall, stumble at the door to the lavatory, peer through the cracks. Is Rauneke still there?

Tschatschan's bed is not in good order. "Kubelik!" – Max calls the cretin by his nickname. The others pass the call on. Tschatschan was in the mess hall. He has taken handkerchiefs, soap, and shoe polish out of Rauneke's locker. There's even a half empty jar of jam among the items of inherited property. The room senior yells at him: "Where in the world have you been hiding, Kubelik?"

"I took the things from Rauneke's locker so that Grünewald doesn't get his hands on them." Grünewald is camp commander Kögl's deputy whom Tschatschan especially despises. Anybody else in Tschatschan's situation would have been beaten half to death by his comrades, but no one resented the fact that this poor imbecile had declared himself to be Rauneke's sole heir.

The commission from Munich arrives just as breakfast is about to be distributed. Our team has to move out to our work detail without eating. Those who have time are able to pocket something edible, whether it is bread, a cube of sugar, or a cold potato still lying in the garbage from the evening meal.

A Scholars' Dispute

One day two physicians were working right beside me in the topsoil. When there was no SS-guard in the vicinity, they would engage in intense discussions on scientific topics. At times they would throw caution to the winds, and when I exhorted them to speak more softly – since we obviously weren't on academic grounds – it would help only for a short time.

Right before the end of the workday, this scholars' dispute flared up to a volume that didn't seem advisable. I looked over toward them and with horror saw two block leaders – their presence concealed by a small pile of earth – standing scarcely two paces behind them. They apparently had been following the conversation in front of them with great interest although probably not understanding much of its medical implications. To one of them who had turned to face me, I gave a caution sign that danger was looming. But he thought that, just like earlier, I was being overly cautious in sending warning signs and punctuated his scientific statements with clarifying gestures. All of a sudden the guards stepped out from behind their cover and stood in front of the prisoners who had paled in their fright.

One of the block leaders asked: "What are you arguing about? You don't understand shit about medicine. The best medicine for you is a smack in the face."

"You said it!" the other chimed in.

"Come over here and stand facing each other, you two, then give each other his medicine."

The two scientists had to face one another and for a quarter of an hour until the end of the workday, they were forced to slap each other's face. The block leaders bent over with laughter. Wasn't it really just too hilarious how two scholars who had shortly before argued passionately about a scientific proposition now grappled with one another on a concrete basis! And hadn't the National Socialists "arbitrated" differences of opinion in all areas – art, science, and culture in general – in just this same style?

THE LORDS IN THE TOWER

The camp also served as a training area for Nazi troops. The seven machine gun towers were so positioned along the camp wall that there was no unobserved point within the camp. Battle ready, the soldiers took up their positions as guards. They carried their own machine gun up to the tower. We detainees had in the meantime developed a thick outer as well as inner skin and weren't easily impressed. We had learned to recognize, even through the hardest of exteriors, the emptiness of the interior.

An attempted escape or even mutiny – everything, that is, which could have brought about the intervention of an armed response – was totally out of the question here. So the heroic poses of the heavily armed black shirts made an entirely amusing impression on us and we called them plant-watchmen. Besides that, for us they were by far the most sympathetic part of the surveillance team because we were safe from them. They were not allowed out of their towers and bored themselves to tears up there. They found victims for their boredom and some distraction only in the newly arrived prisoners who did not yet possess our experience and disciplined nerves. An experienced prisoner simply ignored any call from a tower. A newcomer, however, when dragging his burden past a tower and suddenly hearing a call from above, would suddenly come to a halt and answer – it was awkward. Most of the time such a dialogue was linked to a series of bodybuilding exercises ordered by the lord in the tower as entertainment. When he thought he had worn his victim down, he let him rest or stagger on and searched for a new one.

We older detainees let the tower owls scream as long as they wanted. We went our way, knowing full well that the lord in the tower could only reach us with his voice. He would just have to wait until someone else could be taken in.

Once I got into a conversation with a tower guard, and it turned out that he belonged to the rarer, more humane variety of SS-members. I at first ignored the calls: "Jew! Jew!" Nor did I respond to "Austrian!" You just had to let tower owls go on shrieking. But when he called out: "Sports journalist!" I was taken aback. The man knew me. How? Who might it be? Cautiously, I got closer. The tower guard then asked me if I had forgotten him. But then all of these SS people look just alike.

The voice came to the aid of my memory: "I was the guard in the railroad car that brought you here." Now that was not an encouraging introduction for me and, although I had learned in Dachau not to betray my feelings, my observer must have sensed my alarm. Maybe he himself realized at this point that the memory of this harrowing trip from Vienna to Dachau could not have been very pleasant for me; anyway, he said: "I didn't do anything to you, sports journalist. I never touched you." Apparently he was an athlete who had learned by accident what my profession was. It may be that I owe my life to this fact – who knows? In any case I assured him that I completely understood his good-natured interest in my plight and moved as quickly as possible out of the range of his voice.

A Little Diversion

We were paired up, working at the sifter. This was the most coveted work location, since the sifter was off to the side, almost hidden by the surrounding piles of sand. We couldn't "be observed by the enemy." My partner too was in his mid-fifties, one of the few Jews who had formerly had a seat and vote in the Austrian National Assembly. Somehow a block leader remembered our existence and suddenly appeared in front of us. He grinned scornfully, since it hadn't escaped him how we had winced at his unexpected arrival.

"Have I perhaps interrupted the Jewish gentlemen in their conversation?"

We did what is normally done in such cases: we kept silent and worked away at an even faster pace.

"Come over here, both of you filthy old asses. Stand side by side and open your traps wide!"

We did as ordered and opened our mouths as wide as we could. The SS-gentleman drew his pistol, elaborately releasing the safety catch and rammed it into my mouth. After he had observed me for a while, he let my comrade taste the pistol's barrel. I stared to my right as well as I could in order to see what was going on. Since I had not heard a new order, I continued to hold my mouth wide open. Somehow I found the situation absurd, but all of a sudden my hair stood on end. I saw and heard how my comrade burst out laughing and knew that something horrible was about to happen. To my amazement the block leader pulled his weapon out of my partner's mouth and yelled at him: "Swine, so you think I don't have the guts to pull the trigger!"

Without batting an eye or reflecting even for a second, my comrade answered: "The guts to be sure, but it would be cowardly to shoot a defenseless man."

The SS-guard seemed to ponder for a moment. I had the impression that he was embarrassed. He jammed his pistol suddenly back into his holster and growled: "Get out of here, Jew!"

Although the command was given in the singular, I quickly shut my mouth, clicked my heels together, turned around and hurried after my comrade. Soon we were again standing at the sifter, throwing one shovelful after the other into it. The block leader left without once turning around.

WHITE RAVENS

It would be unfair if I were not also to register occurrences that point to traces of humanitarian feelings, even in members of the SS. I'm sticking with my own experiences, but take it that other comrades occasionally had similar surprises too. Thus there are also a few white ravens among the many black ones in the SS.

As already mentioned, the labor in the plantation, the large nursery outside the camp walls, was generally not very strenuous. Naturally, that always depended on the mood of the nearest guard. If time seemed to drag and if he enjoyed this kind of distraction, he would set out to entertain himself by tormenting the prisoners to his heart's content.

One day I was unlucky enough to fall into the hands of a block leader who immediately began – as the technical expression would have it – "to get on my case." First, he criticized my working speed. Then he ordered me to load a pushcart with a mountain of gravel and, since I still showed no trace of collapse, demanded that I run, pushing the loaded pushcart in double time. I ran and continued to run away from the monster – directly into the arms of a watchman. He was a young fellow, his pronunciation betraying his Austrian origin. He was standing on a mound of weeds that had been collected there. As I felt my energy draining away, I devoutly prayed that the watchman might not finish up the handiwork on me that the block leader had started. Unfortunately, he seemed not to have heard my pleading. The sentry roared at me: "Lay down on your stomach, you old Jewish swine! Crawl up closer, mutton head!"

Inwardly I once again took leave of my loved ones. I was totally exhausted, my heart was beating as if it was about to burst, and I was drenched in a cold sweat. Following his order I had laid down on my stomach and semiconsciously I heard – probably thinking it was a dream – what the guard whispered to me: "Now just lie there until you feel rested."

I slipped into a leaden slumber from which the guard woke me with the words: "Stand up, old man, it's time to call it a day." The SS-man had woken me up after I had slept for two entire hours.

I had a second experience of this kind while working outside the camp. A watchman near me had twice given me the order to increase the amount in each shovelful of earth. The vice-capo, an Aryan detainee from a provincial Austrian city, called out quietly to me so that the guards couldn't hear: "Let the idiot gripe, just keep working away at your pace." The guard who had noticed something, but didn't really know what had taken place, screamed at the man: "Hey you, why are you chatting with the Jewish swine?" Then he took out his notebook and pencil apparently in order to write up the vice-capo. For a moment he was unsure how he should respond. I used the pause to step forward, standing at attention, and to report: "Sir, it is my duty to inform you that it was I who spoke. I asked the capo if I might not get some water." The guard looked around carefully, then came over to us and said: "Well, after all, you are an old man. You remind me a bit of my cousin. Come here and have a drink from my flask. The other guy, get me some fresh water."

The day was one of the hottest that summer. Each hour four prisoners from our work party were assigned the task of fetching water in large buckets. Yet only the Aryans were allowed to drink out of them. The Jews just had to go thirsty.

Except for this one guard . . . !

THE *FÜHRER'S* SPEECH

One day we were told to gather at 7 after supper on the square where roll call was held. The *Führer* was to speak, and whoever wanted to, could listen to the speech in front of the loud speaker. Whoever wanted to come, could come. Stools might be brought along, and smoking would be permitted. This "whoever wants to, could come" sounded so annoyingly ambiguous that no one believed they could remain in the barracks. So, already by half past six, the square was filled with about ten thousand prisoners who were very happy to take advantage of staying outdoors beyond the curfew and being allowed to smoke a cigarette or a pipe. And of course, no one could care less what the *Führer* had to say.

There was even an "entertaining" opening program – the broadcast of a merry evening at a pub in Hamburg. To thunderous applause and convulsive laughter, the master of ceremonies served up genuine Prussian humor. But the applause outbursts and salvos didn't come from those men who sat on their stools around the loudspeaker on the square – they were truly not in the mood for laughing. No, the chaotic clapping and shouting erupted from the sound equipment itself – it was authentic Prussian.

And the witty MC from Hamburg recounted: "Some time ago, a mountain farmer's wife gave birth to a healthy baby boy. Naturally, widespread happiness accompanied the arrival of this splendid newcomer, the youngest of the *Führer's* recruits. After a week the farmer's wife tells her husband: 'Hannes, why don't you take the baby on Sunday to Hochfröhlingen in the valley so that the preacher can baptize him.' On Sunday Hannes puts the baby, wrapped in warm blankets, into his backpack and walks the three hours into the valley to Hochfröhlingen. It's ten o'clock and Hannes reflects: I don't want to disturb the pastor before noon, so I'll have the baby baptized afterwards. So he goes into a beer hall where a merry group has already gathered for a morning pint and drinks his liter. And of course, after this one, then another. And then another one and still another. Suddenly he thinks about the baby lying in the backpack under the table. He picks up the backpack and takes the little bundle out. The baby doesn't move – he's lifeless. Hannes exclaims: 'You devious bastard, didn't I just lug you down here for three hours so you could be baptized in honor of the *Führer*? Now I have to trudge up the mountain again and make sure that our *Führer* gets a breathing brat from my Hildegard.'"

This marvelous, folksy joke was enthusiastically cheered. As always, genuine German humor is only appreciated on its native soil. The prisoners on the square in Dachau, however, just looked at one another without saying a word. Their faces looked even paler in the glare of the spotlights . . .

The intrepid MC then started again: "Schnulch meets Knulch: 'So good friend, what's going on?' Pleased, Knulch replies: 'Thanks for asking. We had a dual celebration yesterday.' 'A dual celebration?' Schnulch asks inquisitively. 'That's right. In the morning we dug a fine crop of potatoes out of the ground and in the afternoon we put our ornery mother-in-law into the ground.' ..."

The rounds of applause faded away. Were they aimed at the program just over or the one to follow?

And now the *Führer* spoke.

And, after we had heard this broadcast as well, we took our stools and went home. It was only Willy who couldn't control himself. His critique was short and to the point – with as much force as he could muster, he spit out: "Disgusting!"

Camp Punishments

For the detainees a concentration camp is a life of terror concentrated upon them. There were mitigations and escalations. The camp punishments were the terror of terrors. Nobody was safe from them. Complete dedication to the forced labor that often went beyond human powers, the most scrupulous order and cleanliness in the barracks, the most precise observance of all rules – even all this provided no immunity from punishment. The presence of one's own will power could not even be hinted at. Even the most unassertive attempt at refuting accusations of a capo or an SS-guard – mostly pure inventions – was entirely outside the realm of possibility. An objection was unthinkable. Naturally this was true for Aryans as well, only that during my time an Aryan's torments – in all but a few cases singled out for special harassment – were less persistent and intractable.

When the inspecting block leader asked: "Why are you smiling at me like that, you mutton head?" we just had to stay silent – even when nothing seemed more remote to us than to smile at this sadist, quite apart from the regulation that prohibited Jewish prisoners even from looking at a passing SS-guard. This regulation may have been issued so that a look from a Jewish eye might not besmirch the paradigm of the Aryan race or perhaps it originated from a more profound psychological insight. Still a human glance from a subhuman eye could, by chance, fall upon one of these black-clad fellows. But it was precisely stipulated how we were to look away when we were forced to pass by such a barbarous divinity. If it were somehow possible to avoid, none of the prisoners let it happen anyway, since whoever got by with merely a punch or a kick, could count himself lucky. It only got really bad when the block leader "reported" the infraction that he had allegedly observed. That meant certain punishment.

The talent that our torturers had in inventing novel ordeals and traps was just as inexhaustible as it was wide-ranging. Again and again they created possibilities of "offenses" that provided an occasion for punishment. Punishment was the Alpha and Omega of the entire operation. They were successful in turning all of camp life into a permanent state of terror. At every moment we had to be prepared for torture, infirmity, or death. Not for a second could we feel secure, and that was apparently intended.

The water in Dachau was fresh and good. After the hard labor it was very energizing. The cold water intended for washing our bowls and plates was less satisfactory, especially on days when the soup contained whale meat or something similar. The grease formed a crust on the sides of the bowls that was difficult to dissolve and the cold water simply made the layer of fat even harder. The bowl, however, had to be completely cleaned and scrubbed until it shone before it went into the locker. The block leader couldn't give a damn how you got it clean.

Out of fear of certain punishment the poor prisoners came up with the most ingenious ideas. The cleaning had to take place quickly. One waited behind the other at the water outlet. What to do! The bowl could only be gotten clean with a brush. Every remaining spot of grease could mean "twenty-five" – pain, injury, mutilation. Prisoners tried toothbrushes and shoe brushes and I saw a few in their mortal fear who made use of toilet brushes to get their bowls clean. This fear displaces the borders in no small measure between what one considers hygienic and what appetizing.

There was a kind of "procedure," a typical sham or eyewash, to which these sadists, strange to say, attached great importance. Maybe it is an oversized cowardly streak, perhaps merely another documentation of their inferiority complex, but in any case, they try to find "legal" cover for their brutality in empty formalities. They make great efforts and even enjoy finding a "lawful" basis for their coarsest acts of bestiality. The procedure was, in reality, entirely one-sided. The prisoner who had been written up was marched in front of the camp commander or his representative a few days later to be "examined." The examination consisted of the prisoner being charged with his alleged offense, a charge to which he was then to remain silent if he did not want to make matters even worse. Then, a few days later in the evening after work, he was ordered out in front of the Jourhaus where his punishment was meted out.

The Tree

In the language of the camp, being tied to the "tree" meant being tethered to a martyr's stake and tortured. The hands of the victim were tied behind his back and he was hoisted up in the air until just his toes touched the ground. He had to persevere in this dreadful position from one to two hours. During the war this method of being bound up had been the most severe disciplinary punishment in the Army. It was, however, practiced in a much milder form and for a shorter period. There was as well a regulation that a supervisor and, if possible, a physician, had to be present. In the concentration camp, it was not a method of punishment, but of torture. Anyone who saw the human wrecks after this torment – staggering as they dragged themselves back to the barracks with swollen wrists – cannot have had any other thought than unappeasable hatred when he thought of the SS-torturers. The final insult of this ignoble procedure was that following this torment, the victims were forced to drag the "tree" – a kind of gallows – back to the place where it was stored. The image of another tortured Jew who was made to bear the instrument of his martyrdom to Calvary arose in the mind's eye of not just a few of us . . .

A young Viennese attorney was one day ordered to the office of the camp commandant. The *Hauptsturmführer* yelled at him: "You've had communist gatherings at your apartment!" The man asserted his innocence and assured me later that he had never been politically active. Somebody who perhaps had ties to the Party must have denounced him, I thought. He attempted to convince the Grand Inquisitor of his innocence, but naturally he was immediately cut short. He was led away and first tied for an hour to the "tree." After that he was again summoned and asked if he now wished to confess. He declared that he had nothing to confess since he had, in fact, done nothing, and he then received twenty-five lashes with the bullwhip. So it went for three days. Since the victim, however, had been strong enough, and would not make a false confession just to escape the ordeal, the matter was dropped.

In our barracks there was also a landholder of large estates from Upper Austria. He came to me one day, white as a sheet, and asked for my advice. He had just been summoned to the camp commandant Grünewald. At headquarters there was a letter in which a former laborer demanded 25,000 Marks from him as compensation because he was allegedly wrongly dismissed. It's simple to figure out that 25,000 Marks amounts to more than twenty years of full pay for a laborer, but the camp commandant had ordered the man to immediately write home and instruct his wife to pay the laborer the 25,000 Marks. The prisoner asked me what he should do. My advice was: "Pay up!"

Even if he still had money remaining, it would in any case be taken from him in the long run. If they wanted to make the effort to find excuses, the Nazis could find any number of them, but with Jews it wasn't necessary at all.

But the man didn't follow my advice. Instead, he first wrote to his attorney and asked him to find out whether he had ever had a laborer or employee by this name who might now be demanding 25,000 Marks from him. The censor gave the letter to *Hauptsturmführer* Grünewald who promptly sent for the landholder and dictated a letter to him that the landholder then sent to his attorney authorizing him to pay out the 25,000 Marks immediately.

Because he had not followed the first order to write to his wife instructing her to do the same, he was bound to the "tree" for two hours.

In our room we had a very dear and special comrade. Still half child, yet a courageous fellow, his name was Faray and he came from Burgenland. Tall, pale, blue-eyed, he was a handsome man with winning manners that he didn't forget even in this domain. One day the block leader visited the room. We were at work. He pushed Faray's locker open and, screaming, ordered the room senior to write him up for interrogation. What crime had Faray committed? None! He was known as being orderly, and everything in his locker was bright and spotless. The block leader, however, needed a demonstration of the diligence in which he carried out his work and fortuity had decided against the good man Faray. It could just as easily have been someone else. Deeply disturbed but still collected, Faray read the room senior's notification. He knew that it meant twenty-five lashes or an hour in chains on the tree. The thought of either, the fear and terror of it, could curdle the blood in your veins. Poor Faray! Men much stronger than he had been prey to such thoughts. Either the one or the other punishment had been the ruin of many others. How often the black beasts had loosened cripples and the dying from their shackles on the scaffold or the tree!

Faray's sentence: to the tree! And it was to be carried out after work hours.

A sorrowful mood prevailed among the prisoners gathered around the supper table. Everyone's thoughts were with our comrade who, like Christ, was at that moment experiencing the inhumane torture of the "tree." Leo stood in the corner, his face in the darkness, his folded hands motionless. I ran in agitation back and forth in the room, as if I were trying to escape the thought of this Golgotha. Will this weak, delicate youth survive? Some couldn't stand to remain in the room. They waited at the edge of the barracks.

A murmuring approached, the room door flew open. The image that presented itself exceeded their fears. This was Faray? Propped up by two comrades, he staggered toward his chair. What had happened? Had they not gotten their fill of the poor man's suffering until they, for good measure, set the provost marshal's bloodhound on him while he was still helplessly attached to the tree?

Faray's head was a formless mass. The innocent eyes of the martyr blazed outwardly from beneath a crust of blood. But he conducted himself like a hero. There was no cry of pain issuing from his childlike lips. The commotion in the room was enormous. We ran around in confusion like ants. Each of us wanted to do something for the poor man, but no one knew exactly what. Everyone wanted to help the heinously tortured man forget the cruelty that had befallen him by outpourings of love that now surrounded him.

One brought a lemon, another came by with a glass of water, while, in his confusion, a third man handed the nearly unconscious Faray a treasure from his locker, a piece of bacon. The room senior washed the blood off Faray's face with a wad of cotton revealing the waxen face of a dying man.

Faray stammers: "That brutal ape!"

We all know what he means. They not only let the dog of the camp's supervisor loose on the vulnerable Faray, but his vicious ape as well. And just for their "amusement."

We bedded our friend down on a straw sack. "Mother, help me!" he whispered. Then he closed his eyes. Toward morning the room senior heard his death rattle. He went up to his bed. His heaving chest thrust out waves of bloody foam, his face was distorted by pain. The room senior clenched his fist: "Murderers!" And the pale lips of the dying man murmured: "Mother!" – Then he fell silent.

It was a gripping image as the men passed the victim's pallet before leaving for work. Tears welled up in everyone's eyes and their thoughts reached out to those loved ones whose cherished family member was lying here on his deathbed . . .

When the sobbing Willy, who had been bound by a close friendship to his colleague in the Home Guard, stepped in front of the body, he raised his right hand in allegiance.

The next day Viktor Matejka, Hans Schniede, and many others came over from the Aryan barracks to take leave of the deceased . . .

Escape from Purgatory

Suicide was by no means forbidden. Quite the contrary! The block leaders repeatedly offered us ropes and other implements to inspire us to take the step.

The humane advice that we often heard was: "You'll be gone soon enough, you filthy Jewish swine. Do it yourself and you'll spare yourself a great deal." Quite a few obeyed. Just among my good friends there were five who in the first six months in Dachau departed this life by hanging themselves – if the term "life" can even be used for the existence we led. We were able at the last moment to stop a few others from committing suicide. In one case I myself was able to cut the rope just at the most critical point in time. Of course it was strictly forbidden to interfere with a suicide attempt, but we naturally intervened whenever we could, and often with success.

A preferred method for suicide often consisted in deliberately stepping beyond the cordon of guards or the camp ditch. Every prisoner knew that a step behind the chain of guards or a leap into the trench meant certain death. Such an action was taken to be an attempted escape and was acknowledged with well-aimed rifle fire. In the minds of the guards as well as those guarded it was absolutely clear that an escape was unworkable, even unimaginable. There probably was not a single one of us who had not thought of shortening his torments in this rapid manner. On those days of particularly hard physical or mental suffering, death seemed to me like divine deliverance. Only the thought of my wife and children, only my belief in God, and – I openly admit it – my desire for punishment and revenge for these outrageously criminal deeds kept me alive. It helped me as well in comforting others, giving them hope and strengthening their resolve to persevere. I believed that the dictatorship of these scoundrels would soon end, and this thought gave me the strength to endure the most ignoble humiliation.

When we returned one evening from roll call we discovered one of our comrades hanging from the framework of his bed. We were immediately forced to leave the room and wait in front of the barracks until the homicide squad from Munich had assessed the facts. In this case the squad did, in fact, arrive quickly and, led by the camp commandant, proceeded into the sleeping quarters. One half hour later the commandant had us form up. We thought he might perhaps say a few words about the deceased, and I marveled silently that this torturer was still capable of human emotion. He said, however: "When I was in the sleeping quarters just now where the filthy Jewish swine hanged himself, I found a dirty spot under the bed on the floor. So I'm mandating punishment drills for the whole room on Sunday from 1 to 2. Dismissed!"

That was the obituary with which Dachau paid tribute to a man driven to death, and I had believed that this monster was capable of human feelings.

These drills were a collective punishment that was not directed against individuals, but against a group in a room or even against an entire block. It was imposed when a block leader was not satisfied with the overall orderliness of such a group. Such punishment could be tolerable or brutish, depending on the degree of ruthlessness of the SS-guard in charge. The drill took place following our return from work. It consisted of running in place at double-time pace with random commands of "Stand up/Hit the ground" thrown in – a particular pleasure for the SS. But there were no limits set to the fantasies of our supervisor. He could decree that any exercise last for any stretch of time so that a drill lasting for one or two hours might well end badly for older or sickly detainees.

I've already mentioned that going beyond the cordon of guards or stepping into the camp ditch meant suicide and that many chose this path in order to be free of SS bestialities. It was the most reliable way into the afterworld, but there was one person whom it did not lead to this destination. Appropriately, the name of this lucky – or unlucky devil – was Dr. Pechkranz (*literally: bad luck wreath*). He had arrived with the first transport of Jews who had been rounded up at the end of May in Vienna; that is, with Jews who been taken randomly off the street. Until this time in Dachau he had not been harassed any more severely than any of us. He was, like me, fortunate in this regard and had experienced only the normal share of mistreatment and suffering. Punches and kicks – that was commonplace. Just as long as you weren't treated as a "special case," you needn't think of yourself particularly as abandoned by fate – quite the contrary. Everything is relative, however, and all of us had noticed for a few days that Dr. Pechkranz seemed extraordinarily depressed. He spoke very little and even in his free time he kept away from his friends. One night when everyone was already asleep – normally I fell into bed and went right to sleep – he undressed himself, stormed out of the barracks completely nude, and jumped into the camp ditch. A few of our comrades had noticed this insane behavior, but too late. In no time at all the whole room heard the alarm, yet no one dared leave the barracks because we knew that anyone outdoors at this time would be shot by the machine guns in the towers. We waited, our nerves strained with tension, for the rat-a-tat-tat of the machine guns firing, but the shots failed to materialize. The spotlights outside were as animated as usual, yet there was no sound of shots being fired.

To our boundless relief Pechkranz stepped back into the room a few minutes later. But he himself seemed anything but happy. Although despondent, he was highly agitated and his entire body trembled. Part of the reason may well have been the low temperature. We asked and asked until the entire, unbelievable story tumbled out of him. A miracle had happened, but a miracle that he had in no sense welcomed.

He had scarcely left the barracks when the light cones of two spotlights caught up with him and followed him to the ditch. He closed his eyes, jumped and waited for the shots that would inevitably hit him and put him out of his misery. Instead, however, two sentries arrived, pulled the would-be suicide up on the edge of the ditch and gave him a terrible beating. They then asked him for his barracks and room number and led him to the specified address, all the while threatening him with the most dire punishment were he to repeat his attempt. They left him at the barracks door with a parting kick.

Nobody in camp was able to give a rational explanation for this miracle. I'm just repeating how it apparently must have happened.

Unfortunately, Dr. Pechkranz died in Buchenwald in the winter of 1938-39. During a work break as a member of a detachment working outside the camp, he hanged himself.

Sick

When someone got sick, they naturally could not be taken immediately to the doctor. The medical procedures for flushing out phony complaints were strictly followed. If a prisoner had a high fever, an assistant from a first aid station was called in. If he determined a temperature of over 39° C, the patient was sent to the hospital ward. If the patient was lucky he could also be sent to the hospital in an unconscious state – as, for example, with a broken leg or, in general, after an accident that left him in such a serious condition that even a layman could make the diagnosis. In other situations, a patient had to be written up by midday "for hospital," even though he might have gotten sick the previous evening. He was then taken to the hospital around five in the afternoon.

The diagnosis – sometimes a decision between life and death – was jointly made by a member of the SS and the first-aid assistant. Besides being based on how the patient appeared, this diagnosis sometimes rested upon questions put to him. This so-called "commission" decided – and this decision was irrevocable – whether or not it was necessary for a physician to see the patient. If the sick prisoner was given the go-ahead by both examiners, he would be able to go to the doctor on the following morning. There he was treated civilly and like a sick person, but how difficult it was even for seriously ailing, suffering, and desperately needy inmates to get to a doctor! It's evident in the following depiction of my own experience:

At the end of April I collapsed during roll call due to overexertion and the mistreatment I had suffered. Unconscious, I was carried to the hospital ward. Shortly before we got there, I regained consciousness. The first-aid assistant, himself a prisoner, but "established" within the camp hierarchy, asked: "What kind of scoundrel do we have here?" The comrades who had carried me answered: "Fell to the ground, unconscious." "Could have left him on the ground. He would have gotten up again," was the charitable reply. "Get this mutton head out of here!" I was then taken to the barracks. That night I had such a high fever that the room senior allowed me to report to the doctor. On the afternoon of the following day I went to the hospital ward – naturally after forced labor – and got into the waiting line. Consequently, I was witness to one of the "investigations" of medical cases.

First, it was the turn of an inmate who had death clearly written on his brow. The following dialogue took place:

"What's the matter with you, filthy Jewish pig?"

Moaning, the miserable man complained: "An asthma attack, I'm having an asthma attack."

The SS-man replied: "Asthma? I know a good cure. One

hundred knee bends. You'll get better or die. Get out of here!"

The exam came to an end. The sick man was refused access to a doctor.

The next case was a man with a dangerously festering wound that was dealt with even more summarily since the man in his extreme agitation had not reported according to regulations. He received such a kick to the backside that he stumbled toward the door. The next patient was a youngster who reported, rigidly erect and clearly able to stand at attention. The first aid assistant understood in a flash. He said a few hushed words to the SS-man that seemed to contain a magic formula. The man who had not yet even stated his complaint was given permission to see the doctor. During this exam I had retreated carefully back toward the door and slipped away. I left my cure to nature rather than to put it into the hands of this commission. There were many times in Dachau I wanted to see a doctor – you might even say, I was in need of medical help since I had bad fever attacks several times and two severe fainting spells – yet I commended my well-being to God and He saw to it that I survived these times without being hospitalized.

Here I want to make it clear that those comrades who had the good fortune to pass the nearly insurmountable mess of the pre-exam that I've just described – mostly very ill ones – were well treated, in the humanitarian and medical sense, in ramshackle rooms but without racial prejudice.

Willy's Typhus

One day in the middle of June when I returned from work, Leo approached me with a worried look on his face. "What's wrong?" I asked anxiously. "Willy is in the hospital. He seems to have an infectious disease. Fever and vomiting." "I have to go right over and see what's the matter with him. Even a look through the window will tell me something."

And I ran as fast as I could to the hospital. I had to be back in a quarter of an hour since I was a food server. "What's wrong with Willy Kurtz?" I asked the first-aid assistant who was dozing at the window. He looked me up and down without replying. "Is he doing poorly?" Sonnabend – that was the name of this pupil of SS-methods – stepped wordlessly into the background of the barracks and, before I knew it, he had thrown a bucket of hot, dirty water over my head.

I attempted one last method, opened my chemise and shirt, and took a Mark out of the leather bag that I wore. I held it under Sonnabend's nose and snorted at him in a mixture of anger, disgust and fear: "I have to know what's wrong with Willy. After I withdraw some money tomorrow, you'll get two more Marks, but hurry up!"

At that Sonnabend motioned to me to come inside the barracks. Trembling from tension, I walked in and the medic led me in secretive silence into a small adjoining room where Willy was lying in a dark corner. Sonnabend left us alone.

"For God's sake Willy, what's the matter with you? Did Sterzer catch you again or did you run across Kögl?" – The poor man groaned: "No, it's my stomach. I have terrible cramps. They think I'm getting typhus and so they've isolated me here."

"And what is really wrong with you?" – "Shh, not so loud! In reality, I've overeaten horribly. After the punishment drills yesterday I was starving and ate everything I could scrape together in the canteen: three pickled herring and a pound of onions. It was inevitable that that wouldn't settle well with a liter of milk and the four pieces of bread and jam – it all exited my stomach via the shortest route possible. Naturally I let the idiots believe that I was deathly ill. I think I'll be able to rest up here for fourteen days. Will you please bribe Sonnabend with a few Marks so that he'll let some white bread and sardines be smuggled in? Don't worry about coming back, because no one else has dared come visit someone who may have typhus! Don't be afraid – I'm completely all right."

I left the hospital ward in a good mood. "That scamp has the constitution of a horse," I mused while walking back. "And his native wit helps him get past any obstacle. This monstrosity of a man, suspected of being sick with typhus and lying stretched out on a hospital bed, has no other thought than searching out his next food supply!"

DR. BRESS – THE SPY

Just at the time when I myself was relatively safe from the brutalities of the SS, I was faced with difficult problems. There was a German doctor, Dr. Bress, who was suspected of spying for the camp administration. If what my comrades said about him was correct, Dr. Bress was a totally abject character. To me, this dwarf-like figure of about fifty was always conspicuously amicable. The "Doctor," as everyone called him, was one of those who never received any money from home, and I often gave him part of what I bought in the canteen. When the Doctor offered to shop for me at the canteen, a minor – not serious – quarrel arose. It seemed to me to be at odds with the solidarity among comrades for him to offer his services in exchange for a piece of bread and butter now and then. The Doctor believed that I should accept his small favors, however, like washing my bowl or going shopping for me. If he took my gifts without any *quid pro quo*, he would feel like my gifts were alms and consider himself a beggar.

In contrast to my light workload at the time, Willy's situation was miserable. In spite of all his efforts not to stand out, he constantly strayed into the proximity of particularly irate SS-hooligans. He was loaded down with burdens under which he collapsed and was then beaten until he was bloody. As "sport" they forced him to run, throw himself into a pile of dung, and do a hundred pushups. Willy suspected that the "Doctor" had directed the attention of the SS at him.

I decided to put the "Doctor" to the acid test, and coincidence came to my aide. Bress knew how to arrange it so that he was marching next to me the next day as we returned from work. It was a Friday, and he asked if he could talk to me about something important on my next free afternoon. We agreed that between noon and roll call on Saturday I would seek out the Doctor in front of his barracks in order to have our talk.

I wasn't sure what I should make of Willy's suspicion. Up to now Bress had seemed to me to be a particularly pathetic comrade. Earlier, while we were working, he had told me that he had once been a rich man and, as a psychoanalyst, he had had a large practice. He was a Jew married to an Aryan, a woman celebrated for her beauty in his hometown. When the Nuremberg Laws went into effect, she left him, and upon her instigation – as he presumed – he was placed in the concentration camp because of alleged drug dealing. In this way she was able to acquire all of his millions in assets. He had been in detention now for five years and, during this time, had not received a penny from anyone. How terrible for a man who had once lived in prosperity and now had to beg his comrades for a piece of bread!

The next day, as arranged, I went to the Doctor's barracks. Bress began to speak very haltingly and explained that I shouldn't think any less of him because he was under tremendous pressure. I should simply hear him out and then give him some friendly advice.

The Doctor began: "Except for the sad fact – unlike most of our comrades – that I'm not in the fortunate position to receive money from my family, I don't really do too badly in camp. I am, as it were, the secret doctor of most of the young SS-men. I treat those illnesses that they won't admit having to the SS-doctor. The consultations take place in the laundry room in the evening after roll call. Other than the SS-men that I treat, only the block leader of the laundry room knows about these appointments. They've threatened to kill me if I breathe as much as a word of this to anyone else. So I implore you to exercise the utmost discretion in the matter.

But this secret is not the most burdensome one I bear. There's something else even more dreadful, a kind of coercion from which I cannot extricate myself – you're the first person in whom I dare confide. Just maybe you can help me free myself from this bondage because, in the long run, I won't be able to tolerate it."

"I'd be happy to, if I can," I assured him. "What is it?"

"One of my patients is the administrator of the garden area where you've worked before. A totally uncontrollable bastard who gets drunk and beats the hell out of our comrades. As a reward for my successful treatment, he made me his personal valet. I have nothing to do other than keep his blockhouse in the garden area tidy, clean his clothes and shine his shoes, and prepare coffee for his breaks. It's difficult to fill up my days with these chores, so I read books and newspapers in his cabin and occupy myself with scholarly matters. So, relatively speaking, my life isn't bad as far as my physical well-being is concerned.

But there's another facet of my services for this vicious man. He is constantly short of money and insists that I help him out. But since he knows that I don't have any money myself and can never expect any to arrive at mail call, he has shown me a way to acquire the cash for him. I'm supposed to put the touch on the others while guaranteeing them that nothing bad will happen to them in the garden area if they pay five Marks per week. But I'm in big trouble if I let slip that my chief is involved. So, I'm forced to bear the guilt myself for stealing money from my impoverished comrades – money that mothers, wives and family members at home are scrimping and saving in order to make life for us in this hell more bearable! Is it any wonder that for me – whom the others all envy for my light duties – the thought of suicide never leaves my mind? I often think that I can't bear it any longer to be a villain in the eyes of my comrades, and that I could clear myself of this moral blemish only by putting my life in danger!"

"But at least you know that you're accomplishing something for our comrades by getting a return for the bribe you deliver to the thug – which under the circumstances is worth more than the money. In this case where death lurks at every turn, where every SS-guard – whether motivated by a whim, murderous lust, or maybe because he sees in you a mortal enemy – can blot out your existence. It's not, if you consider it carefully, just a trifle that you offer your comrades for their money. Are those whose money you funnel to this shameless bastard, in fact, safe in the garden area?"

"Yes, he keeps his word. He not only refrains from harming a hair on their heads himself, but he's also constantly maneuvering to prevent harm to his charges by vice-capos or SS-guards. Since he ranks higher than any of the sentries, the protection of those in his custody is relatively unproblematic."

"And, naturally, you too are free from any abuse?"

"Well, that's not always the case. When I don't collect enough money, the idiot beats me and threatens to silence me once and for all. He's now been able to get the approval of the camp administration for doubling the number of prisoners working for him. And it's my job to seek out appropriate people for his goals.

From his point of view – that by necessity I must make my own – 'appropriate' above all else in the sense that they are able and willing to pay. The more, the better."

The Doctor had talked himself into an alarming state of agitation and, as he stood there in front of me with a reddened face and despairing look, I felt a deep sympathy for the poor guy who under such dreadful coercion was forced to appear to the most wretched victims of the Nazi beasts as a scoundrel, as a beneficiary of the system.

"Right now you can neither reveal yourself to your comrades nor refuse your chief services as a collection agent of his shameful revenues. But I will attempt, as much as possible and without putting you in peril, to alter your image in the men's eyes from the one they may infer."

"My fate is doubly tragic," Bress continued. "I'm taken, as it were, for a living encyclopedia by the SS. You often hear my name called out by someone, even an SS-guard. 'The Doctor knows everything,' they say. For one, I am expected to write a poem for a girlfriend, for another, explain how to amplify faint photographic plates. For two others, I prescribe remedies by mail for a distant grandmother suffering from hemorrhoids and therapy for a brother plagued by rheumatism. These guys have gotten so used to me that I'm convinced that they would block my release if my turn came up."

I tried to console the poor wretch: "Just like everyone else, your hour of release will come. Can a regime like this, with representatives like these SS-criminals, continue to exist for long? With your connections you have a good chance of surviving this period, and let it be a comfort to you that you are in a position to improve the plight of many of your comrades in camp. The end justifies the means. Apart from all the ethical conflicts that arise for you because of the administrator's financial straits, there is one positive facet: it will inevitably help more prisoners leave Dachau alive. I have only one request of you. Give our comrade Willy Kurtz your support. Try to get him duty in the garden area, and I will see to it that he comes up with the 'fee.' Although physically colossal, the poor guy is at the end of his rope."

After this moving conversation, I walked back to my block

deep in thought. What strange fruits this Nazism bears! Bestiality mitigated by corruption. How wrong Willy had judged this doctor! While he thought that he benefitted from his comrades' suffering, his situation was in truth among the very worst.

Politics and Camaraderie

It wasn't easy for me to talk about politics with Willy because he talked almost exclusively with former members of the Home Guard and closed himself off to those dissenters with whom I liked to discuss political topics.

There were representatives of all of Austria's political parties in camp, which, unfortunately were quite a few: Monarchists, Socialists, Communists, the Clerical Party, the Home Guard group, the Peasants' League, and Zionists. And in each of these groups there were two kinds of men: those who merited respect and those who didn't.[9]

I once said to Willy: "Characters here reveal themselves, just as they really are. In this constantly perilous atmosphere, a human being displays the naked truth about himself to the eyes of others. True honesty discloses itself with just as much clarity as cowardice and base selfishness."

I have seen men with noble dignity and heroic valor collapse under the abuse of the SS: the Christian-Social mayor of Vienna, Dr. Schmitz, the Home Guard envoy Gorbach, the Monarchist, Court Counselor Werkmann who was secretary to the last Austrian Kaiser. Also: the Zionist Stricker and the Socialist Dr. Dannenberg. And conversely, there were others, Socialists and Monarchists alike, who debased themselves by pleading for mercy from their tormentors. Some wrote letters home in which they paid tribute to the Nazi regime, like the German Jew who wrote to his wife about the intrinsic merits of National Socialism. These merits were so clearly expressed in the marvelous camp organization, he declared, that if he weren't Jewish, he would himself profess allegiance to

---

[9] Viktor Frankl always emphasized this difference in his works and lectures as well.

National Socialism. This groveling was even too much for the SS who had been trained in mendacity. The block leader consequently read the letter of this Jewish Nazi aloud to the others.

Consolation

The day the mail came was a holiday in camp. Letters from home let you forget everything bad that had happened during the week. I waited for Mautzi's letters with great anticipation. These not only gave me new strength, but similar messages from loved ones were also the source from which others, sick with worry, gathered new hope. May had come and gone without bringing the liberation that Mautzi had forecast. I had to summon all my skills in oratory and writing in order to demonstrate to my comrades that the examination of the files – as Mautzi wrote – just had to be completed. At that point the releases would occur in large batches. It was not easy to assure them. It was apparently cathartic for those inmates who had languished in camp for many years when they tried to convince the others that they would themselves be released long before the Austrians who had "just" arrived. But I was always able in my "Sunday sermons" on the camp street to rebut those dreary prognoses of our comrades "from the Reich." The Austrian question was one that required special treatment. The Austrian inmates in protective custody had not been citizens of the German Reich before 1938 and therefore could not have broken German laws. And after Hitler's invasion? "It was then that we were arrested," I explained. "At that time we hadn't had any possibility to break the laws of the Reich!"

I myself was not at all so persuaded of the logic of my words because I had clearly learned the hard way that the rule of law had disappeared since Hitler was in Austria. It was almost miraculous what effect my words had on my comrades and how they surrounded me when I appeared on the camp street on Sundays. I seemed to radiate a wave of reassurance. There were ministers, reputable scientists, and writers present who were used to examining closely the words spoken to them. Whether in their state of demoralization they simply could no longer summon the energy to test the content of my speeches or whether – as one comrade told me – they took me for a representative of the priest whose solace they were refused, it was enough that they believed in me and my promises. More and more I was convinced that it was my calling to lighten the oppressive lot of my comrades. In spite of the leaden heaviness in my limbs, I would often lie awake for hours at night trying to think of new ways of saving others from despair. "If summer, then fall and winter would come, what then?" I often thought. "Will God give me the strength to sustain these unfortunate creatures?"

And summer came and then fall. We saw nothing of nature's transformation in the camp. Not one blade of green grass was seen inside the barbed wire fence, nor was the chirping of a bird heard.

New transports arrived from Vienna. They brought people who had been rounded up on the street and in the coffee houses. They had not even been allowed to take leave of their families and were brought directly into the concentration camp. One of my colleagues was among them. He brought firsthand news from Mautzi. She and the children were all healthy, and he had seen them all three on the day I was arrested in front of the house. If he had only suspected that he would be brought here! I was delighted to have such good news. One of Willy's Viennese neighbors confirmed that Mia was running the business and – so it was said – that an SS-officer had helped her arrange things. There was a widespread rumor in Vienna that Willy had died. Mia hadn't received mail for weeks and was thrust into frenzied dismay by the rumor. Willy should immediately write to her . . .

Time passed. It often seemed to me that everything that was now happening had an otherworldly quality. Had I died, and was I now atoning in Hell for the sins of my life? When in the early morning hours this parade of ten thousand ghosts poured from the camp street onto the roll call square, the unfortunate figures seemingly floating free of gravity in the fog rising from the marsh – didn't this image come from another world?

Or when we were gathered in the square around the place of execution where human beings were tied on racks and whipped by the SS-beasts! Oh, the whimpering of those being flogged, suffering and humiliated! And the camp commandant stood there – or was it the devil himself? – braying like an animal!

I absorbed hundreds of these images that appeared to me like visions. And how often a shot rang out in the middle of the night!

Once again someone had been released from his suffering. Every such shot meant that one of those in misery had stepped out of the dark barracks into the glare of the spotlight. The cracking sound of a rifle firing from one of the seven machine gun towers followed instantaneously.

Isolation

One day we were told that our block was to be isolated. We had to return to our barracks immediately where the windows were closed and no one was allowed to leave the block. We were horrified. Then a real panic broke out. Many began to prepare for their departure into the hereafter, and I openly admit that on this day I lived through the most critical moment of my stay in Dachau. To this point I had been able to stay calm in every situation and helped many of my comrades to regain their mental equilibrium. As the word "isolation" was spoken, my nerves failed as well. I had just enough self-control not to deepen the despondency of my comrades. I had enough energy to hold off my collapse until I had reached the sleeping quarters. Once there, I hid behind the beds, but then I could no longer hold myself together and broke down sobbing. I had hit bottom!

After a time I calmed down and returned to my comrades. They were all pale, terribly agitated, and apprehensive.

Why did the command "isolation" stir up such terror?

Others had told us about a punitive isolation that had been imposed on all Jewish blocks six months before our arrival in Dachau. It had lasted three months. The following is a report by one of those affected:

"One day we were told at roll call that untrue rumors about Dachau had once again appeared in the foreign press. This was before the annexation of Austria. Horror stories had been spread. The most slanderous depiction of conditions in the Dachau camp had been published in a Viennese Jewish newspaper where there was even talk of the mistreatment of detainees. The camp administration had decided for this reason to isolate the Jews in the camp until the foreign press ceased publishing its untruthful dispatches about Dachau. Beyond this there was, at the same time, a six-month suspension of releases for Jewish prisoners.

We didn't know then what isolation meant and went to our blocks without being particularly upset. Three months without forced labor was something that didn't seem terrible at all. What SS-excesses we would be spared! We would soon learn how mistaken we were.

A letter was dictated to us that we were to send to all our family members. The letter stated that they were forced to counter the reports of atrocities since these could only make things worse for the prisoners.

An hour after roll call Aryan detainees appeared. They sealed off the windows of our barracks and pasted paper over the windowpanes so that we sat there almost in darkness. The block senior had us all assemble in the main room in order to let us know the further consequences of isolation. We were not allowed to open any windows. Any attempt of this kind would be met with machine-gun fire from the towers. Both the receipt and sending of mail was suspended for the period of isolation. Shopping at the canteen was forbidden as well.

We sat there and could do nothing except wait. Being barred from the canteen was not difficult for us. The theoretical consideration – that since we were free of hard labor, we could survive with less nourishment – helped us over this barrier. Besides that, we could either sit or lie down at our own discretion. On the other hand, the announcement of the mail ban was a terrible blow to us. And we were soon to realize the full horror of isolation – the most invidious of torture instruments even in this environment.

Because our barracks had been sealed off, the air had less and less oxygen, and breathing became harder and harder. The moisture of our perspiring bodies rose to the ceiling and hung there until it trickled down the walls. We began to suffer from dizziness, vomiting, and bouts of asphyxiation. Our heads felt as if they were in a vice and our veins about to explode. It was only possible to endure these horrible conditions while resting. We lay on our mattresses during the day and gathered nights in the laundry room. We opened the water spigots and stood head to head around the flowing water, drinking and wiping ourselves off with the refreshingly cool water, inhaling the small amount of oxygen that the water brought with it. This water saved our lives.

Can anyone imagine what it means to survive three months of this? Still today I suffer from the nightmare. In my dreams I see my comrades in front of me, sitting on their mattresses and literally panting for air. It's my worst memory. Martyrdom was an everyday experience for us!"

This is why our knees turned to jelly when we heard the word "Isolation."

There we sat on our stools, our heads buried in our hands, and no one was capable of uttering a word. Suddenly a block leader appeared at a window and shouted: "Open the windows!" For us it was a liberating fanfare. We could breathe again. Color returned to our faces. It apparently was not a punitive isolation. A few minutes later we learned that we were to be isolated for several days because there had been an unexplained death and the suspicion of spinal meningitis had arisen.

A Discussion about Religion

I saw the concentration camp as a reformatory. Not as an institution for re-educating prisoners – although that was the officially stated central theme – but rather as an institution refining and perfecting the training of the SS-youth. Measured against earlier German and Austrian standards, the educational level of these 17- to 20–year-old youngsters was incredibly low. This was, however, more than overly compensated for by the arrogance and pretension with which these juveniles imparted advice or worldly wisdom in overblown phrases to older, more experienced men, some with world renown. It was sometimes difficult not to burst out laughing.

I was once present at a lecture given to a prisoner by one of these smart alecks who otherwise had trouble signing his name to a report. The lecture's theme was of a religious and philosophical nature. The crux of his wisdom was that the Catholic religion was a colossal bunch of nonsense like everything the Jews had concocted and only existed in order to addle people's minds and make them easy victims for the Moses' gang. Any contradiction or objection was impossible. Even such friendly SS-boys who lowered themselves to this kind of discourse could become unpleasant if the thread broke in the monologue they had learned by rote. When "intellectual" arguments failed, these were immediately replaced by violence, a kind of argument that was no more convincing but more painful and which the prisoner preferred to avoid. The prisoner in this scene was a former professor at the University of Vienna. He at first listened to his SS-teacher without batting an eyelash. Only when the boy spoke of "Jesus, son of a whore," did the professor – humiliated by his role in being forced to listen to a cretin – dare mutter an objection: "But, but . . . Sergeant!" That, however, enraged the boy even more and, imbued with the wrath of divine conviction, he screamed: "What else was this holy Magdalena other than a whore? And who was the father? That Jew!"

Our professor was forced to capitulate to this historic reasoning. When he told this story on the parade grounds on Saturday, all of Dachau laughed. This SS-bumpkin seemed too dumb for us to be outraged. Yet when we thought about it more carefully, the goal of Nazi-"education" again became so crassly evident. Shying away from no lie whatsoever, zealously alienating their youth from every religion, future generations of Germans would march into a boundless barbarity, void of knowledge, humanity, or belief.

The Slipper-Tragedy

Again and again I must emphasize that it's not the large-scale barbarities that can make life unbearable. It's almost as if it were quite the opposite: the ceaseless strain on the nerves, those – in actual fact – meaningless needle pricks driven under the skin with machine-gun precision, injuries more of a psychic than a physical nature. It is these that drive us to despair, that wear us down, and finally crush the moral wall of resistance erected and maintained with such effort until it collapses. The "system" is well aware of this and is quite innovative in the ways it finds not only to constantly terrorize and brutalize the prisoners, but also to torment and harass us incessantly.

Before we entered our room in the barracks we were forced to take off our shoes. Here we were allowed to move around only in our socks, but if we wanted to go into the lavatory, or if, within the barracks, we wanted to go from one room to the next, we had to put on our wooden slippers. Every prisoner had a pair in his possession. When we returned from work, we first had to clean our shoes and then walk into the room in our socks. Naturally we were fatigued and used the fifteen minutes until roll call resting on our stools. But if an individual wanted a glass of water, then he first had to pull on his slippers before going into the lavatory. When he came back, he had to clean them before putting them in his storage chest. Then the command would come: "Report for roll call!"

Shoes were quickly pulled on but afterwards had to be cleaned again. This cleaning wasn't such a simple thing when there was bad weather, especially since the block leader would cast a particularly critical eye on the shoes during inspection. If he found a speck of dirt or grain of sand either on the upper part or on the sole as well, the consequences were severe!

Two buckets of water stood in front of the barracks. Each of us could clean our footwear with this water and a brush. It often happened during our daily work routine in the topsoil that our shoes and clothes would become covered with a layer of mud. To remove it required not only rigorous scrubbing, but a substantial amount of time as well. The two buckets of water had to suffice for fifty pairs of shoes. But if the weather was bad, the water was already murky after the third pair and, a short time later, so dirty that the shoes whose turn came still later were even filthier when they came out of the water than when they went in. As a result this procedure also became a constant source of fear and strain on our nerves.

One evening when we returned from work our wooden slippers had disappeared. The room senior told us that the block leader had burned them because they were a danger to the cleanliness of our room. From now on, wooden slippers were banned and only felt slippers were allowed. They could be purchased at the canteen for 1.6 Mark. Naturally, we all heard a hint of punishment in this new arrangement and bought ourselves the new canteen-slippers as quickly as possible because no one wanted to attract the block leader's attention in an unpleasant way.

If it was dry outside, most preferred to spend the time outside between returning from work and roll call, just to save ourselves this shoe cleaning. When it was raining hard, we naturally tried to get into the barracks as fast as possible. It then could happen: we would clean our shoes and walk into the barracks. At the command "Fall in!" we would pull them on again and hurry outside. For some unknown reason roll call would be postponed, and the command "Fall out!" would follow. That meant, of course, that we again had to clean our shoes and move into the barracks. The order "Fall in!" would resound a final time. We would rush outside and, after roll call, once again into the barracks!

THE GRAVEL PIT

"Report to Sterzer!"

Block leader Remmele's Prussian snout puckered into a devilish grin. I was the object of the command. Remmele's raspy voice had exploded with the order, and thousands of eyes had looked to their left to see what poor devil had gotten the death sentence. A murmuring went through the rows as I was recognized as the delinquent.

I had a stabbing pain as my verdict was spoken. But I hid my agitation. I marched erectly to the corner of the roll call square near the administrative barracks, the assembly point for Sterzer's labor force.

A group of living corpses was moving under Sterzer's command toward the gravel pit. I was the single neophyte; all the others showed signs of lethal mistreatment. Two wore bloody bandages around their heads, while most hobbled along groaning with pain while two crept behind like kicked dogs. They were barely able to move from the spot, yet every time Sterzer looked back and rasped "Tempo, tempo!" these poor bastards attempted a kind of quickstep moving along on both hands and feet.

Sterzer ordered them to stop at the gravel pit. He seemed to be having a good day since he had not yet touched even one of his victims. The prisoners – who all knew each other extremely well by this time – made a run for the tools and snatched up the shovels and pickaxes. I had paused for a moment and was immediately punched and knocked head over heels by a blow. I fell down the steep embankment into the gravel pit where the water was more than a meter deep. A pickax slung down by Sterzer plopped into the muddy pond not more than six inches from my head.

Since the pickax had missed its target, Sterzer drew back growling like a lion whose leap had fallen short of its victim. I crawled out of the pit and mingled with the others. One of the detainees, his green patch revealing his criminal background, whispered to me: "Just a hair closer and you wouldn't have had to eat the intestine goulash today."

Sterzer was apparently busy with something else, because we didn't see him for an hour. But then he appeared, carrying a cherrywood cane in his boot. He was singing a little ditty and seemed quite cheerful. The others hacked away at an insane pace in the stony sand – without pause. I too raised my pickax high above my head so as to pound it into the earth with all my strength. He observed my vigorous efforts with apparent pleasure. "That's the way to do it," he bleated. "You've still got marrow in your bones – but you haven't worked for Sterzer yet. Ha ha! Just take a look at this ghost!" And he pointed with his cane to the poor Osio who had defied the tortures of this fiend now for two weeks with a tenacity bordering on the superhuman. "Just look, see what this guy can take!"

Sterzer had smashed the cane down on Osio's skull with such force that the poor man fell bleeding to the ground. I started to leap to his aid, but a kick in the stomach taught me that Sterzer had no tolerance for interference in his abuses. So I stopped. Sterzer seemed to have fallen into a murderous frenzy. He bounded through the ranks of his charges, bringing his cane down on their heads in a blind rage.

A young fellow I had known from the gardens collapsed to the ground. The next one was the senior civil servant Wielmann who lay motionless on the ground, his face buried in the gravel. Jonke, who had four times made futile suicide attempts, now seemed to have his wish granted. On his knees, his body resting on his arms, a death rattle issued from his gaping mouth.

I felt a warm flow trickling from my nose down to my chin. Stunned, I looked around this circle of hellish images as tears of compassion streamed over my cheeks.

As I looked up, I saw a miracle! Osio, the human wreck, stood up on his own power. Blood was running from his mouth and nose; one ear on his deformed head hung loosely, but was still attached by a scrap of skin. And – a shiver ran down my spine – Osio was laughing!

As if he shot up out of the earth, a *Sturmführer* suddenly stood in our midst. He barked at me, seemingly enraged: "You filthy ass, how did you get here? Report to capo Wundsam's stomping squad immediately! Wait just a second – I'll help you change work assignments on my own!" Turning to Sterzer he shouted: "If this guy comes to you again, chase him back! Understand?"

I stood there, stunned. A knight in shining armor had again appeared, a knight at the hour I feared would be my last. And I ran to Wundersam's stomping squad at a pace comparable to my best years of active soccer competition.

The signal for lunch had just sounded. The stomping squad was returning. Willy already stood at the corner of the barracks. This massive man blurted out a howl of joy as he saw me coming – and in relatively good shape. He grabbed me under the arm and nearly carried me to the room. I lost my composure, laid my head down on Willy's chest and wept. "Dear, dear Willy! The crimes are too immense for human beings to avenge. But God cannot let them go unpunished."

I thought about the entire episode. Who was this *Sturmführer* who had now saved my life for the second time? The longer I pondered, the more certain I was that the SS-man who had today snatched me from Sterzer's deadly grip at the moment of gravest danger was the same man who had intervened for me again and again during that night of horrors on the train from Vienna to Dachau. Just where had I seen this face before in the course of my life?

Who was this *Sturmführer*?

Images from the past formed in my mind's eye. I had brought dreams of a lifetime to fruition in 1936 by challenging Vienna's ardent soccer youth to take part in a student tournament. The success of my efforts exceeded my boldest expectations. School teams formed up on nearly every courtyard and tenement square and on every grassy patch of Vienna's outer belt. The organization of the youth teams, all registered by the individual schools, was an enormous undertaking. For weeks, from early in the morning to late at night, team captains visited me to have their questions answered. I fully shared the pleasure of the youthful players. All of Vienna's soccer clubs made their facilities available at no cost for the tournament. Both the state and the city began to take an interest in the event when, after reading the reports, they realized its magnitude and significance for the youth of Vienna.

Then the big day of the drawing arrived.

I was standing on the platform. The boys were glowing with excitement and I – aware of my role as architect of this venture and dispenser of this happiness – stood there, beaming with pleasure myself.

And then, after a few words from the world famous club captain of the Austrian soccer league had brought the enthusiasm of the youth to a boiling point, a tall, fair-haired and blue-eyed youth stepped up timidly. Awkward and urged on by the others, he spoke a few words of gratitude that had a highly emotional appeal in their simplicity. I could feel tears in my eyes.

I now saw the boy in my mind's eye in front of me again. I sensed his voice and movements. Feature by feature the image of the fair-haired captain stepped clearly and well defined from the dark recesses of my memory. And the light of comprehension dawned on me: this fair-haired captain had developed into one of the few truly human *Sturmführer* in the Dachau concentration camp.

When my Patience Wore Thin

The summons to the Records Department meant we had half a day free. We were required to state our personal information, then be photographed, and thoroughly interrogated by the SS-staff sergeants of the Auditing Department. When this summons came, we marched in groups of about fifteen to the Records Department and later returned in the same detachment back to our work areas. This group procedure took about half a day. It was an entirely pleasant break because the Records Department office was one of the few places in camp notorious for the absence of prisoner mistreatment.

When it was my turn to go to the Records Department, a group of sixteen of us under the command of a block leader moved out to the office. There we had to remove our shoes so we might form up in the anteroom. In the interrogation room there were two desks manned by officials so that two prisoners could be questioned at the same time. I had learned the art of giving short military answers and employed this technique here as well although the examining block leader gave every effort to pump out of us as much as possible. He often made what were supposed to be amusing interjections. At least they seemed that way to us mainly because they lacked any dangerously menacing tone or scornful derision. The mood swing that occurred when the block leader touched on the topic of military service was therefore even more unpleasant for me:

"Did you take part in the War?"

"Yes sir!"

"Were you decorated?"

"Yes sir, *Herr* block leader"

"You're lying! You obtained the awards by fraud or bought them. Did Austrians actually do service as soldiers? A flaccid society all together – Jews and Christians – a cowardly lot that we have always had to dig out."

It might seem foolish but who can say why just *one* drop can cause a barrel to spill over, why that happens sooner than later. In any case, that was the moment when I forgot wife and children as well as my firm resolve to survive this camp. I flew into a passion and yelled: "*Herr* block leader, you're only twenty years old, so you cannot know that from your own experience. I was an officer in times of peace and war for eight years and have to say, that the Austrian officer and soldier are inferior to the German neither in terms of courage, honor, nor morality . . ."

I certainly would have risked my life, if the SS-man had not cut me off. "Dismissed!" he shouted and I left, once more happy to have gotten off so easily. The turn that the conversation had taken had apparently been embarrassing for the examiner.

One Man Who Liked Camp Life

The fact, that when he was to be released after two years of internment, he stepped forward and requested to be able to remain in some capacity, characterizes this man better than any lengthy description. He said that he felt an aptitude to complete any assignment in the camp according to the camp commander's wishes. And, after a petition to Himmler, he was, in fact, granted permanent residence in Dachau. He was given the function of an administrator. He is not able to leave the camp, but may freely move about its grounds; he receives better meals and is directly subordinate to the camp commander. And this long-term civil servant is one of the cruelest brutes in the Dachau camp, a place not otherwise lacking in bestial behavior. The prisoners in the "bunker," whom he brutally abuses, are under his custody. He also keeps watch over those prisoners sentenced to the "stake." The bloody noses, the swollen eyes, and the missing teeth of these unfortunates are demonstrative proof that Himmler found a congenial pillar of strength in this volunteer. In his free time he takes the camp commander's pets for walks – a large, black cur and a chimpanzee. The four-legged beasts were dangerous as well, and whoever found himself near this infernal threesome, made a wide arc around the executioner in the bright red shirt. We knew from experience that it wasn't advisable to come too close to him. Rating this trio from the standpoint of their humanity, the two-legged beast would take last place.

Church Service

One day at roll call it was announced over the loudspeaker that a priest would hold Catholic Services in camp on the following Sunday. Those prisoners who wanted to take part should tell the block senior. This was also made known to the Jews since there were many Catholics in the Jewish blocks. In many families only two of the grandparents were Jewish, in some only one.

After we left roll call for the barracks, we sometimes were not allowed to go immediately to the evening meal. Instead, we were held back in order to be given some sort of instructions – or to collect our mail. That evening the sergeant didn't dismiss us since he had an important announcement to make. He began: "On Sunday, as you have heard, there will be a Catholic service. Whoever wants to can sign up. But for my block, the following will hold: whoever does register will be drilled so hard that his ass will be dragging. Anybody who signs up will never have a free Sunday again. If you have time to pray on Sunday, you have time to work. So, go ahead and sign up if you want. Dismissed."

The block senior was a decent guy who had never reported anyone except at the express desire of the block leader; i.e., under compelling pressure. The SS-tone of his threats surprised us, but later I learned from his subordinates the real reason for the sergeant's threat. The following is a reasonably accurate reproduction of a conversation about this topic:

"It's unbelievable how the sergeant has learned the manners of the SS. Such scare tactics to keep our comrades from attending church services are outrageous." "Don't repeat it, but the sergeant has a heart of gold. He knows about an earlier, similar situation where men who had signed up for church service were horribly harassed and so he wanted to scare us off." "The end justifies the means, you're saying?" "Exactly right."

The block seniors of the other blocks must have sounded similar warnings, but by the next morning 300 prisoners had signed up for church services.

In general, most inmates preferred to do their devotions by themselves, unobtrusively and quietly. Some orthodox Jews fasted even on minor holidays despite the hard work. The high Jewish holidays of the New Year and Yom Kippur fell during the first days of our stay in Buchenwald. On the evening just at twilight before these festival days, all believing Jews stole out of their barracks to block sixteen. We still had not received any caps and so the attendees of this improvised service covered their heads with handkerchiefs tied in knots at the four corners. A young rabbi from Vienna took over as prayer leader and everyone followed his lead in a low voice.

Although the prayers lasted almost an hour they were not disturbed. A few hundred prisoners from the Aryan blocks stood quiet as mice around the group of Jewish worshippers. A grand starry night arched over this somehow indescribably sublime and eerily unsettling scene of mutual worship. Conjoined by their suffering, Jews and Christians prayed to the singular eternal Being, the God of all humanity.

WILLY'S APPARENT DEATH

The detainees had Sunday afternoons free. Their leisure was seldom disturbed. Only once the devil sent out one of his black hounds to frighten them. As Willy and I had just settled into a political discussion with our comrades, one of the block leaders on duty suddenly stood right in our midst. He had emerged from one of the narrow barracks streets on his bicycle. Luckily, he had not heard or perhaps not understood my words: "All this commotion will be over in six months."

But the fact that prisoners were standing together was reason enough for the block leader to intervene. "Aha, you wretches – maybe you're planning a mutiny? You do know that the punishment for mutiny is death, don't you?" We stood silent and motionless. "You, big fellow," he turned to Willy. "Seems to me that you're the chief here, right?" And before anyone knew it, he gave Willy such a blow to the head that he fell over, stiff as a board. He lay there like a dying man, his eyes open and turned upward. A rattling noise came from his chest and a shiver ran down my spine. But the whole sequence that had been played out in front of a crowd of witnesses also seemed a bit fishy to the black hero.

He thought for a minute. I believed I could read his thoughts. He was apparently undecided whether he should now sound the alarm and lead the whole group away on some kind of pretext – for treasonous discussions or something similar – or try to squirm his way out of the whole situation. "Carry the idiot into the room and let him lie there until he kicks the bucket. The big lout had a heart attack, understood? Whoever says otherwise will have to deal with me."

He swung himself up on his bike and rode off in the direction of the command center. While one of our comrades ran off to get water, I knelt down, opened Willy's undershirt and shirt, and pressed my ear against the dying man's chest in order to listen to his heartbeat. I suddenly jumped up and skipped around in circles like one possessed. "That beats everything, everything!" I shouted and laughed and laughed and was beside myself with joy.

The others thought I had gone crazy. What had indeed happened? When I had knelt down toward Willy, he had whispered to me: "I'm not even considering dying, not just now anyway! Has that scarecrow gone?" And then he raised his head, looked around and laughingly called out: "That's right, boys, I'm good at dying, and no one can do it as well as I can. I learned how to do it during the latter years of my boxing career, and I always 'died' when I couldn't go on, when I was completely out of breath."

At that point I remarked: "How could I have forgotten! How could you have fooled me so completely? Wasn't I the one who wrote about you giving up in your last appearance in the ring: "Willy Kurtz, dead for the third time." At that everyone was convulsed with laughter.

The Secret Mail Carrier

It was Sunday and we were again strolling on the camp road. It was a quiet day. Suddenly Willy said: "Lately, in so many of the letters there's been such a clear but painstakingly concealed undertone of hopelessness. What's really going on at home?"

"Just for once we ought to be allowed to write everything that we really have to say, for once something more than those empty phrases that are never believed: 'I'm fine, I'm in good health.'" The block senior had expressed this thought. Everyone remained quiet for a moment. Then all of a sudden, capo Stups chimed in: "We ought to think about that and see if something couldn't be done."

"Do you really think so?" – "What do you have in mind?" – "I'd spend my last penny for that." We all shouted at the same time as we crowded around Stups. But he anxiously fended us off. "Boys, boys, don't cause a stir! I don't think it's possible, but let me sleep on it."

Deep in thought, we went our separate ways. Stups was a clever guy who even had a certain standing with the SS. Could he pull it off?

At the end of July he came up to me and asked – in strictest confidence – whether for a fee of fifteen Marks I'd like to get a letter to my wife which could be put into her hands without going through censorship. In the same way and totally without risk I would receive a detailed letter from her in which she could write anything that was near and dear to her heart.

I agreed without a moment's hesitation to come up with this fee on the very next day I got my hands on some money. I was inwardly exultant at the thought once again to be able to say to Mautzi – in place of those phrases prescribed by the camp commander – how deeply I believed in the future and the liberation of Austria, as well as to hear from her about plans to rescue the children as quickly as possible from the milieu of Nazism that was so detrimental to morality and spiritual faith.

We agreed on a day when I would give him a letter as well as the fee, both of which would then be given to a member of the SS to manage and transmit further.

The next day I looked up Stups in his barracks in order to talk more about the arrangement. Besides that I wanted his opinion about something I cared deeply about.

"Is it possible," I asked him, "that our mail carrier would also deliver the letters of other comrades for the same fee?" – "Of course," Stups whispered. "The more money he pulls in, the more secure his business will be. But we have to be extremely careful; otherwise we've all had it. If you are aware of others whose discretion you can rely on, invite them to take part in our transactions. But don't accept any letter without the fee!"

On the following two days I ran from one barracks to the

next to bring them the good news. Almost everyone accepted the risk in spite of the possibility that it might be a trap; i.e., that the SS go-between might pocket the money and destroy the letters or even betray us. Was there any greater torment than when we had so much to tell our loved ones, yet were able to express so little?

I knew from my own experience what it meant for the others, just once to write down candidly all their thoughts, to be able to relate all the signs they had observed concerning their own liberation, as well as those concerning the deliverance of family members. How often I would lie awake on my mattress, in spite of my fatigue, wondering how I could write Mautzi – especially about the future of our children – without having the letter ripped apart by the camp censor!

During all those months of our confinement there had rarely been such excitement among the detainees. They pondered day and night what they should write in this most important "letter of their life" as they feverishly anticipated the big event.

It was agreed that the letters would be written on Sunday afternoon and given to Stups in the evening. It was too dangerous to write them ahead of time.

The great day had finally arrived. A passionate desire to write was palpable in all the barracks on this Sunday afternoon. I had arranged it so that even those who had no money at all made it known to the others that they too wanted to take part. So informed, these comrades let their own loved ones at home know of this situation, information that was then further passed on to the loved ones of the impecunious detainees. So it happened that there was not one Viennese – it was only a matter of letters to Vienna – who got left out.

And then the great moment arrived when I had gathered up all the letters and gave them to Stups. All the letters had to contain the following stipulation: "Please hand over to the bearer of this letter a detailed letter in response and one hundred Reichsmark." Who among us would have hesitated to attach this comment, even if double or triple this amount would have been demanded?

Days of worries and fears now followed. Will the SS-messenger really deliver the letters to the addresses written on the envelopes? Will he bring the answers into camp and let them land in our hands? When one of the band of "letter conspirators" was called to the Jourhaus or accosted by an SS-guard, the hearts of the others beat in unison. Was the camp administration already aware of the letters? Had the strange messenger held his tongue? One thing argued in favor of the letters reaching the addressees: this was the fact that the main chance for profit for the courier was in the response letters.

The suspense was enormous. How could it have happened that I had managed to make such an arrangement with someone from this pack of criminals that – according to everything I had experienced since the Nazi revolution – possessed no visibly human impulses? But what if this one man simply made off with the cash and betrayed us all? Wasn't that really what we ought to expect from him if, as a Himmler robot, he were true to his character?

More than fourteen days had passed since we had heard anything about the letters' affair. Passing by Stups, I asked him: "Do you think we will be hearing anything soon?" "Probably in a week," he responded, "since the mail courier has two weeks vacation in Vienna." – "And do you think that everything will run smoothly?"

"Oh yes, I think so. I figured it out that there will be a five thousand Mark profit for the SS-courier. So it pays off for him for once to keep his word."

On Sunday there was one flap after another. All kinds of rumors were spreading: one was that an SS-guard was sitting in the clink under suspicion of being linked to prisoners. Then, that Stups had been taken away. Then one detainee, his knees shaking, sounded the alarm: "Stups has admitted everything."

Willy and I tried to convince each other that nothing was true about the rumors. Yet it did trouble us that Stups, who usually appeared on the camp road about this time on Sundays, was not yet there. And it was almost time for supper. We sent some people out to look for him. He wasn't to be found. The panic was incredible. Groups formed everywhere. One man said tearfully: "We'll get the death penalty!" Old Katzenstein began to weep.

Stups burst right into the middle of this uproar. Everybody pressed around him and wanted to hear the liberating word from his mouth. "Don't do something so foolhardy as congregating here at this one spot! Everything is in fine shape. The letters have already arrived in camp and you'll each get yours after mealtime. But now get back to your barracks so that you don't attract attention!"

I began to worry again, however, about the difficulties Mautzi might encounter if the conspiracy were discovered. But after the meal as I went to find Stups, he came over to me and gave me a long letter, Mautzi's response. It was impossible for me to read it that evening. The possibility of a surprise was too great. So I put it into my money sack that I wore under my shirt. But I was so disconcerted that I couldn't sleep.

The next morning – it was Saturday – I shoved the letter into my shoe. Time just didn't want to pass. We had afternoons free and so I wanted to find a spot where I could enjoy Mautzi's response at my leisure. But I was so excited and the suspense was at such a pitch that for a moment I forgot all caution, hid behind a bush and took off my shoe. I just wanted to cast a glance at the lines to see if Mautzi and the children were in good health.

The blood in my veins curdled when I heard a voice right beside me: "You swine, what are you up to?" An SS-guard was standing in front of me. I was incapable of uttering a single word. I had had just enough time to stuff the letter quickly back into my shoe. "You wretch, why did you take off your shoe?" – "There was a pebble in it." – "Is that so? In that case take off your other one and run ten times through the puddle over there and back. But on the double!"

I did what I was told. Meanwhile the guard stood only two steps away from the shoe that held the message for which I had gambled my life. I ran and ran some more. My head was feverish. My lack of self-control had gotten me into a pretty mess! If the guard found the letter, all was lost, and my comrades would have to suffer along with me . . . My knees were shaking and I thought I'd faint.

"Now, put your shoes back on, you mutton head!"

With lightning speed I first slipped on the shoe that held the treasure. When he saw me struggling to tie the shoelaces with my trembling hands, the guard screamed at me: "How long is this going to take?" Finally it was done and the danger eliminated.

After returning and gobbling down lunch, the blissful moment had arrived, the time when I could unfold Mautzi's letter while lying in the semi-darkness under my bed. I read:

"My dear one,

The messenger was here and I responded according to your wish. That was finally another day filled with light! I only slowly realized what your letter meant for me and what mine meant for you. Words from you that had not been written under duress – and when I hear from you that you have read my response, I will have reached the heights of happiness. The beam of sunlight that has found its way into my heart allows me to look into the future from a perspective filled with strength and confidence. Up to now I haven't made any headway with my requests at various agencies, but my experiences have convinced me that our separation will not last long. I hope that your detention will be of much, much shorter duration than you think. We are healthy and the children are not having difficulties in school although I still endeavor to bring them into the company of decent human beings. I'll keep sending you the fifteen Marks every week. And don't worry, Thilde and Marie are helping out quite adequately. We longingly send you our kisses and pray for you. Mama, Traudi, Etti.

P.S. Last Sunday Mia Petersen married that SS-man with whose help she 'rescued' Willy's business from Aryanization. Help comfort Willy!"

MIA'S BETRAYAL

These letters had powerful consequences. Here in camp we were twice as vulnerable to joy and suffering, and it was easy to read in the facial expressions what the SS-courier had brought to each of us. Fate wrote in a mere few lines its cruel tragedies. Leo's daughter wrote that, due to the excitement, her mother's nervous system had been negatively affected and she had gone to a sanatorium to seek help. Yet the poor man was spared the worst news. He was not told what many of us had known for weeks: his wife had committed suicide in the sanatorium and was now at rest in her grave.

Löffler received an envelope from his brother: it contained nothing more than the death certificates of his four-year-old boy and his mother. This poor soul did not suffer long. An hour later we found him hanging near the tool shed.

A number of our comrades got letters that reported the meetings of their wives with the secret police in which they were promised that their husbands would soon be released. The spirits among this group were understandably heightened. Several of them found the money for the return trip enclosed in their letter. They were so excited they could scarcely speak. They expected to be released at any moment. Unfortunately, however, they were all disappointed.

Poor Willy came up empty-handed. Stups had nothing for him. He walked as if in a trance from barracks to barracks. He asked everyone: "Did you perhaps hear anything from my people?" To this point I had remained hidden from him. The first thing I had to do was to concoct a strategy to reveal the horrible truth to Willy in a cautiously circumspect manner.

Willy had already twice been at Stups' door. He finally confronted him. When he whimpered, "My good man Stups," the good-natured capo could feel his pain. "You know that I got no answer to my letter. Can't you ask the courier what's going on? And if he wasn't able to meet with her at all? I gave him the apartment as well as the business addresses!" Stups softened a bit and promised Willy to find out and asked him to come again after supper.

What Willy learned an hour later did not dispel his fear. Stups had actually talked to the courier who reported: "That was a risky episode. I, of course, went to the address I was given. I rang and a *Sturmführer* opened the door. I quickly left the house while stammering some lame excuse. The next day I sent my friend there again with appropriate instructions. This time a lady answered, but over her shoulder he saw the *Sturmführer* again so that he also quickly invented an excuse and was able to breathe a sigh of relief only after escaping. Under these circumstances you must understand," he had told Stups, "that I gave up . . ."

At this news Willy became even more crestfallen. At the end this shattered giant made a pitiful impression. "I am sincerely grateful, Stups," he groaned and slunk into his room.

It was clear to me that Mia Petersen had deceived Willy in the most shameful way. She had arranged to play his assets into the hands of her lover and then married him. She had been successful in realizing her dream of moving into Willy's luxurious home as the lady of the house. She now had his money, his residence, and his dog "Sherry." Under these circumstances she was quite happy to abandon Willy himself.

How was I supposed to reveal the entirety of this monstrous truth to Willy? Would this colossus of a man with the heart of a child be able to bear up to this new blow of destiny? This fate erupted like a storm upon the poor man – the betrayal of his loved one and the loss of his fortune. Meanwhile the story of Mia's betrayal had already made the rounds in camp. How was that possible? I had not breathed a single word of it to anyone.

Eisenstädter came to me that evening: "Something terrible has happened. Mia Petersen has married the SS-man with whose help she stole Willy's possessions. My wife wrote to me in detail about it. Here, read!" And he put the letter in front of my face that confirmed everything that Mautzi had told me.

I decided to tell Willy everything. It was better if he learned about it from me since, after the questioning and the absence of an answer to his letter to Mia, he had to be nearly overwhelmed with anxiety. "Maybe I can convince him," I thought, "that Mia is not worth his love."

Before going to bed I said to Willy: "I have something important to talk to you about. Try to work next to me tomorrow in the garden area. There we can talk about everything in peace."

Willy Learns the Facts

On the following day Willy was successful in joining the "weed whackers'" work party by bribing the vice-capo Paul with a pack of cigarettes. At first there was no chance to talk to him since we were working at the street's edge where we could constantly be "observed" by the guard as well as from the machine gun tower. But after an hour we had worked our way up to a hedge where we could risk – without pausing and looking up from the ground – exchanging our thoughts. I had had enough time to organize my thoughts and find the words in order to expose Willy to the terrible truth little by little. When the moment to speak had arrived, however, everything that I had intended to say seemed so vacuous and callous that I refrained from speaking. But by the time we had stood behind the hedge for a while, I realized I could no longer remain silent.

Then Willy himself abruptly began to speak and I believed I could hear in the tone of his voice a certain peace and composure: "Tell me, Max, can you comprehend the whole story? After what Stups told me yesterday evening, it slowly began to dawn on me." – "What did Stups say?" And Willy recounted the conversation with Stups with a sense of calmness that I marveled at, but which also reassured me as well. He came to the conclusion: "You know, I think I'm completely in the picture now. The *Sturmführer* is the man into whose hands Mia transferred my business, my home, and my fortune. And the bastard is now collecting his reward. She seems to have surrendered up herself totally to him and, as an honorarium for his services, he is now demanding Mia herself. Doesn't it seem like that to you too?"

I was flabbergasted. Then I said: "I always suspected that Mia was only after your money. Now that she has it, she is abandoning you. She has never loved you. Otherwise she wouldn't have forgotten you so quickly and been able to carry out the deception so ruthlessly by . . ."

I stopped for an instant. "By what?" Willy asked. "By marrying him, as Mautzi has assured me in her letter."

Suddenly I was again aware of our surroundings where any loudly spoken word could attract the attention and retaliation of a guard. So I added in a pleading voice: "Please control yourself, Willy. In any case, this woman is not worth wasting one more word or thought on."

Indeed, Willy did not explode into one of his fits of rage but couched all of his feelings in one single word that he spat out: "Monster!" He then took his rake and stepped into an area in front of the hedge where he couldn't be seen by the guard or the "tower owls."

The bestialities of the SS could apparently be traced back to schools in which they were specially prepared for service in concentration camps. At least this was the conclusion I arrived at, based on their consistently surly behavior. Every one of them had the same limited vocabulary and used the same terms of abuse and expressions. They seemed like robots in their spiritual emptiness. They had been taught early on that there were more important things than education and knowledge. Although our supervisors outside the camp during work hours changed daily, I had the impression for the longest time that it was always the same sentries. The degree to which they resembled one another was remarkable. Naturally there was just one form of address for us: "Filthy Jewish swine, filthy ..." Even the little tricks by which they tried to entice us into traps – totally lacking in individual variants – had to some extent been drilled into them.

Medicinal plants were cultivated in the large garden center that we called the "plantation." I worked there for a few weeks. The guards stood so far apart in the plantation that they could no longer observe one another. This made it possible for a few of the SS-youth to engage in conversations with the prisoners without fear of being overheard by the others.

When one of us had to answer nature's call, he had to get the guard's permission: "Sir, the Jewish prisoner X in protective custody dutifully requests permission for a toilet break." The guards used these occasions for special harassment that they called "playing sports." Most of us would rather endure the most intense physical discomfort in repressing our bodily needs than risk this harassment. It usually began when the guard replied that the request had not been made loudly enough. He had the prisoner step back further and further away and shout out the request to relieve himself at an increasingly louder volume. When he was finally satisfied with the sound level, the guard ordered the supplicant to march at double time in little circles around him. The prisoner often became so dizzy that he collapsed. He was then helped by kicks to get on his feet again, the heel of the SS-guard's boot landing haphazardly – in his face or on his shinbone. He often allowed himself the jest of "tickling" the prisoner with the bayonet that was always attached to his weapon. A guard liked to impose up to one hundred knee-bends in this situation. On the other hand, it happened once in a while that the seventeen- to nineteen-year-old sergeant began a conversation with one of us. At that point we were often asked tricky questions which we had to answer very carefully. I had had such an unavoidable conversation with one of the youngsters in the garden area that I found so embarrassing that I always avoided every approach of an SS-guard. During the weeks I spent there I never asked to be excused to empty my bladder or bowels, and worked at places – insofar as the capo could accommodate me – where there was little prospect of catching a guard's eye. But once a guard called to me from such close proximity that it was impossible for me to pretend I didn't know that he was calling me. I ran over and stood at attention in front of him.

"Where are you from?"

"Vienna."

"How old are you?"

"Fifty five."

"How do you like it here in Dachau?"

The young man had such a clear and open gaze that I became more talkative than I had intended and said something like the following: "Sir, you surely can't expect me to tell you how much I like it here. How can I possibly like it? Just because I was an Austrian, I was thrown out of my profession, separated from my wife and child, and am treated here worse than a poor dog . . ." – "How so like a dog? You all have enough to eat and drink, and the work is not bad at all. And you really can't complain about your treatment here."

I was numb. Was this youngster doing duty for the first time today? Had he not gone through the special school? Didn't he really see how his comrades all around him were torturing the prisoners to death? I became even more agitated: "Sir, all of your comrades are not as humane as you. Most of them take great joy in demeaning us, in mocking us, in beating and kicking us. They drive us until we collapse from their games."

"Well, well, just no exaggerations! Once in a while somebody may be amusing himself, but it's not so bad after all. The food is good, the work bearable, and you all get 15 Marks per week from home – with that you can afford all kinds of things. Just consider: we get up like you do and have duty as long as you work. We too are verbally harassed – you really can't envy us."

Didn't this fellow really know what it was like to be a prisoner in Dachau? There couldn't possibly be one living soul in this camp who didn't know about the numerous crimes committed daily, even hourly, against the defenseless prisoners. I threw caution to the wind: "Sergeant, are you trying to mock a man who could be your father? Not one day passes here in which innocent men don't receive crippling injuries or die. It's simply impossible that you've noticed nothing of this!"

"Is that really the case? I've been here just four days now and have had duty only in the garden area. It's true that the *Sturmführer* just yesterday said that we were to antagonize you, but nothing else. Nor have I hit anyone. And I would not assault any older person."

I lost all restraint. When I think about it now, I fully comprehend it. This young SS-man must have been sent to me as a messenger from another, better world where even the SS have human characteristics.

"Sergeant, how in the world can you hold your own in the SS with such notions?" I almost felt sorry for the youth. "You are a human being. How did you get into this mess?"

"Don't think that I'm the only one who thinks like I do. We arrived here last week, about 200 Austrians, and I can't believe that even one of us will persecute any of you."

Gradually I could make sense of what he was saying. These were the young men who had worked together in the Socialist youth organizations who suddenly weren't able to find anything to eat at home and were forced to join the National Socialist associations in order to survive. Hunger drove millions into the arms of the Nazis.

Suddenly he said abruptly, but not in an unfriendly way: "Get to work. We'll talk more about it the next time."

As I was leaving, I saw the officer on duty approaching the fence in front and hastened to put as much distance between us as possible. I never saw nor heard from this odd SS-guard again.

Every day, for as long as I worked in the garden area, I kept my eye out for him. He never came again. I can't help but wonder what happened to him.

NEWS FROM VIENNA

A new shipment arrived on Saturday evening. These poor unfortunates had to stand on the roll call square until after midnight and experience the customary reception ceremonies. Sunday after roll call we naturally hurried over to the barracks where the newcomers were housed in order to learn the most recent news from Vienna.

I went together with Willy and Leo. All of a sudden I felt a hand on my shoulder: "Hello, uncle Max!" My nephew Erwin stood in front of me. I blanched and had to lean on Willy so I wouldn't fall over.

So now they had even caught this poor guy! "Erwin, why in the world did they bring you here?" Why? Still in the act of saying it, the absurdity of this word occurred to me. Was there even a "Why" in the vocabulary of these deniers of justice?

We were naturally eager to hear the latest from Vienna. He knew very little about Mautzi and the children, except that they were in good health. But it was horrifying to hear what he had to say about the general situation in Vienna.

"You knew Colonel Deloge, didn't you?" he asked me.

"Sure I did. Has he become a collaborator?"

"No, no! Even though he helped run an anti-Nazi journal, they put him in charge of one of their papers. Ostensibly, he accepted. But on the day after he began work, he was found dead at his desk, a revolver in his hand. There was a slip of paper in front of him with the words: 'I cannot serve these godless beasts.' There have been masses of suicides, but they have been kept quiet so as not to create martyrs. The counsel for the district court who lived in our house poisoned himself, his wife, and four children. He pasted a large sheet of paper on the window of his ground floor apartment – so that it was visible from the street – with the words: 'I can't take responsibility for submitting my children to this spirit of disbelief and criminality. God forgive me!' By the time the Gestapo stepped in and removed the poster, the entire neighborhood had seen it and, in two days, all of Vienna."

"You know Dr. Dedekind, don't you? Well, Mrs. Bauer's cute little boy had run across the street and been knocked down by a motorcycle. He was lying there with blood all over him when Dr. Dedekind drove by. Someone stopped him, and he bent down over the boy's bloody head. Then, as he was about to get in his car again, he suddenly said: 'That's the little Jewish boy from house 11. It would be better if you'd get one of his own people.' And he left the poor little suffering mass lying there and drove off."

"The people did their best for the child. They called another doctor, but by the time he arrived, the unfortunate little boy was out of his misery – he had bled to death. The women wept, but no one dared protest out loud . . ."

As Willy now heard about the ravages of the Nazis in Vienna, he slowly began to realize how profoundly Mia had betrayed him. Every time it was mentioned, he grabbed his head and said: "How could I have been so blind!"

Willy underwent an amazing transformation in these days. Apparently it was the awareness that he no longer had to look after himself for the sake of someone else that calmed him down. And, through Stups – who thought highly of him – he had the good fortune of acquiring a quiet job as a foreman in the carpentry shop.

SS-men as Prisoners

At that time I was doing duty as a food server and was going into the kitchen to get the meal. All of a sudden I noticed an Aryan prisoner across from me, smiling, but not daring to speak to me since a block leader was standing quite near. That often happened, I thought, so why was it particularly disturbing this time? I recognized the prisoner's face, but who was he? There was more than a pleasant memory of a fleeting acquaintance behind this smile. I couldn't place him, however, and during the day's activities the trivial incident that had moved me more than I was able to comprehend faded away. Only that evening as I was lying in bed and just about to fall asleep did the scene reappear in my memory. Then I suddenly realized how I knew the smiling prisoner and how he knew me. At first I still had doubts, but the longer I thought about it, the clearer the image became in my memory and the more convinced I became. In the following lines I will depict an experience in the camp that I had had about three months before this meeting.

I had been assigned to a so-called swamp-express. There were several of these, and each consisted of twenty men who formed the lead team of a large wagon on rubber tires that was loaded with all kinds of cargo and pulled into the camp. In general, this was not difficult duty, although guards always marched along with us, and it depended on their disposition and mood whether we had to pull the wagon at a walking gait, a trot, or a gallop.

One day we got the job of picking up empty tin cans from the kitchen and delivering them with the swamp-express to a dump situated at some distance from the camp itself. As we left camp, one guard took command of the detail that included us and four other guards. The man in charge was what in normal times we might call a "handsome fellow." He was a good-looking young man and, at least temporarily, acted quite friendly toward us. When we arrived at the dump, an area surrounded by a board fence, he had us arrange the empty crates scattered around as chairs. He, along with the others in the guard detail as well our capo, then sat down. Next he inspected the prisoners and chose a few – myself included – to sit on the still unoccupied crates. He then strategically posted two other prisoners outside the fence and ordered them to signal us immediately if an SS squad should approach. The prisoners were therefore temporarily elevated to the rank of "sergeants of the guard."

Our leader gave us cigarettes that we had to smoke on the spot. He asked about our families, and following the custom of the SS, he made remarks about wives and daughters that were not always of an innocent nature; in short, he led an animated discussion. For the prisoners, the whole thing was a fully unexpected diversion for which they were grateful and one of the finest afternoons in Dachau that they spent on a work detail.

Big piles of old newspapers were lying around at the landfill area. Among them were bundles of the *Schwarzer Korps*[10] that some of the prisoners opened and browsed through. Suddenly one of my comrades held up a newspaper and called out my name in a loud voice. Months earlier my picture had been published in the *Schwarze Korps* and my comrade had accidentally stumbled across the old issue where it had appeared. I cringed as I saw the troublemaker waving the newspaper and signaled to him to hide it, but it was already too late. The commotion had attracted the attention of the man in charge of our detail, and he demanded to see the newspaper. I wasn't feeling well about the situation, especially because I had not observed one of the most primitive security measures in Dachau and was sitting in close proximity to the SS-guard. I was convinced that our camp idyll would now find a quick – and for me, painful – end, but I again experienced a pleasant surprise. The guard looked at the picture, then at me, read my name out loud, and finally said: "Aha, just look at this! What an honor, we have someone of prominence among us. My regards to you sir, 'editor dedicated to atrocity propaganda.'"

He laughed loudly at his own joke, and we all shared in his merriment. My laugh was particularly vigorous, since moments before I had been certain that I would have absolutely nothing to laugh about. Finally, however, the situation became uncomfortable for the SS-guard. He suddenly stood up from his crate and gave the order: "Fall in!"

I was now sure that the prisoner who had smiled at me by the kitchen and this SS-guard were one and the same individual. My memory didn't deceive me. The rumor was soon circulating in camp that the head count of prisoners had experienced an interesting growth spurt due to the addition of four former SS-men. I was later to learn why these four had been added to our number.

It was suspected that their political views were not entirely correct and so they were inconspicuously monitored. Their arrest demonstrates how cleverly this all was staged. The four young men had met and become friends with four young girls at a dance. They met again at an inn where the young "ladies" suddenly inserted political tones in the conversation that might be heard in Germany

---

[10] The *Schwarze Korps* was the official organ of the SS.

in the most intimate circles but almost never outside one's own four walls and never within audible range of any one who was not absolutely trustworthy. When the girls began mocking Hitler and the bigwigs around him in radically negative language, the young men felt better than they had felt for a long time in the company of these like-minded females. It felt wonderful just once to be able to speak frankly and to abandon the constant hypocrisy. Just before they were about to go their own ways and toasting another meeting as well as a happier and brighter future, several squad leaders in the room, armed with carbines, suddenly stood up. With that insistence characteristic of the SS, one that tolerates no challenge, they demanded that the young men follow them out the door. It was in this way that they – once members of the SS – came to Dachau as prisoners where they had been guards shortly before.

The Strong Hero

When someone's job or mandate is to seek out reasons for imposing punishments, it surely isn't very difficult to find any number of them, especially when this person is also arbitrarily able to fabricate the facts of the case. Those being punished, the prisoners, are not allowed any objections. They are merely entitled to hear the accusations and the imposed punishment. If at times a timid objection might be raised, this "revolt" would result in an additional penalty.

The SS and, as mentioned before, some of the capos who tried to copy their bosses' actions, were always thinking up new ways to torment us. And, it must be said, they were often successful at it. There was, in particular, no work pace that was fast enough. If an SS-guard had it in for a prisoner, this poor devil could work himself to exhaustion in setting a record pace – it was all in vain. The guard often stood over him for hours, driving him on, abusing and taunting him with such a show of stamina that it was unbelievable.

Our tormentors' lexicon of insults was extremely limited. One seemed to parrot the other, and it was only an exception when one of them succeeded in creating something novel. And the harassment was so similar, no matter who was in charge, that we were in fact unable to distinguish one from the other. They were a group, not individuals. Their training was, however, clearly identifiable. They were trained "to attack people." But how could we have distinguished one from the other, since we were forbidden to look the block leader or his subordinate in the eye? We could be sure of being punched or kicked if we suddenly crossed the path of an SS-man and, while lost in our thoughts, unintentionally looked him in the eye.

One day I was assigned to an easy detail, working on the road between two barracks. The earth was being tamped down and had to be watered. My task was to carry water from a well without stopping and douse the soil with it. When there was no SS-guard in sight, I had no reason to rush and sometimes stayed at the pump longer than absolutely necessary to catch my breath. On one of these occasions I became witness to a scene that illustrates perhaps more than any other the brutishness of these new German masters.

The well was on the narrow side of the garden area. There was a path, about 500 steps long, leading from there to the Jourhaus, the building where the camp offices were housed. At about the same level as the well was a pile of gravel that a work party was transporting with wheelbarrows to the Jourhaus where an annex to the camp kitchen was being constructed. On one side of the path, a column of prisoners in single file pushed their wheelbarrows to the construction site, while on the other side they filed back with empty carts. Two SS-guards stood every fifty meters along the way making sure that none of the prisoners set their carts down even for a moment.

The usual amusement of these merciless peasants was goading the workers with kicks and physical blows. Today this sport didn't seem to put the slave drivers in sufficiently good spirits, until one invented a new parlor game that I – fuming with rage and almost numb from pity and anguish – was forced to watch. After all, I was not only a Jew, a human being, and a prisoner myself, I had also been an athlete – and among other things – president of the Austrian boxing association. Every nerve in my body rebelled and I struggled against an overpowering urge to vomit.

The SS-monster bet his comrades that he could lay out with

one blow any Jew they would pick from the group pushing the wheelbarrows. For fully an hour they selected one victim after another. Those chosen had to place themselves in front of the huge SS-man who ordered them to stand at attention. He then punched each one of these creatures, all weakened to the point of exhaustion by the forced labor, with the full force of his fist directly in the face. He gloated with delight over this series of glorious knockouts. What heroic deeds! In the inferno of this concentration camp I have experienced a large number of truly horrible things, but this sight brought tears to my eyes for the first time, and I sobbed like a child. It was a long time before I brought my nerves under control again.

Of the literally hundreds of examples that I saw with my own eyes, I will recount only two. Just like the incident sketched above, they signal the depraved nature of these beasts – the words human beings are out of place here.

On work details outside camp boundaries we were watched over by 17- to 18-year-old young men. Quite naturally they did their best to emulate the block leaders, their role models and bosses, as exactly as possible. Thus they hassled the prisoners in the most malicious ways possible. At times though, one of them would lower himself to our level, start a conversation, and even seem to show an interest in our previous lives. Not a few prisoners felt themselves honored by such interest and casually began to open up without thinking a lot about it. The capos often warned us about getting involved in a conversation with the guards. Even if these young SS-men sometimes disguised themselves as friendly, they still remained our deadly enemies. Everything that we said had to be well thought-out. A trick question might be hidden behind the mask of amicability. It had happened that prisoners had been severely punished for information they had revealed in such conversations.

One day when one of my comrades and I were turning over topsoil, a guard who seemed particularly friendly spoke to us. He even came up with a few words of regret regarding our fate. He inquired about my comrade's profession, if he planned to emigrate in the event he was freed, etc. Suddenly a *Sturmführer* was standing behind the guard and fired off the question: "What's the matter with this filthy Jewish swine?" Immediately it happened just as the capos had always predicted. The "soldier" in black tried in the sleaziest way possible to extract himself from the affair by answering: "This guy was loafing, and I was reprimanding him." The result: my comrade was severely punished, and we learned a lesson about the treachery of these "heroic guards."

I myself didn't personally experience the events in the following story but reliable witnesses confirmed it. It took place in the Buchenwald camp at the end of July 1938. Just as in Vienna, raids were held in Berlin and in all other German cities in May and June. Perfectly innocent Jews, destitute and beaten, were interned in Buchenwald. It was here that the following prank made its rounds among the sentries. It was strictly forbidden for those working outside the camp to cross over the cordon of guards. This command was given so often that every prisoner was quite familiar with it. As if in jest, the guards would snatch the caps of individual prisoners and throw them over their shoulders. Laughing out loud, a guard would then call out: "Fetch your cap, Jew!" If one of them was naïve enough to follow the order, he was simply gunned down. He had crossed over the cordon of guards and was therefore shot "while attempting escape." At that time in Buchenwald, 117 prisoners had already fallen victim to this dirty trick.

Caps Off!

A few weeks before our departure from Dachau a new commandant arrived. His reputation didn't give us much reason for hope, although after we got to know him better, the moods of this military "lifer" amused rather than scared us. One of his first "reform measures" concerned the way the prisoners were to salute him when he appeared on the square for roll call. The ceremonial salute was to proceed in the following way:

When the camp commandant entered the camp, the guard posted in the tower over the gate announced:

"Tower A has nothing new to report!"

The report was always the same, no matter if someone had been killed in the gravel pit or whether someone's leg or chest had been crushed by an overturned block of stone – for the machine gun tower, it was always: " . . . nothing new to report!" The powerful figure moved closer to the mass of a thousand prisoners and the command of the sergeant in charge rang out: "Caps off!"

At that signal we removed our headgear with our right hand.

"You bunch of pigs! That's not the way it's done in the military! Block seniors, report to me!" Those were the words the new commandant used to answer our mass salute.

The block seniors received the order to instruct us next Sunday in removing and putting on our caps – a procedure that was to happen rapidly and without hesitation. On Sunday then, we practiced for two hours: "Caps on – Caps off!"

When the block seniors had screamed until they were hoarse and we could no longer hear the command, we were dismissed. During these two hours I saw an image over and over in my mind that had been imprinted on my memory when I was still a young boy. It stemmed from an organ grinder who was accompanied by a monkey dressed in pants and jacket with a little red cap on his head. Every time someone passing threw a coin on his metal plate, the monkey yanked off his cap, not once, but ten or twelve times. "Cap on – Cap off!"

At the next roll call, the salute deserved a spot in a Popeye the Sailor Man film. At the command "Caps off!" thousands of caps flew off. It was like the wings of a giant bird flapping, and just like such a flapping would cause a whirlwind, a similarly stiff wind went through our hair. The organ grinder was quite pleased with his monkey that day.

The Czechoslovakian Crisis and Plans for Escape

The threat of war with Czechoslovakia in September 1938 brought agitation and concern for days into the lives of the prisoners in Dachau. Some went around wailing, while their teeth chattered: "They'll kill us all if war breaks out."

Most of us were glowing with restrained enthusiasm and happy anticipation. At roll call it had been announced that the prisoners would be allowed to hear Hitler's speech. After the evening meal, we were to appear on the square with our stools and sit anywhere we wanted around the large loud speaker. Smoking would be allowed.

With the exception of the very old and sick, just about all of the detainees in the Dachau camp were assembled this evening on the square. My friends and I had spread the word: "Not one critical word. Spies are everywhere!"

Hitler's speech boomed into the dead silence of the roll call square. He demanded "War!" Our group had arranged ourselves close together, but no one spoke a word even though our hearts were overflowing: War! That would be the best opportunity to be liberated. As we returned to the barracks carrying our stools over our shoulders, the word spread from ear to ear: "Tomorrow in front of barracks 6 after the evening roll call."

I couldn't sleep. In case of war, what would the Nazis in fact do with the prisoners? Maybe they would use us to build bunkers. It was already dark in the room and no one was stirring. I sensed someone coming toward my bed, then sitting down on its edge.

"Who is it?"

"Stay quiet, it's me." I recognized the voice of the room senior, Hans. "We have to talk today about what we're going to do if war does break out overnight. Reiß Herbert, the sergeant from number 4, thinks that we have to take some action in order not to be killed or not to starve. Since food is already so scarce, they won't want to feed a thousand people here if war breaks out! Herbert said that all of the very young SS-guards were already replaced with older men this afternoon. Among those, the majority are leftists and will potentially meet the same fate as we do. Two of our older men are going to try to speak with them tonight. Kaupe thinks they'll leave the gates open so we can escape."

"And what happens if we do get out?" I whispered nervously. "Don't ask that question! When we're finally out, there will be a way forward. At least if we're out, there's a bit of a chance we can fight our way through. We'll surely die if we stay here." – "You can count on me!" – "Okay then, more tomorrow after we return from the evening roll call!" And Hans disappeared just as quietly as he had come.

Morning arrived, and nothing in camp life had changed from

yesterday. Except for one thing: I was able to convince myself that older squads of SS-guards had really replaced the younger men. One stood at the gate, fat and dull. Up on top of the machine gun tower, another one, sporting a moustache, looked down on us from beneath his helmet, his facial expression lacking any malicious intent.

As the work detail for the garden area moved out through the gate, I was amazed at the unusual calm. The sentries who met us there and were to accompany us were all reservists, overweight and lethargic. They didn't shout or hit or kick us. The war was starting rather nicely! Our labor turned into a period of pleasant loafing that was in no way disturbed by our guards. They stood together in pairs and gossiped away the morning while leaning on their rifles.

They truly looked as if you could talk about this or that with them. I already imagined myself on the other side of the barbed wire around the camp borders. What then? The room senior was right. Only after we're outside will we see what to do next.

After lunch, as I was approaching the barracks, I saw Herbert approaching on the camp street. He was walking slowly, his head bent toward the ground. He stopped in front of me. "Where's Hans?" – "Inside in the sleeping quarters," I answered. "Don't you want to go inside?" – "No, have him come out here!"

When he came out, his pale color betrayed his inner turmoil: "What's the matter, Herbert? Has it started?" Herbert's face twitched and his eyes filled with tears: "No, it's over. The dream is over. The Sudeten German territory has surrendered to Hitler without a fight! And my sixth year of internment has just begun."

A depressing atmosphere of sorrow prevailed among the prisoners. At least we enjoyed the blessing of our "wartime guards" for two days, but these veterans were replaced once again by the young, brutal and pitiless SS-monsters. The familiar horrors then gave our workday back its normal routine.

AN SS-JOKE

As I've said before, our clothing was miserable. The prisoners' uniforms rarely fit properly and were made of inferior material.

Underwear, as far as it existed at all, was in even worse condition. Around the end of September they suddenly took everything away that still looked passably useful and attired us in "uniforms from old supplies." We were, in fact, wrapped up in rags. We were issued tattered denim trousers and a strange amalgam of military blouse and cutaway as jackets. Even our former prisoners' garb was put together in such a subtle manner so as to give us the look of wandering scarecrows. But compared to our new outfits, it could almost be called elegant. It had been so riddled with holes and seemed so unattractive that it was impossible to get it into a condition that approximated what we mean when we say clothing. These rags were so rotten that when one hole was mended, two new ones inevitably opened up at the sides. We really weren't vain in Dachau. We had become so used to our scarecrow-masquerade that we didn't notice it nor did it even bother us. What they did with us now was again something new. Even though it had gotten noticeably chilly in the past few days, they took away our underpants so that we were even colder. Our bodies shone blue through the holes of our so-called uniforms. And the torturous uncertainty about our future depressed us as well. But like with everything else, we made the best of it.

It was rumored that we were being shipped to Buchenwald.

It was suddenly announced that we were to all line up to withdraw some cash for a remarkable shopping spree. Regulations about shopping at the canteen were put on hold until our decampment, and we were allowed to make purchases in the quantity we wanted and take them all with us to Buchenwald.

Once more a bit of happiness in our glut of suffering. At least we could stock up on tobacco and snacks for our trip to Buchenwald. Everybody rushed to withdraw the cash. Needless to say, no one received even a penny that wasn't his own; that is, that his relatives hadn't placed on deposit for him. After withdrawing the money we went to the canteen and our depressed mood gave way to a cheerful, bustling activity. We supplied ourselves with travel provisions, and those eternal optimists – a group to which I belonged – were immediately prepared to draw their conclusions from the new situation. We reckoned that we were to be living in more favorable circumstances in Buchenwald since we would not otherwise have been allowed to supply ourselves so amply. At this point our Aryan comrades reported that they had heard that Buchenwald would be only a kind of "switchyard" for us from where we would be sent home as quickly as possible. There were often these kinds of rumors, the kind that always spread with amazing rapidity through the camp because they were so willingly believed. Now the mood was almost euphoric.

On the evening before we were to ship out to Buchenwald, I was a witness to the following scene: a block senior had his group fall in outside the barracks and addressed them with the words:

"Comrades! It was very uncomfortable for me, when I first was ordered to take over a block of Jews. I had hardly ever had dealings with Jews and knew them only from hearsay. And what I had heard was not positive. But in the five years of my confinement in Dachau I've learned to judge people by the way they conduct themselves in difficult situations. My experiences with Jews here have been the very best. It's a myth that the Jew is dirty. My Aryan comrades don't value cleanliness any more than you do. I have often been shaken by the Jewish readiness to help others, not only other Jews, but Aryans as well. A 'green' prisoner who went begging for bread to a Jewish barracks has never been chased away empty-handed. Most Jews here – who have suffered tremendously under the SS – have preserved their masculine pride. With this I take leave of you, my unfortunate comrades. Hold your heads high! Whatever awaits you in Buchenwald, stay true to yourselves. Better days are coming, even for us. Farewell comrades!"

His words "heads high, dear friends" faded away in a sob. He then turned and disappeared into the barracks. We, too, had been moved to tears and crept into the barracks. What humanity! This simple man, who himself had been imprisoned and tortured for five years, had dared not only to have these feelings, but to express them in words. There would have been hell to pay if the SS-monsters had gotten wind of what he had said! No one knew that better than he did, and yet he tried to give us comfort.

Suddenly we heard: "Fall in!" Quickly we took leave of the room senior with a handshake and then packed our goodies from the canteen – real treasures for us – in boxes and bundles and fell in on the square. Goodbye to Dachau! The moment almost seemed ceremonial. There were many who had come with us who were now missing at this roll call! No, it wasn't possible that we had an even worse future ahead of us. One thing was sure: whatever was to come, Dachau was behind us forever . . .

Suddenly there was movement in the crowd. It must have started somewhere over there at the other end of the column. What's going on there? We weren't long in the dark. Four block leaders were approaching, followed by capos pulling two carts. The purchases we had just made are being loaded onto them. We have to hand over all of our boxes, bundles, and packages. The camp commandant then arrives with a few words of farewell for us:

"What were you thinking, Jewish pigs! That you would be allowed to take these nice things from the canteen along with you? Wrong – they are staying here for your Aryan comrades." These stirring words were followed by the block leaders' tumultuous cheering, as well as their loud laughter rewarding the witty humor of the staff officer.

On the Train Again

Even during the train ride to Buchenwald we had a foreshadowing of what lay in store for us. We were put in freight cars in camp and shunted off to the Dachau station. In the First World War such cars were often marked: "forty men or four horses." This was in case of a general mobilization, and it was never thought these forty men would have a comfortable trip. Yet at the time it was customary for the sliding doors either to be left entirely open or at least partially. 120 prisoners, however, were jammed into one such cattle car, the doors were sealed shut, and off we went to the Dachau station. The entire procedure – squeezing us aboard, shunting us from camp to the station, unloading us – probably lasted about an hour. If it had taken even fifteen minutes longer, I don't think that even one of us would have gotten out of these steam chests alive. We were subjected to this ordeal of near suffocation in doses, so that most of us were still barely conscious when the familiar commands resounded. We climbed out – how we must have looked! Streams of sweat ran down to my shoes. How I found the energy to pull myself up into the passenger car that stood there waiting I'll never know. I only know that I fell like an empty sack onto the bench and that all my comrades had a similar experience. The trip from Dachau to Buchenwald lasted the whole night. It was not the same journey for everyone. In some compartments, the SS passed the time by beating the half-dead and defenseless victims, while in others it was more peaceful. In my compartment the guards were in a tolerant mood and bellowed Viennese *Lieder*.

BUCHENWALD

The misery of Dachau now lay behind us. Many of our comrades had remained there permanently. The physical memories of Dachau will remain with us our entire lives. Buchenwald, however, was incomparably worse.

Even the very first impression was devastating. The camp area is impassable. There is no camp road at all. The barracks into which we were led were partially dilapidated shacks. They are situated in hilly terrain and even the fissured path to roll call is dangerous, especially for older men in the evening twilight. In Buchenwald there was no trace of the hygienic measures in Dachau. On the very first day we found the WCs closed. Only in the evening were they opened for fifteen minutes. There were, however, two other latrines about 200 steps from our barracks. Ritual battles often developed around the individual spaces there. These were understandably of a particularly bitter nature in the morning after reveille. For 11,000 prisoners there were only these two facilities with the possibility for relieving one's bowels limited to fifteen minutes per day! Even Dachau couldn't match that. Buchenwald clearly held the record among camps for making life miserable for its inmates.

Our first evening roll call took place in complete darkness. We formed up in rows of twelve in front of the barracks and had to hold hands so that the columns weren't uneven. The terrain made it fully impossible to line up in formation, since every minute or so, one of our comrades had to be lifted from a ditch or someone fell over a tree root.

The deputy camp commandant[11] was a flashy but worn-out looking young buck with a pale, doll-like face. Only hardened Dachau inmates could have endured his words of greeting to us without getting the creeps:

"Don't for a minute think you'll have it as good here as in Dachau under Grünewald.[12] Here you're going to slog away until the water in your backside boils over.[13] And we don't shirk from handing out twenty-five lashes like they do in Dachau."

Nor was the evening meal arranged so as to put us into a happy mood. Food in Buchenwald was handed out every 24 hours. First, there was a bowl of soup that had to be consumed immediately. Beyond that there was a half loaf of bread, a bit of margarine – about 30 grams – the same amount of marmalade, and a piece of cheese. The latter had to be divided up so that it lasted until the following evening.

Sleeping was out of the question since there had been absolutely no preparations made for our arrival, and for every three of us there was one straw mattress.

The next morning we had no opportunity to wash up. The water had been turned off. The battle for a slot at the latrine was fiercely fought, although a heightened mood prevailed due to the rumor that England and France would come to Czechoslovakia's aid in a war against Hitler.

HELL GETS HOTTER

When we arrived in Buchenwald, there were already thirty old wooden barracks, eight two-story brick buildings, and workers

---

[11] A certain Hermann Hackmann who went by the name "Jonny" or "Johnny."

[12] Grünewald was this dandy's counterpart in Dachau. He too was the commandant's deputy, later becoming camp commandant himself.

[13] This was one of the most used phrases in the limited vocabulary of the SS.

everywhere were doing excavations for new buildings. I have absolutely the most unpleasant memory of Buchenwald. On the one hand, a planned process of dilapidation was clearly visible, while on the other hand, the aforementioned feverish construction was under way in order to enlarge the camp's capacity. Four of the brick buildings were already crammed to the ceilings with beds, always stacked three high. At the time I wasn't able to understand why Dachau and Buchenwald had been combined. Had it been intended to give the impression that the Nazi educational policies had borne fruit and that the Dachau camp had become superfluous? Why then this increased construction activity?

After the events in November things became much clearer to me, and I'm convinced that by October they were already determined to prepare for larger concentration camp populations. The murder of Rath was then the welcomed external occasion that, in any case, could easily have been fabricated.

A few days after our arrival in Buchenwald – we were at evening roll call – around 800 men in civilian clothing were deployed on the terrace above us. I recognized a few of them: the State Secretary Karwinsky, the Procurator General Winterstein, the Privy Councilor Friedmann, the journalist Ostry, and to my greatest horror, the well-known Viennese shoe manufacturer Klausner, Director General of the DELKA shoe factory. His appearance was especially disturbing, because Klausner had previously been held in Dachau and had been released to return to Vienna only a few weeks ago. In camp for the second time! We knew Klausner as a good comrade and so we regretted his plight even more. The group was introduced to us as "police prisoners" and was to be billeted in isolation. We were threatened with the severest punishment if we had any contact with them. The poor souls didn't have a clue what the night would hold for them. We heard a report about it the next morning.

The gigantic barracks that was to house this group had not yet been completed. The SS didn't worry at all about such details. The 800 men whose journey from Vienna to Buchenwald had not been a pleasure trip – as one can easily imagine – were ordered to fall in and left there standing in formation overnight . . .

It might sound exaggerated but is nevertheless true: already after the first hours in Buchenwald we were yearning to be back in Dachau – Dachau, despite its unlimited possibilities, its unimaginable degradations and medieval tortures.

The Most Infernal Hell

I carefully weigh every word I write. And I declare: Dachau was almost a summer resort compared to the hell of Buchenwald. The sadistic practices at Buchenwald were, however, organized differently than those at Dachau. In order to ensure more and crueler punishments as well as a smoothly running mass production of martyrs, all refinement and sophistication was abandoned. Even the formal suggestion of a legal system – an arraignment or interrogation, as the Dachau sadists called the farce – was out the question in Buchenwald. Here there was only a sentence and its execution. Every formality ceased to apply. The guards apparently had instructions simply to administer beatings and to subject the inmates to torture in order to reduce their number.

If a block leader was of the opinion that a prisoner was working "halfheartedly," he simply took him to the square where executions were performed and administered twenty-five lashes on the spot. It was not only that there were large numbers of punishments, but also that they were constantly being doled out. Often prisoners had to wait behind a dozen others until it was their turn. While in most ways none of the torments here might be categorized in any sense inferior to those in Dachau, the twenty-five lashes were, however, of somewhat milder quality – instead of a bullwhip, a Spanish cane was used. This didn't cause the same horrible wounds as the torture instrument in Dachau.

On the other hand, punishments in Buchenwald were meted out in a much less scrupulous manner than in Dachau, if this kind of terminology has any meaning at all in such a milieu. The prisoners were bludgeoned and trampled or mowed down with no effort to hide these actions or to construct any provocation, no matter how specious. Although ruthless, the guards in Dachau would often fabricate a rationale for killing. In Buchenwald it was the rule rather than the exception that the SS-guards would run amok and club their victims to death on the camp road.

Many of our Aryan comrades and not a few Jews maintained their humanity and preserved their human dignity.

'Toe Inspection'

As the prisoners in barracks 16 slept – exhausted, half-starved, their bodies covered with sores and scratches – a sudden screaming around midnight jolted them from their only respite. "Just remain quiet in your sacks! Anyone moving will be shot. I'll warm all you queers up!"

The *Hauptsturmführer* was the one who had switched on the lights. Apparently he had stumbled into our barracks by mistake. Shocked awake from our slumber and blinded by the light, the blood had congealed in our veins. We watched as this drunken camp leviathan staggered from one bed to the other. As he lurched through the room he waved his revolver in front of our noses. Beads of panic-induced sweat stood out on our brows. We knew full well how easily a weapon could be discharged in the hands of such a bastard in a drunken state.

We started to breathe a bit easier when "Johnny" – as this full-blooded beast was called – moved closer to the exit. In his anticipation of surprising "love birds" he seemed disappointed. A scoundrel's thoughts spring from his own true nature. Johnny himself was that kind of homosexual: groomed, rouged, and thoroughly dandified. Suddenly he stopped: "Every one on their backs with their feet over the bed's edge! I pity anyone who has dirty toes!" And he marched up to the first bed and shone his flashlight on the occupant's feet. Because he roared out his furious rage, he didn't hear the sound of the assiduous activity that began in the beds a little further away. No one had apparently been convinced of the capacity of his own toes to pass inspection. One prisoner spat on his handkerchief in order to begin an emergency cleaning while another one grabbed his pants hanging from the bed in order to wipe his toes off on them. One fellow who had a particularly bad conscience slipped under the bed of his neighbor. Another one used a clothes brush in a last ditch attempt at cleaning his toes. But "Johnny" remained totally oblivious to all of this. He blurted out absurd nonsense in his drunken stupor, made menacing threats referring to death and Satan – yet in mid-sentence he seemed to forget why he was there and asked the room senior if everyone had received all their mail. The latter realized what was happening, tore open the door through which this nocturnal visitor then took his leave.

We soon pulled our ice-cold feet back under the warm blankets. One vented his anger with the curse: "I hope a stroke sends him to his final rewards on the holiest of holidays!" An angry retort from the far corner of the room seconded the curse while intensifying its terms: "Amen! But I'd be satisfied with any weekday!"

A Voice from Above

Naturally there was a confinement area in the camp. It was called the "bunker." Usually a prisoner was sent there in connection with a camp punishment – the stake or twenty-five lashes – and stayed there for up to three months. Some were taken from the train car in which they had arrived at camp directly to the "bunker." Since I never observed anything myself I can't say with certainty what happened there.

One evening we were standing at roll call. The camp commander had just appeared and given the order: "Caps off!" The 11,000 men stood erect and as still as salt pillars since the slightest movement would have called down on us certain punishment. All eyes were turned toward the Jourhaus, from where the dreaded figure emerged to receive the report. The bunker was situated just to the right of the gate. Suddenly breaking the deathly silence, a powerful, almost threatening voice resonated from one of the tiny, heavily barred bunker windows:

"Jews, have no fear of these devils! Your God will liberate you . . ."

The eerie scene ended abruptly with the rattling of windows and a mad howl. At roll call, the count of the prisoners proceeded normally.

When we returned, we learned more about the voice from the

bunker. The man we had heard at roll call was the Protestant minister Schneider who had been incarcerated since 1934. He had been put in the bunker because he had refused to render his respect toward a swastika banner. It hadn't been his first attempt to address his comrades, but each time he had been horribly mistreated. A fellow sufferer and neighbor of the pastor in another of the cells in the bunker, one who later had been released, reported that, on the very evening he called out to us, the poor man had been visited by the camp commandant and two SS-officers. His heartbreaking moans had been audible long into the night.

JEHOVAH'S WITNESSES

Nazi Germany created its own new terminology. All political movements with an anti-Nazi core are branded either as Jewish or Communist. In more sophisticated party circles they are more simply termed Judaic-Marxist or Judaic-Bolshevist. In camp language the designation Jehovah's Witnesses was used for all religious sects that opposed war. In the concentration camp known as Germany they are considered traitors, and it's no wonder that, in Dachau, they are considered particularly dangerous enemies of the state and treated accordingly. They would always be sent to a barracks in isolation and remained there. In Buchenwald, on the other hand, they got by relatively easily, and I even worked together with Jehovah's Witnesses. It's difficult to imagine the boundless decency of this sect. If they are assigned to duty as capos, they do everything conceivable in order to protect those comrades under their supervision from punishment. They never take on the role of boss or overseer but act as the prisoners' advisors and counselors, inconspicuously giving them tips about looming threats. Of course they often place themselves in danger since, if they are found out, they are subject to the same cruel punishments as the others.

In Buchenwald I was once under a capo who was a Jehovah's Witness. We recognized them by the violet triangle on their shirt and pants. He saved my life by rescuing me from the clutches of a block leader who was just about to "take my measure" with a club. Swearing wildly and bellowing like a demon, the capo lunged at me and, with a series of histrionic blows that I barely felt, he drove me out of the reach of the real adversary. Later I had a long conversation with the capo about the principles and worldview of Jehovah's Witnesses.

He declared: "Humans have to do good." As he explained this basic principle of his faith to me in the middle of the Buchenwald nightmare, his face was transfigured. He took on an inspired eloquence. "We reject clericalism as it's found in Catholicism and Judaism. The cleric puts himself between the believer and God. It is only the alliance of the Old and New Testaments that produces the basis for true belief. We oppose non-belief and so we are opponents of National Socialism which is wicked and antagonistic toward faith as well as God. Here in camp as everywhere else we see that our task is to act morally. As you have seen, there is no lack of opportunity. We fear neither punishment nor another human being nor even death. If we suffer death, it was God's will and thus right."

He had become ecstatic. Our conversation had turned into a sermon, or more correctly, a statement of faith. To me he looked like a saint standing there – passionate, inspired. I now understood why Jehovah's Witnesses were put in concentration camps. They preached goodness and love; they were human beings determined to live their Christianity and so couldn't be allowed freely to walk about in the Third Reich. It was too dangerous for the rulers of state.

This was truly the domain for the faithful. It was here too that many an unbeliever found his way back to God, albeit *not* that emergency exit so often taken to the Almighty.

The thought often occurred to me when we were marching off to work at the crack of dawn in the undulating fog banks and everything seemed unreal, disembodied: "Life has long been over. You are here to atone for your sins before the real and truly emancipatory death releases you."

I know that many thought this way. Fate proved many correct. They died. Did these deaths take away their opportunity to be given back to life, or did they achieve genuine freedom only with their actual deaths?

We brooded a lot in Dachau and Buchenwald. We philosophized a lot. We prayed, we believed.

We emigrants brood a lot. We philosophize and talk politics. We pray and hope and would desperately like to believe.

The Miracle

From the first day on, even in Dachau, my role had been one of offering comfort and consolation, and from day to day I had – unconsciously and without intention – increasingly grown into this role. The Nazis are right. Dachau *is* a reform school. I was never interested in politics, but was always an outgoing, helpful person who enthusiastically carried out his professional duties, who lived for his family and his simple pleasures – especially sports. As far as anything else, I asked for little except to be left in peace just as I left others in peace. The concentration camp had turned me inside out like an old glove and strengthened me in a sense. Now I am passionately interested in politics. I was, I believe, a good comrade.

Often, even on days when I had escaped death by a hair's breadth – for example in the gravel pit under Sterzer – I consciously tried to have a smile on my face when I returned to my comrades. I believe that I helped several men over the roughest spots by comforting them and reminding them of their responsibilities, even saving them from suicide. What responsibilities? Their responsibility not to despair, to cherish life even when death seemed so enticing, as well as their duty to exert their last efforts in the battle against this regime.

There came a day in Buchenwald, however, when I needed someone to console me. We were carrying large planks. First, we ran up a slight slope of about 200 meters at double-time. Returning, we were burdened with massively heavy loads. Each pair of men carried two planks that were so heavy that I could scarcely walk. My partner was not at all suited to this hard labor. He was a frail, hunchbacked man who had already collapsed twice. For me the excessive strain caused a terrible pain in the area around my heart. I was on the verge of collapsing at any moment.

We had delivered our load to the carpenter's shop and were setting out on the return trip. The little hunchbacked man faltered and fell but the capo caught him. The *Sturmführer*, an SS-officer, observed the scene and cursed the capo for still supporting the sloth of these Jewish swine. The poor cripple pleaded imploringly to rest just a bit since he was tubercular and his energies were exhausted. The only answer he got was a scornful laugh:

"I'll give you a break, you Jewish pig! Capo, load the deadbeat up with another plank!"

The capo led the work gang back to the stack of planks and then did something that could easily have cost him his life. He reassigned the hunchback to the task of stuffing straw mattresses. He said to me:

"Unfortunately, I can't help you. If I let both of you off the hook, there'll be hell to pay for all of us."

I surrendered to my fate. I knew that I would inevitably collapse under the added burden. I knew that my heart would no longer hold up. I had concluded that only a miracle could save me – as it had happened another time in camp – could save my life that I already believed was lost. And it happened again!

At this very moment a number was announced over the loudspeaker: "Number 9374, come to the gate immediately!"

It was *my* number – one out of 11,000 – that had been announced. As if by a miracle, I had escaped certain death for the second time.

Both Willy and I Are Called to the Gate

Willy's order to report to the gate had come at the same time as mine. On the way there I said to him: "I dreamed about being home a few days ago. Mautzi and the children were standing around a festively decorated table on which there were beautiful, fresh roses. They were all staring happily at them. And the little girl suddenly said: 'Papa will be here soon!' You know, Willy, I really have the feeling that our release will soon become a reality."

At the gate, however, I was made to stand motionless – the tip of my nose touching the wall – until the workday was over.

This standing position was one of the camp punishments. It may seem easy, but before you come to this conclusion, you should try it yourself. For prisoners already exhausted by the grueling forced labor, this stressful standing at attention – which could be expected even of the best-trained troops for only a very short time – was a genuine ordeal. It was often the case that one of the prisoners made to stand at the gate would collapse. What came of those who failed in this way depended entirely on the mood of the SS-guard on duty. Sometimes the man who had collapsed would be doused with a bucket of cold water, sometimes revived with a powerful kick to his midsection. If this first aid didn't have the desired effect, those still on the ground were left there until the command "Dismissed!" was heard. They were then carted off to their barracks by their exhausted comrades. When I was allowed to return to my barracks, the sergeant in charge gave me the order: "You are to report back here tomorrow right after early roll call!" That didn't sound at all like my release might be imminent!

Willy was anxiously waiting for me. "How come you're still here?" He called out from the open barracks' window: "I saw your release documents in the office!" "They told me to come back tomorrow morning. But what's your situation? What's happening in the Jourhaus?" I asked.

"It's a nasty affair! Apparently, it's some kind of slander. The *Hauptsturmführer* himself interrogated me. He wanted to know if I had established some kind of illegal contacts in Vienna from the camp. 'I've written to only one and the same person – my fiancée Mia Petersen – and only on mail day.'

'Right! But what does this mean?' he asked me as he extracted a letter from a file.

To my amazement, I recognized my own handwriting on it. It was apparently one of the letters that I had written to Mia. At that point he started to read from it: 'When you meet Noldi, tell him to go ahead with our business in the way we agreed.' Rödl suddenly screams at me: 'Who is this Noldi, and what kind of business is this?'

I had to control myself in order not to suddenly laugh out loud: 'Noldi is the secretary of the boxing association where I'm also on staff.'

'*Was*!' Rödl said maliciously. '*Was* on the staff,' I corrected myself. 'And I meant for him to finish up association business in the way we had agreed.'

'We don't regard this business quite so innocently. This Noldi – whose real name is Arnold Wawerka – is already under arrest in Vienna. Now get out of here and back to your barracks!' I wasn't able to say another word. Tell me though, how did this letter get into Rödl's hands?"

I thought the affair no less puzzling and no less dangerous although I tried to calm Willy down. "The letter was probably not even sent but kept back by the camp censors."

Visibly upset, Willy countered: "That can't be the case. I received a response from Mia herself that she had spoken with Noldi and that he would proceed as we had agreed. And you know Wawerka! I've always thought he was a Nazi."

I tried to comfort Willy: "I'm sure it will prove to be just as harmless as it is in fact." But since it was time to begin his duty, he went off into the main room pensively shaking his head.

FREE!

The next morning I again went to the gate and this time my release was confirmed.

Everyone gave his best efforts to facilitate my departure from Buchenwald. I'll pass over the numerous unpleasant experiences that I went through between my notification and my actual discharge, the kicks, the blows, and the torments of all kinds. But they were now so meaningless! I *was* free!

As the news of my release got around in Buchenwald – as always happened in such cases – many of my friends, both Aryans and Jews, came to take their leave from me. The very bleakness of their misery seemed even more pronounced in contrast to my imminent liberation. I looked both backwards into the oppressive darkness in which they were condemned to a continued vegetative existence and forwards into the revitalizing rays of the sun of my release. They crowded around me, each imploring me to convey a message of consolation to his loved ones. "Take care, comrade!" was the message that echoed in my ears from every direction as I made my way to the camp gate. It was a salutation, a request, a challenge, and I silently vowed I would do everything in my power to make good what had been perpetrated against these men.

The last man who shook my hand in farewell was an old Aryan camp inmate. I had paid little attention to him since I had only been in Buchenwald for a short time and he had not stood out in any sense. He kept hold of my hand and almost ceremonially said:

"You are leaving. You are Jewish and that means that you can leave Germany and have your freedom. Don't forget about us! Tell the people the truth wherever you may travel. Tell them we must die here because we believe in God and love."

On top of the gate a black shirt appeared.

"Take care!" I heard, before the apparition disappeared and I went out into a joyless liberty . . .

"Take care!"

Was there anything that could have made me more blissful than the deliverance from such agony than the return home to my loved ones? And yet the joy was not untarnished when an hour later the guard led me through the gate to the border of the camp and with outstretched hand pointed me in the direction of Weimar: "You're free," he said to me unambiguously. And yes, he actually addressed me with the formal pronoun "Sie" rather than the informal "du!"

I cast one last poignant look back into the camp where so many others remained with whom through our common suffering, I had formed an unbreakable spiritual bond, and who were forced to undergo yet further agonies in the concentration camp – for how long, no one knew.

Wavering between bliss and fear, I walked along the narrow trail through the meadow to the wide forest avenue that led to Weimar – the path to freedom, freedom that didn't seem to me to be release . . .

The moment had come that I had longed for with such indescribable passion, that I had so often experienced in my dreams. How I had resolved to celebrate! To fall onto my knees, to embrace the earth and kiss it. How I wanted to thank God for His mercy. I had feared that I would go insane with joy, and I had seen myself exulting and dancing, screaming with elation.

Once again reality was something different than all the visions that I had imagined. I still wasn't thinking about my wife and children. In my thoughts I knelt and gave thanks to God, but not in the form of a prayer, but rather as a sacred vow: in my lifetime to have but one single thought – to bring this cowardly, murderous mob to justice.

I tramped through God's magnificent forest of beech trees, but my ears were still filled with the whimpering of those poor, badly injured men stumbling into the barracks after work.

I was walking home, but my thoughts were shackled to Buchenwald, as if in chains. I thought of my comrades and wept. I had thought I would shed tears of joy on my release. I was weeping, but certainly not from joy. An infinite sadness engulfed me. *I* was free!

It was in this state of mind that I arrived in Weimar. What resonance this name had once held for me! Goethe's city! I scarcely paid any attention to it. Hitler had cast a shadow over Goethe. I had received money from Vienna and could have bought all the good things that I had for so long done without, yet I didn't waste a single thought on them. Since my clothing had not yet arrived in Buchenwald when I was released from Dachau, the clothes of a supervisor had been given to me on loan for the trip home. These included a suit of cord velvet and an open shirt with no collar. Because I had no cap or hat, my shaven head betrayed my status as a released "convict." Waiting for my train at the station in Weimar, I walked back and forth on the platform – three hours, back and forth. But it was only my body in motion since my mind was still in camp.

Then the train arrived and I climbed aboard.

I had to change trains and wait once more. A railway employee approached me:

"What's your destination?"

"Vienna."

"Do you have money? You still have some time. Come into the lounge with me and have a beer."

They all knew that I came from Buchenwald. The shadow of this site of horrors hangs like a black nightmare over the entire area, over all of Germany.

I declined with a sincerely cordial expression of gratitude. Are there in reality still human beings out there?

An older gentleman, a worker moved up close beside me:

"Hey, Buddy, do you need something? Tell me. I'll help you."

At that point the sun rose for me again. The future opened up before me. These aren't Hitler's creatures. These are comrades. These are your brothers, just like those you just left behind.

So it was really true what my pals had told me in camp:

"There are still many human beings out there!"

And I was *free!*

In Vienna Again

My first thought the next morning is to look through all of the addresses and phone numbers of people I now had to visit to bring news of relatives in camp. I organize a list according to districts. I am under way from morning to evening on my visiting day and at first manage to meet very few. Many parts of my journey were in vain. "Relocated, location unknown," "deceased," "arrested": this was all there was for several on my list. For those I did meet, my appearance itself was comforting. I avoided questions that had to do with our treatment in camp. A haggard seventy-year-old asked me: "How can my poor husband hold up under such terrible drudgery?" My answer was: "I can assure you that he is doing wonderfully well, better even than many a younger man. He's plagued by only one worry: how you are bearing up."

One of my first stops was the house of the elder Kurtz, Willy's father. I wanted to find out how he had died and if I could learn more about Mia Petersen. I knew that the owner of a large flower shop lived in his building, someone by the name of Kauba, if I remember correctly. The business was closed and the man was in the military. I was lucky to find him at home. He had leave since his wife had just given birth.

Naturally I had to be careful. It wasn't out of the question that I might not be welcomed at such a time or even be faced with a worse reception. I only knew Kauba from Willy's stories. In my awkwardness, I lied: "Please excuse me, but can you tell me where I might find the old gentleman named Kurtz? The apartment is closed." "Oh my, the poor man has been dead for two months. Unfortunately we knew nothing about his affliction since he was always so tight-lipped and shy. Otherwise we would most certainly have come to his aid. We only learned the sad truth when he was taken to the main cemetery, him and his poor housekeeper Nedelka."

The way the man spoke revealed such honest empathy that I abandoned all reserve and casually remarked that I had wanted to bring him greetings from his son. Kauba pricked up his ears and scrutinized me. Then he closed the door to the next room. "You've been with Willy?" he whispered in excitement. "Is he still alive? Haven't the bastards hounded him to death like his poor father?"

"He's still alive," I answered, "and I hope he will survive imprisonment."

"Oh, my God, how the old man suffered. You know, Willy was his pride and joy. Why don't you sit down, Mr. . . . ?" – "Reich is my name." "Mr. Reich! In my experience, the story is one of the most disgraceful chapters in liberated Austria. With the help of her SS-lover, Mia was able to get her hands on the business. The old Kurtz didn't get one cent from her. He would have starved if Nedelka, his housekeeper, had not taken care of him. I did something to make his situation even worse. I advised him to apply to *Gauleiter* Bürckel for a small portion of the business. He did it. Instead of a response, he received notice to vacate his apartment. One day a couple of guys showed up with a truck and carried off everything except his bed and a living room chair. He resisted having the pictures taken off the walls and put up a fight. At that point they hurt him terribly. From then on he was completely apathetic and lay in bed without stirring. He seldom had any more lucid moments. And during those few moments it was heartbreaking to hear him call out: 'Willy, Willy, can't I just see you one more time!'

Nedelka took care of him a short while longer. But then it seemed that her savings had run out. On July 15 she opened up a gas connection and that evening both were found dead."

I was shaken by this tragedy. "This Mia! Long after his father's death she was still writing poor Willy passionate love letters." I sputtered indignantly: "She must be the epitome of maliciousness!"

"She certainly was! But there's more! She handed Willy's letters to the Gestapo and ascribed quite another meaning to them than what was actually there."

I squeezed Kauba's hand in gratitude – there are still good people in our beloved Vienna.

Now I could finally turn my attention to my own family. It was a terrible thought that we soon would be forced to leave the country, a country that every one of us loved with all our heart. But, on the other hand, there were things that lessened the pain of leaving. Above all else it was the desire to extricate the children from the quagmire of the Nazi youth. When possible, I avoided people unless I was absolutely sure that they had not undergone a change of heart. But guided by the microcosm of population in our close vicinity it seemed to be advisable – and the sooner, the better – to flee with the children to a country in which anything evil was not given a stamp of approval simply because "the *Führer* wanted it that way."

After the mean-spirited and pointless harassment that sprang from the same origins as the elaborate system of mental torture in Dachau, the completion of all the documents necessary for our departure to America with a stopover in England seemed at hand. We were expecting the paperwork in the next few days. Our journey was set to begin on the next Wednesday – barring, of course, any unforeseen obstacle.

We were expecting our passports at any moment and, as soon as we had them in hand, we wanted to leave immediately.

Traudl had taken the *Gymnasium* leaving-exam without any problems at all in school and, since the final exam was based on materials that had been taught for 8 years, she remained untainted by the new curriculum for Third Reich high schools that were to go into effect during the following school year. She had been told that I had mistakenly been arrested instead of another man of the same name. And, that clearing up the mistake would be a protracted process, but I would soon be set free.

Since her exam she had lived with Mautzi's brother. The idea had come up since she had graduated together with his daughter, a close friend of hers. As it turned out, however, both the sons had been illegal members of the Nazi party. Wasn't it possible that this setting could have had repercussions for Traudi?

For the first time since the disaster of March 11 my will to survive in order to take revenge was shaken when I heard this. Again and again I caught myself thinking about fleeing the emotional torments inherent in the situation by committing suicide.

When I discussed with Mautzi the horrifying picture of the future I had painted in my mind, she attempted to comfort me by reassuring me that this environment had not rubbed off on Traudl in the slightest. Her firmly rooted character had remained unaffected and she had not deviated from its inborn direction. But she added: "It would, however, be good if you would talk to her openly about it."

Up to this point we had not spoken a word in the children's presence about the barbarism I had seen and experienced during the past few months. Slowly, however, I began to allude to such things in Traudl's presence, and while we were on a walk together I described various episodes of my life in camp. She looked at me with horror in her eyes and, for a long while, remained speechless. It was certain that she had understood immediately!

Our Nephew

Events that seemed calculated to make our departure less painful now came fast and furious.

One of my nephews was engaged to an Aryan. A visit by the bride's father had just been announced, and the nephew was making positively festive preparations for a reception in his new apartment. Mautzi had furnished this residence for him with furniture from our own home. His apartment, which had formerly belonged to a Jewish physician, had been assigned to him by the "Party." He defended himself at Mautzi's reaction to his bargain-rate price as follows: one of his colleagues who had paid *more* than the price stipulated by the medical association had been threatened with concentration camp for a violation of Party discipline.

This incident had put a considerable chill in Mautzi's relationship to this nephew who, from the cradle on, had enjoyed her special affection and favor. Now, however, it was about to cool down even further.

While Mautzi was busy arranging the apartment and making preparations in the kitchen for the grand gentleman's visit, her nephew suddenly came up to her. At first he acted embarrassed and stammered something about his future father-in-law's strict adherence to the Party line. He finally came out with it: naturally, she was herself most welcome to attend the party, but he asked her not to bring Traudl along.

When Mautzi told me this story, her memories of the scene brought her into such an emotional uproar that she exclaimed – with tears streaming from her eyes: "At first, I didn't believe my ears. Then I asked: 'Okay, but why in the world shouldn't Traudi come along?' And then that scoundrel had the nerve to say to my face: 'Well, you know that my father-in-law is a firm believer in race theory. After all, Traudl is of mixed blood . . . ' I got so angry that I took the roast and cake that I had spent so much time and energy preparing for this jackass and threw them on the floor. I've never been so enraged in my entire life. I grabbed my coat and my hat from the rack and ran out of there."

Mautzi was terribly depressed by this experience that she had to endure just before leaving her homeland. She told me in a voice filled with melancholy: "It almost seems as if these people have been infected with some kind of disease. How can this change be explained in any other way? Even in Marie I've noticed signs of the puzzling transformation. I can no longer read in her eyes what's going on in her heart. You know how kind she was to me and the children while you were gone and how she now supports all of us, especially you, right? But then! There's a shadow that's fallen between us. The only thing that brightens my hopes for the future is the worried plea that she almost shouted at me: 'For heaven's sake, you can see how I'm suffering – don't force me to endanger the happiness of my children.' I can't get the words out of my head."

MEETINGS

In the concentration camp I had learned to look calmly and directly at even the most horrific sight. But these last days in

Vienna had undermined my fighting spirit and exhausted me. I had only one wish and that was to be gone from here and to live among people who could say what they think.

I had once more been on the prowl for travel documents and came home in a good mood. This time my mood wasn't a pose to cheer up Mautzi, but was based on my experiences that morning. To begin with, I had run across Horwath, the international soccer star, on the *Wollzeile*. At first I intentionally glanced to one side so that I wouldn't set off any pangs of conscience. But to my absolute delight as well as amazement, he embraced and kissed me. At the same time he called out so loudly that everyone around us stopped in their tracks: "I cannot believe that you're acting like we don't know each other! Don't you know that we athletes have stuck by you? You've always been honest in your commentaries. No athlete will ever forget that." Truly moved by this greeting and acclaim, I replied: "My dear friend, I thank you from the bottom of my heart for your friendship and, wherever I end up, I'll never forget our meeting today – but please, let's lower our voices! You must be aware how easy it is to slip up these days and, if they arrest just one of us, it will undoubtedly be *me* again." As I said these last words, I was laughing, and Herwath soon echoed my amusement.

At this point another athlete arrived on the scene, a broad-shouldered, blond giant of a man who was a European boxing champion. He shook my hand with such warmth that I couldn't move my fingers for a time. "Such a pleasure," he called out – again in an alarmingly loud voice. "Mr. Reich! I have thought about you so often while you've been away. But now I hope you're staying here." – "Not possible, my dear friend; we'll soon be taking our leave again, this time maybe forever! I've still got a number of things to do, but hope to leave by tomorrow or the next day."

"I wish you all the best, but I really believe that we'll see each other in Vienna again soon. What's happening here surely can't last forever," Horwath said. Lazek chimed in: "There's nothing to eat, denunciations occur constantly, and there are now more lies told in a quarter of an hour than there used to be in a quarter of a year."

The words of these two splendid fellows warmed my heart. I interpreted them as the voice of the people, and they strengthened my belief in the future. Shaking hands, we parted. Horwath was crying like a baby.

And on *Stephansplatz* I ran into someone else I knew.

Here was another friend standing there with whom I had spent my youth. As boys we had played together on the youth team of the same club and later made countless tours together as members of the same ski club. I spotted him from a distance and eagerly made my way towards him. And then I saw that he recognized me. He stopped, unsure what to do next. He turned away and quickly went off in the other direction. My mood sobered and I simply continued on . . .

As if to round off my final experiences in the Third Reich, I stumbled upon two other acquaintances. The first was a man I had known in the military. My memories of him were not at all pleasant ones, and I would rather have avoided him. But he greeted me in a very friendly manner and began to tell me how well he was doing. His brother Julius had been a secret member of the SS for years and was held in such esteem that he was able to send all kinds of business deals in his direction. He said with a laugh: "We used to think that Julius was a nitwit, but it's turned out that he's the cleverest of all the brothers."

Finally, I ran across the path of a graphic artist whom I had formerly employed and held in high regard. I took the initiative and addressed him: "Good afternoon, Mr. Polsterer. How are you?"

The man looked at me as if he were seeing me for the first time in his life. Looking me straight in the eye, he lied: "You seem to be in error, sir." I had quickly calmed down however and said as I went my own way: "Oh, excuse me please, you're right. I have no idea how I could have made such a mistake."

The Last Day

It was now time to say goodbye to the house and garden where we had spent half a lifetime. Again, everything happened differently than Mautzi and I had imagined. A policeman had been there that morning. He had brought along a new arrest warrant, and I had just barely had enough time to climb out the kitchen window into the backyard and flee.

Our hour of departure, a time that should have had a ceremonious feeling, had become an hour of fear and alarm. Mautzi stayed at home alone, and I was to go directly to the train. I had to sneak out of my own house like a thief. The bloodhounds were nipping at my heels again.

While I was looking through the garden fence to see if the policeman had left, the old caretaker, Kopetzky, was suddenly standing next to me. He had seen my escape through the window and had hurried after me in order to wish me luck on my travels into a murky future. The old man pressed my hand warmly: "I wish you happiness in whatever comes into your life and hope you end up in a free land where you can finally find peace after so much suffering. I am grateful for all the kindness that you have shown me and my wife over all these years."

The good man's eyes were filled with tears. I was deeply moved as well. "My wife," I said, "has told me how you came to her aide, how often you courageously protected her from harassment by stepping in at the right moment. I'll always remember you for this. We will hold dear the memories of both you and your wife as living proof that humanity and the meaning of justice in our Austria have not yet been completely wiped out."

He declared quite simply: "I'm a Socialist and have done nothing more than uphold my human obligation." We then shook hands like two old friends.

The Departure

As the doors closed and the train finally began to move, I saw – as if through a veil – those people on the platform crying and waving as they gradually disappeared in the fog. Exhausted, I sank into my seat. We went through border control in Aachen and sat tensely scrunched together. Now the final test began. Suddenly someone cried out: "All Jews, out of the train!" Perplexed, I looked at my wife. Should I get out and should she stay seated? An SS-guard appeared. "Are you a Jew?" – "Yes, I am!" – "Then see to it that you exit the car!" He looked at my passport and then took my wife's. "Are you related to this man?" – "Yes, he's my husband." –

"Then you get out as well!"

We were herded along with hundreds of others into a narrow passageway. There we had to line up in single file. Next we went individually into the booths for physical examinations. My wife went into the women's booth. I was forced to completely disrobe, but found the procedure otherwise inoffensive. Getting dressed again, however, went too slowly for the guard and so he helped me along with a few kicks. When I emerged into a glass veranda where we were led after the exam, my wife came in from the other side. We could see on the faces of other people that things hadn't gone quite so well with them: there were swollen eyelids and some were bleeding from their eyes and noses. My wife's smile had a calming effect on me . . .

Postscript to Buchenwald

Maximilian Reich wrote the following chapters on the basis of detailed conversations with a friend – also a prisoner – who was released in 1939 and initially emigrated to England.

Organized Thievery

The normal Nazi corruption was already mentioned in my report on the camp at Dachau. It became even more and more extensive in Buchenwald. It was an everyday occurrence right from the start that the prisoners were forced to buy large articles from the SS camp contingent at excessive prices, some items of low quality and most of them quite unnecessary. Once it was a batch of socks, another time, so-called woolen waistcoats. The procedure was always the same: certain items had to be bought, and those prisoners who had more money than others were forced to help pay the bill of their poorer comrades. It could happen that a pair of the cheapest socks was priced at several hundred Marks. But that was a milder form of corruption.

Communists and Social Democrats were the oldest residents in all the concentration camps, and it was from these groups that most of the room seniors and capos were recruited. In Buchenwald many of these were not barbarous enough for the SS-sadists and were gradually replaced by "greens," essentially, one would have to say, well established and seasoned career criminals. By the end of 1938 they held all the positions filled by prisoners, starting with the posts of camp senior, camp police, medical aides, block and room seniors as well as capos and office assistants. The first "green" camp senior operated a reign of terror. The entire camp was linked in a consolidated network of corruption. There were fixed fees and rates for every advantage that a prisoner could possibly acquire. Food, tobacco, even alcohol could be bought – for a price. A release from hard labor could be bought, better underwear purchased. For hard cash, a prisoner could even get his bed made or buy a shoeshine. For these criminals, the extortion practiced on the poor and defenseless prisoners was child's play. They had been appointed to their duties just because they were so eagerly ready – in accord with the camp leadership and the SS – to make life into a living hell for the prisoners if their own plights could be made just a bit more tolerable. The real skill of these criminals was in managing the transfer of the prisoners' funds into their own hands, since apart from smaller sums – small at least in the eyes of these gangsters – the assets of the prisoners were in the custody of the camp administration. But the "green" organization had connections that went beyond prisoners' circles. And the prisoners who were in possession of deposited funds were in fact successful in obtaining permission to withdraw larger amounts. The appetite of the crooks grew with their success. They were ingenious in incessantly contriving new means to squeeze out every last Mark from the prisoners' accounts.

The main meal in camp was soup. Before the soup was passed out, the "greens" had anything removed that looked nutritious. Pieces of bacon or other meats or vegetables were separated and had to be paid for with hard cash by the prisoners as "extras," that is, if they had the financial means. A pauper would receive only the broth. Naturally, the imprisoned Jews were the main targets of these robberies. Just like muggers on the street, it was "your money or your life." The criminals knew no mercy in practicing their extortion. Among prisoners, on the other hand, there was absolute panic. It's no wonder then that the situation deteriorated into orgies of corruption that finally led to them being exposed.

These "green" camp demons cut off the prisoners' water supply and handed out a cup of water only after a payment of 5 to 10 Marks. If they wanted to drink, the dehydrated prisoners had to pay. The price for a cigarette was several Marks as well. On the other hand, if someone could fork over 100 to 200 Marks, he could buy himself "sick" into the infirmary where he could relax for a few days.

Since there were "greens" in the administrative offices as well, the chief gangster also knew exactly how much money a prisoner had on deposit, and this information channeled the raids in the most promising directions. The villains kept an eye out especially for so-called "police inmates." These inmates were allowed to retain their own clothing and keep everything that they had on them at the moment of their arrest. Their money and their valuables were soon in the possession of the crooks. Among this group there were naturally those totally depraved and those of less brutish character. The Jews who were taken into custody during the November pogrom simply had to pay for everything: blankets and shoes, food and water – in short, everything made available by the camp. In addition, the number of so-called "comradely thefts" grew steadily.

As the corruption took on the scale described above, the bandits – which the camp director had deployed as guardians of discipline and order – began to get unpleasant for him and his SS-comrades as well. Brutality, merciless treachery, a perverse delight in causing suffering – these were commendable characteristics even in prisoners, yet they must not be allowed to develop into a disruption of business.

SS-Corruption

As previously mentioned, the prisoners were victims of extortion by the "greens" as well as the "blacks" – the SS – although the latter used different methods. The thievery practiced by the organized criminals was played out openly for all to see. That set in motion by the SS-criminals was also easily recognized, if one had access to the correspondence in the office or the accounting records. The most innocuous maneuver was double billing. The same delivery of bricks and lumber was simply posted twice, once for the troops' garrison and once for the prisoners' quarters. Rödl, the camp commandant, demonstrated an incredible ingenuity. During the many festive evening celebrations where spirits ran high and where expensive champagne was imbibed in large quantities, large deficits always arose. Rödl simply covered these through contributions that he imposed on the prisoners. At various times, blankets, then dishes, then underwear, then woolen garments had to be replaced. This was accomplished by simply charging each barracks a collective purchase price – i.e., contribution – of, for example, 300 Marks. The prisoners had to raise this sum – how, that was their business.

Rödl pulled off a minor masterpiece of extortion during the Christmas season. For their amusement, the SS arranged a snowball fight between two groups of prisoners. This mischief-making took place on the square where roll call was held. On the edge of the square stood a cage containing the so-called camp menagerie where an eagle, two buzzards, and a wolf were confined. On the day after the snowball fight the wolf had vanished from his cage. Rödl announced that the wolf had been killed by a snowball and assessed a damage compensation of 8,000 Reichsmark, that the Jews in camp had to raise.

One day, under threat of the most severe penalties, every bit of money that the Jewish prisoners had been able to hide from the "greens" was squeezed out of them by the camp administration. The promised credit voucher never came – the poor devils had simply been robbed.

It was clear to us that several members of the SS worked together with the "greens" and profited from the revenue of this corrupt economic system, although we had no evidence of this. This came only later after a huge scandal when the "greens" and the SS marched together into the clink.

Corruption Collides with Corruption

Unlike the wisdom contained in the German aphorism, one crow will indeed peck out the eye of another crow – that is, once the one crow can no longer turn a "blind eye" to what the other is doing. The two-tracked enterprise of corruption finally led to a momentous – and, for the prisoners – a liberating collision. The "green" reign of terror came to an abrupt end.

The widespread corruption involving extortion as well as the arrival in November of an appalling obsession with tormenting Jewish prisoners led to a rapid decline in job performance and productivity. Jews were made to stand at attention for hours in freezing temperatures: noses, fingers, entire hands and toes became frostbitten. Even in the event of such physical affliction, it was not permitted for Jews to be treated by physicians. It was even forbidden to dispense drugs to Jews. Moreover, it was also strictly forbidden for incarcerated physicians to render any aid whatsoever to fellow inmates. It did happen, however, but with the most severe punishment for all involved. Food rations – already meager – were cut in half, a ban on smoking and writing spoiled the last bit of pleasure and stole the final mental support. Suicides were daily occurrences; hundreds died and others wasted away. The ability to work and – as a result – labor productivity sank to a minimum. Both physically and psychologically debilitated, the prisoners bought themselves out of every chore they could. In spite of the most severe punishments – hours of exercise and the flogging of every fifth prisoner – the most pressing jobs remained unfinished and Rödl began to feel uneasy. He had to account for a certain amount of work accomplished by the prisoners to the highest Gestapo offices.

The "greens" had also learned from their role models and bosses about the utilization of their booty. They overlooked nothing that could be bought with the extorted money and celebrated with drinking binges. The alcohol bought with the blood money flowed in rivers. The insolence of this criminal mob seemed to have no limits after they were able to "placate" the SS-guards on duty. On their inspection rounds, the Black Shirts passed by the barracks where the carousing was in full sway without even being tempted by the drunken bellowing to take a look inside.

But at some point, things were bound to go too far. After a huge squabble, the scandal broke open. Some pilferage of the SS kitchen had taken place. This was followed by interrogations and, directly thereafter, arrests of some "greens" and SS. Surprisingly, Rödl imposed few individual punishments, although a few of them were flogged and some "green" as well as "black" thugs were imprisoned – instead, the camp commandant took steps toward a radical modification of the organization. Above all else, the camp senior and chief gangster Richter was dismissed as well as other stooges from the criminals' ranks. Under torturous methods of interrogation, one of them had betrayed hiding places where large sums of money were found. A block senior had a packet of hundred Mark bills that went unclaimed in camp. Two thousand Marks were found under the floorboards of one room. These "professionals" knew how to hide rings, watches, and other valuables in the heels of their shoes. Almost forty arrests were made and even a novel kind of punishment introduced: the so-called "black bunker."

The windows in block 3 were boarded over and the prisoners had to spend many days in complete darkness. In spite of the freezing winter temperatures, those in the "black bunker" were given neither beds nor blankets. Their meal rations were reduced by one quarter, and each received 25 strokes of the cane every day. Squad leader Sommer monitored the implementation of these punishments. One night a number of these "greens" broke out of the "black bunker" and forcefully entered a Jewish barracks. Threatening to expose the occupants as accomplices, they demanded food. Out of fear, the Jewish prisoners in block 15 gave them a few provisions – a certain Goldstein gave them everything he had. The room senior sounded the alarm, the SS troops appeared, and soon led the "greens" away, taking Goldstein with them. They were all put in chains. Goldstein committed suicide. A few of the "greens" died as well, including Richter, the former camp senior.

A Change of System

As mentioned before, Rödl had ousted all of the criminal types from positions as room seniors, block seniors, etc. He replaced them with "reds" or political prisoners. The camp commandant apparently realized that he now had to protect his own skin. If he himself didn't want to fall out of favor, he had to see to it that the mandatory work outcomes could be reported since inspections could happen any day. It could only be guaranteed that the work would be done if the supervisors were incorruptible. By trusting the "reds" with the task, Rödl – probably unintentionally and unconsciously – paid them the highest compliment. And he must have assumed that they wouldn't let themselves be bribed. The

Communist Bartel, a clever and fearless man, was appointed camp senior. He was sufficiently courageous to be able to extract benefits for the prisoners from Rödl's embarrassment. As the leader of a delegation of block seniors he was able to arrange a meeting with Rödl where he presented him with a memorandum in which the following demands were set out: the abolition of corporal punishment, Sunday rest, greater liberty after work hours, better food, and no collective punishments.

The entire camp awaited the return of this heroic delegation in breathless suspense. Some feared that we'd never again lay eyes on our model comrades, but the miracle happened and the camp commandant accepted Bartel's memorandum point by point.

The camp became almost fit for human habitation compared with the previous hell on earth. Corporal punishment was banned; Sundays were to be free of labor; and on Saturdays, each man was to receive an extra sausage ration at mealtime. The men began staging simple cabaret acts – there were plenty of prominent artists in our group. The corruption ceased, and the labor output increased by leaps and bounds. This luxury, however, lasted only three weeks. All of the privileged treatment was suddenly abolished. Rödl was apparently relying on the honesty and the incorruptibility of the "reds" and that they would pass inspections even if the improved conditions ceased to exist. He wasn't afraid that the earlier corruption would return.

But Rödl went even further and organized the old social evenings, that is, the drinking binges. He also returned to his old system of covering deficits by savings on prisoners' food. At least once a month he personally announced over the loudspeaker: "Due to the poor work performance there will be no meals at all on Sunday."

SPOTLIGHT ON THE GALLOWS (DECEMBER 21, 1938)

The effects of Nazi propaganda on camp life were unmistakable. The Nazi addiction to gigantic stagings of terror spectacles never surfaced so clearly – neither in Berchtesgaden nor in Munich – as it did in the staging of poor Peter Forster's execution. He had escaped. He and his comrade were the only ones who had been able to escape Buchenwald. One of the brown-shirted guards might have arrested both desperate men or shot them down if he had had time. He had collapsed while giving chase, but still had been able to gun down Forster's comrade. What a disparity compared to the tens of thousands of slow, painful murders in which the guard himself had been involved! Forster escaped over the Czech border where he was granted asylum as a political refugee. September passed, then October. Forster was not granted asylum by any of the powers that now had flung Czechoslovakia into the maw of the Nazi juggernaut. The Czechs resisted as long as they could until, finally, they were forced to surrender Forster. The brown beast savored its triumph and staged it in the most grandiose Nazi style.

It goes without saying that Forster was given the death sentence. I don't know what they did to him before the sentence was carried out, although my own experiences lead me to fear the cruelest treatment imaginable. Death held no terror for any of us. On the contrary, most of us longed for it. I, as well as others, resisted dying in order not to do our tormentors the favor of giving in to their efforts; that is, we hoped to "take revenge" on them by the mere act of maintaining our will to live. But above everything else the desire for retribution sustained us, the unyielding drive to be there when, in the future, scores were settled.

The gallows were set up on the roll call square a full week before the execution. The execution itself took place at night. All the prisoners had to form up. We stood at attention in the dark and thanked God that at least our presence was only pro forma and that we wouldn't be forced to be witnesses. During daylight hours, closing our eyes or looking away would not have been possible. The SS-guards silently moving through our ranks were sure to fish out and punish with clubs those of us who were not assiduously fulfilling our duty as witnesses. And whoever came away with a couple of blows to the head could count himself lucky.

But we had underestimated the directors of this atrocity. Suddenly floodlights all around us were lit up and illuminated the gallows and the onlookers in a flood of light. At the base of the scaffolding stood a group of SS men surrounding Forster. Our heartbeats faltered, yet given the steely tranquility of the main person we soon calmed down. Forster stood quietly there with his gaze directed upwards. During the following excruciating minutes, his steadfastness and fortitude never wavered.

The state prosecutor spoke a few short sentences in the typically staccato manner of the Prussian military. He set forth Forster's crimes and closed:

"Consequently, I consign the prisoner who has been sentenced to death to the camp commandant for further legal action."

Once again the camp commandant stood there, visibly affected by the alcohol he had consumed. His retort resembled babbling more than an order: "Do your duty!" We couldn't figure out whether it was a wish or a command, but the scene was unforgettable.

The hangman stepped forward. It was the camp's oldest political refugee. He approached the gallows and began winding the rope in a coil. At that moment we didn't realize why this was happening. Then he grabbed Forster and pulled him closer, put the noose around his neck and hoisted him into the air. When the body of the poor man was high enough that his feet swung back and forth in the air over his head, the hangman jumped up and grabbed Forster's knees. The jolt from the sudden weight on the dangling body must have broken Forster's backbone. Himmler's faithful lackey leapt back down and now it became evident what he had intended with the coiling of the rope. The hanged man began to rotate at increasing speed – the energy of the coiled rope accelerating the rotation of the body – while spotlights bathed the grisly scene in light. A few minutes later the performance ended and we marched off.

Shaken to the core by the gruesome scene and plodding laboriously, a man next to me remarked to his buddy: "Can God let this go unpunished?"

"Not a chance," the comrade whispered: "God's retribution will follow."

New Years in Hell

Roll call on New Year's Day dragged on for an unusually long time. It was so bitterly cold that everyone waited for the "fall out" command with eager anticipation. Time seemed to stand still while we stood freezing in the frosty morning, waiting for the announcement from the loudspeaker. What kind of diabolical idea did the camp commandant Rödl have in mind today? No one in camp had yet seen Rödl sober. Whenever he came into view he was obviously under the influence of a large quantity of alcohol.

Finally we heard his raspy voice coming from the loudspeaker. "Yesterday, workers in the SS-canteen smuggled alcohol into the camp and a group of irresponsible individuals drank themselves into a stupor to celebrate the New Year. Now I intend to stage a New Year's celebration for you that is more to my taste."

What happened that night on January 1 – 2, 1939 on the roll call square of the Buchenwald camp is unique and unrivaled, even in Buchenwald, a camp unique in its horrible excesses. The 12,000 prisoners were made to form a huge square and the 250 inmates accused of smuggling alcohol were marched into the middle of the formation. An SS-guard ordered them to count off and every fifth man was ordered to form up to one side. We all were shivering and not just because of the cold weather. We believed with certainty that those fifty men selected were to be shot. Floodlights illuminated the scene to daylight brilliance. I've experienced a lot in the camps, but nothing nearer to insanity than what happened on this January night. For a time, they let those fifty men and all of us in doubt as to their fate. There was absolute silence over the scene, interrupted only now and again when one of the victims was unable to suppress a loud moaning sound.

In the meantime the camp band of inmate musicians had marched in. The camp commandant Rödl himself indicated where they were to take their position. Fifty sawhorses were set up and the chosen few were tied to them. While the band played, fifty SS-heroes took up their posts, each one at a sawhorse, and began their handiwork of whipping their quarry. The bullwhips lashed the naked bodies of the victims to the musical beat. At times their heartbreaking whimpering drowned out the music entirely. Rödl walked from sawhorse to sawhorse and seemed fully satisfied with the first part of his belated New Year's celebration. We breathed a sigh of relief when our sorely beaten Comrades were unfastened and could stagger back into our ranks.

Compared with this sadistic overture, the continuation of the punitive program trailed off considerably. Those in black (indicating an unwillingness to work) and violet (the color of Jehovah's Witnesses) were forced to put on a jousting tournament. A pair of men from each group – one pair after the other and always with one man on the shoulders of the other – entered the ring to do battle. At full speed ahead each team ran towards its opponent. The winning pair was the one whose top man could remain "in the saddle."

I still remember the solemn final act when camp commandant Rödl, goose-stepping to the sounds of the Buchenwald hymn by Hermann Leopoldi, marched by the cordon of 12,000. The German officers can indeed be proud of this comrade! The march back to the barracks was ordered at 5 minutes past midnight.

EMILIE REICH

WHEN MY HUSBAND WAS IN DACHAU

I never thought I would ever write anything other than letters or entries in my book of household accounts. I was completely happy for the 25 years I lived together with my husband and our children. I'm not at all ashamed to say that quite openly – happy. Not that life hadn't dealt us some difficult situations! My husband was in the First World War and I simply waited at home for him with the children. I was afraid for him and full of hope as well. Afterwards there was a long period when he wasn't employed. We weren't doing well at all, just like many others. Death took my beloved son, my only boy.

During those last years I was particularly distressed by a number of things. My husband fell ill with a serious heart condition. But it was not only the illness nor just the frequent turmoil in Austrian life. We quickly adjusted to this volatility. There were alarming rumors coming out of the Third Reich. Whether it was rooted in experience or denial, we simply didn't want to believe what was being reported in German newspapers. Even when acquaintances and friends living there came and reported events in person, we tried to pretend that we were hearing individual distortions or perhaps naïve exaggerations. It simply wasn't possible that human beings could treat, torment, humiliate, and even torture other human beings to death. At the time it still wasn't clear what kept me from sleeping, what it was that depressed me. I knew only that it was a nameless fear. And the fear was summed up in the nagging question: Are they coming to Austria, or not? But, with my husband's support, I was always able to calm myself. My brothers and sisters did their best to allay my fears as well. The chance that National Socialism might take root in the hearts of Austria's easy going, jovial and pious farmers and peasants seemed remote. And it seemed self evident that the

Austrian workers who represented more than half of Austria's population would reject it. And yet things happened quite differently.

I come from an old Austrian family of good reputation. We can trace our family tree back to the 16th century – I say this not because I'm tainted by some sort of racial theories, but to the contrary. I say it to show that the Nazi racial madness with its frenzied hatreds does not concern itself with such details. My father held one of the highest offices in the Monarchy.

I sit here in England today and can't understand that so many million Englishmen do not know, do not want to know, simply cannot comprehend that millions of human beings are being enslaved, martyred, and killed. And it's happening so close to us. In the middle of a country that many British tourists still visit and extol so enthusiastically . . . And yet when I think back, I have to admit that even I often thought that the reports we heard in Austria about the atrocities of the SA and SS in Germany just *had* to be exaggerated . . .

My husband, a sports journalist, was never politically active. Anti-Semitism was discernible in his publishing house, although he was never personally a victim. On the contrary, he enjoyed the greatest respect and his work received all kinds of critical acclaim. He considered the hostility to Jews at the place where he worked – a business run by the government – as tactical anti-Semitism designed to take the wind out of the Nazis' sails.

But just as suddenly as the Deluge, the calamity broke in upon unlucky Austria. It's not as if there hadn't been forewarnings, but those of us living here convinced ourselves again and again that the danger would pass us by. We had all participated in this delusion. The "world" could not permit our country – a small but internationally known and respected nation – simply to be overwhelmed. We had full trust in Schuschnigg. He was an honorable man and a brave soul. And then we heard his farewell address on the radio. We no longer heard the speech of a fighter as in Innsbruck – "Red-White-Red to the death!" – but rather the speech of a resigned man, a betrayed man. It turned my heart to ice and I burst into tears.

A person naturally always thinks first of him- or herself. I'm no exception. I reflected what was likely to happen now – whether the upheaval would mean the loss of all the rights that my husband had earned in 30 years in an honorable career. What consequences would this have for my children?

The next day my husband was asked to come to the office of the publishing house's newly appointed Nazi commissioner. There he was showered with compliments and recognition. In view of the situation at the moment, it was suggested he might take a four-week vacation. This strengthened my hopes and those of my family that National Socialism in Austria would take on milder forms in Austria than in the Reich. How soon we would be disabused of this fantasy in the most brutal way possible!

Horror stories arrived hourly. We scarcely dared to go on the street anymore. We heard about the arrest of journalists who were friends of ours.

Our doorbell rang at 6:30 p.m. on March 17. I went to the door. Two men were standing outside who established themselves as Gestapo officials and asked to speak to my husband. He walked out of the room as pale as a sheet. The men requested that he come with them and then searched his clothing for weapons. They assured me that it was simply a matter of setting straight a few facts and that my husband would be at home again on the following day. I heard the bolt in the door fall and I was alone . . .

The following night was a nightmare. My sister, a girlfriend, and our doctor were very concerned about me. To get me past the initial shock they tried to ease my pain with comforting words but even more with medications. I remained semiconscious. The daylight finally, finally arrived. An exhausting battle now began, a battle between two unequal powers. I, a woman deprived of all rights, fighting for her husband and father of her children against the machinery of the Nazi persecution. On the one hand, the commitment of a love that would stop at nothing, on the other hand, a brutal power that would not shrink from any wickedness.

I learned that my husband had been brought to the police prison on Rossauerlände. I packed some clean clothes as well as some provisions and set off for the prison. I was not allowed to see him nor were his parcels accepted, and I trudged back home. My sister tried with gentle persistence to find some kind of sign for me that my husband was still alive. It was just a short while ago that the doctor had ordered him to take better care of himself. How would he be able to bear up under this tension, this terror?

In the midst of hundreds of women I stood daily in front of the prison. Nothing! Finally, after ten days, I received the first message from my husband, a postcard with the words: "Don't despair, I'm holding out okay." And we received instructions to bring clothes for our husbands. What a relief! At least I now knew that he was alive and that his heart had tolerated the stress.

Both of my girls – ages 10 and 18 – had been with relatives for a few days. The older one was just about to graduate from high school. I brought them both home again at this point. Although it seems idiotic to me today, because I had initially been so anxious, I could scarcely look them in the eyes for the first few days. To have thrown Max in jail – without being charged, without being interrogated – a person who had never done anything dishonorable, let alone committed a crime – this was outrageous!! What was I supposed to tell the children, how could I make it comprehensible for them? I was thoroughly ashamed of the clowns who were holding him.

My eighty-four-year-old mother who had lived with us for the past eighteen years had to leave since I wanted to spare her the terrible upheavals that now filled my days.

Once more the wives were standing in long lines in front of the prison. The mob scorned us, but not a single one of us moved from the spot. Finally, in the second week, I saw my husband. A policeman had left the gate open for just a moment. I saw him smiling for happiness when he caught a glimpse of me, but then the gate was slammed shut again. I stumbled home in tears, envied by the hundreds of women who shared my fate but to whom even this meager happiness was denied. At the time I didn't know that 24 hours after this short "reunion" my husband, as a so-called "security detainee," would already be – together with 150 fellow prisoners – on the train to the netherworld of Dachau as a so-called "security detainee."

Totally unsuspecting, I again brought clean clothes for him. They told me that he was in the prison hospital. So that was it: his bad heart had failed. There was no longer any hope. Almost insane from dismay, I went to the prison hospital. I was turned away. But I persisted in pleading for admittance. The SA-guard at the door however just grinned obscenely: "If he has died, you will be notified."

I still have no idea even today how I then got home. Crying, I crept through the streets. It was a long way, but I couldn't take a tram since it was impossible to be with other human beings. Human beings? These weren't human beings. They were cowardly murderers, all of them, a cowardly mob of killers! They all wore the swastika, the symbol of heartlessness, the emblem of a murderer on their lapel.

For ten days I heard nothing from my husband, nor was I able to find out where he was. For ten days and nights I didn't know if he was suffering or even if he was still alive. The brutal laugh of the SA-guard rang in my ears for ten days and nights: "If he has died, you will be notified."

I finally received a double postcard. His handwriting! He was alive! He wrote: "Be brave – I am well. Write often!" I was overcome with happiness. Then I took a look at the second card and almost collapsed. The message on this card began: "Your husband has been in the concentration camp at Dachau since April 2 . . ." I could read no further. A haze settled over my eyes. Only when I fully regained consciousness did I grasp the shocking truth. The horrible truth dawned on me that in Hitler's Reich even insanity progressed to higher and higher levels. I screamed so loudly – I was told later – that everyone in the whole house heard me: "He hasn't done anything. He can't be punished for doing nothing!" As if the question "why" were still valid here! By chance, a gas company employee happened by and witnessed my despair. He persuaded me to be brave for the children's sake and that it would all turn out well. My sister arrived later. I broke into a fit of rage when I saw her – the person I had loved most deeply before my husband and children with a swastika on her coat – contaminated by the pestilence of Nazism. Finally, my anguish at my husband's plight prevailed, and I wept in the arms of my sister, the best friend I had ever had.

Other than in Germany where only party members wore the swastika, everyone in Austria who was "entitled" to it, had one in their buttonhole. In this way all non-Aryans were immediately recognizable and exposed to the foulest insults. Foreigners wore the flags of their countries to fend off abuse and serious mistreatment.

The next day I started my marches from one authority to the other. I sought out every person who might be able to help my husband. I attempted to make clear that he was the victim of an error, since it was well known that he had never paid any attention to politics. A package that I sent to Dachau came back without any letter. A few days later, my husband's picture appeared in some trashy Nazi rag and – as I later found out – at the same time in the SS-periodical, the *Schwarze Korps*. Here I myself saw for the first time the ruthless techniques of Nazi propaganda. My husband's photograph had been "touched up" until he was unrecognizable. It was a terrible caricature, no longer a photograph, and if not for the caption, I would never have recognized him myself in this "image." The text matched the picture: "The Jew Maximilian Reich – he too danced merrily along with the rest of the atrocity-propagandists and agitators." I remember as well that this publication, which should have filled me with fear and horror, didn't really scare me that much. It was partly because I was already so worn down that my distress could scarcely be heightened, but partly as well because I convinced myself that I now had proof in my hands that it must be a case of mistaken identity. My husband had never written a political article, so it was impossible that he had been an agitator or written atrocity propaganda. In this spirit, based on the publication in the *Schwarze Korps*, I now sent petitions to the Gestapo in Vienna, to Hitler, Bürckel, and Himmler, as well as to the Gestapo in Berlin. The answers were all the same: "Will be forwarded."

Thank God that a letter and a card arrived every week from my husband, and even if they couldn't relay anything substantial, they were proof that he was still alive. That spurred me again and again to feverish searches for ways to bring about his release. This constant speculation about ways to help him – whom we might seek out, which direction we should turn, this hurrying back and forth from office to office, always in vain – this was a great strain on our nerves. And yet it was the only thing that sustained my will to live. I say "our" because my lot was by no means unique. And as an Aryan I had it much easier: I was pushed around less and not abused at all. I had access to officials who remained unapproachable for others. I had it a lot easier than most of my fellow sufferers. I almost had to laugh when I tried to imagine that my situation was "better," since it seemed so terrible to me. But then I thought of the others and had to admit that they were much worse off. Unbelievable, but true.

A futile request, the denial of a petition or interview had ceased being occasions for despair. One failure after another simply meant that a new path had to be explored. My life was totally focused on the one goal: getting my husband released.

After many attempts in vain, I succeeded in getting an interview at the end of May in the office of the Viennese Gestapo. I talked with the head of the press bureau, a polite and proper German. Above all, he promised me material help so that I could at least acquire the basic necessities for the children and myself. In spite of the promises made by the chief of the *Vorwärts* publishing house – who should have been obligated to pay my husband a large sum of money – I had not received one penny. When I explained that my husband was innocent and that he ought to be freed, the official said that this was regrettably not possible at the moment. I should hang on, and my husband would definitely be home again by the end of July. This was devastating. It was now the end of May. Another two whole months! 60 days filled with anguish and worry! But I finally consoled myself with the thought that at least I had been given a definite date to look forward to. The promise had been made with such sincerity that I didn't doubt its truth, although very soon things happened that ought to have made me leery. But a person will gladly believe what he or she desires, and I needed hope in order not to collapse.

The allocation of assistance pledged to me by the Gestapo press relations' officer was not granted. The district office referred me to the Israeli Cultural Community, although they were well aware that as Catholics my children and I had no right to claim support from that source. In those weeks, I had visits from many women whose husbands were also languishing in Dachau. They gathered strength from my comforting assurance that the period of martyrdom would be over by the end of July. I always found new paths to new agencies in my search for information, and the others followed these paths as well. I later found out that my husband played the same role as a dispenser of solace in Dachau. Released prisoners – there were only a few – sought me out and told me. Mercifully, they kept quiet about everything else. We really knew nothing; we had no idea *how* terrible the conditions in Dachau were. Yet even the little that we did know drove us again and again to try everything possible to get our husbands released.

My husband told me later that it was my letters that made it possible to strengthen his fellow inmates with hope. Particularly those letters in which I alluded to the promised release date were passed around in camp and bolstered their optimism.

Horror stories were now leaking out of Dachau as well. It became possible at least to get a vague impression of the brutalities being committed there. Our worries concerning the lives and health of our family members increased, as did our worries about the future, the fear for our own lives, as well as those of the children – the hardships became more and more acute. It also became clear to me that my husband would not be able to remain in the country when he was let out of the concentration camp. The newspapers proclaimed legal ordinances supporting this realization. Again I was plunged into abysmal gloom. I am too old to start at the beginning again. My heart clings to the Austrian homeland with its every beat. I was a part of it, it belonged to me, and I to my native soil. My old mother, my brothers and sisters . . . no, no, no, I cannot leave. Just imagining it pierced my heart like a knife. Then I thought about it again. This pain could also be borne if only my husband were back. Yet how could we establish a new future?

Once more in my distress, an unimaginable piece of good fortune smiled down on me. Just as in a fairy tale or in an operetta: a genuine "rich American uncle" turned up – one of my mother's brothers had emigrated to America fifty years ago. We hadn't heard a word from him for a long time. We knew that he lived in New York, but he had so completely disappeared from our sight that, immersed in our concerns, we had not even thought about trying to contact him. Suddenly he was there. While traveling in Europe, he had recalled that one of his Viennese nieces had married a Jew. She might be having difficulties. Setting off with American haste, he now stood on Viennese soil. My situation unsettled him, and he promised to help my husband. Above all else he would send us the necessary affidavits and provide for us during our initial stay in the USA. A miracle! And one miracle after another! He was a man of his word. A few weeks later the affidavits were there.

Maybe now cutting through the thousands of threads that bound me to Austria would be easier. It just had to be that way, and slowly I began to take leave of everything that had been dear to me in my native land.

My life had become a kind of a rambling hike, not one through forests and down mountain slopes, but through pebbly streets, from office to office, from one station of suffering to another. Again and again I met women whose husbands shared the same fate as mine. It was only then that I saw how much better I had it than many tens of thousands of others. Above and beyond the horrible ordeal and distress that we all shared, the brutish torture of Austrian Nazi excesses – much worse than in Germany to this point – weighed heavily on them. I myself saw how they were dragged from their houses, how they were forced to wash the sidewalks with a caustic lye solution that ate away at their hands, all the while surrounded by a jeering mob. These unfortunate women were compelled to sit in shop windows exposed to the mockery of ruthless mobs. Adolescent youngsters insulted every woman who didn't display the swastika. I only later learned that reports of some of these infamous actions had made their way beyond Austrian borders because some foreigners had been among those hundreds of Jewish women injured by the dreadful beatings. Those SA- and SS-members who were informed about which families might have money, understood how to force the last financial secrets out of these women even after robbing them blind. They first confiscated all their jewelry and valuables, even the furniture from their homes; then they took the children. This was the most effective instrument of torture, and I heard and observed countless tragedies! The children were picked up, taken to a public park or to a large courtyard where they were forced to do gymnastic exercises. We later learned that this was the least severe form of persecutory methods used in concentration camps. Frightened to death, the poor mothers tried to follow their abducted children but were beaten back. The children were abused until they collapsed. They were roughed up and battered. At this point the parents were told that their children would be picked up for "gymnastic exercises" every day if a certain payment was not made. If their children were to be saved, this ransom money had to be raised somewhere and someway. But then another gang of the brown gangsters would often continue the cruel game of cat and mouse.

The stories of suffering that I heard were unbelievable. I stayed in constant contact with women I had gotten to know during the long hours in front of the agency doors and gates. As soon as one of us received a scrap of news that held out any kind of hope, we were on the telephone. I often literally spent the day spreading such comforting rumors by phone and mail. The women were almost without exception the wives of men who had been in the first, so-called "Transport of the Prominent" to Dachau: officials from the office of the Federal Chancellor and the military, as well as politicians and journalists. "A sorrow shared is a sorrow halved." Since we all bore the same burden, it was, in fact, easier to endure when we met and poured our hearts out to one another.

I often had visits from officials who tried to talk me into divorcing my husband who was, after all, Jewish, so that I might share the benefits that an Aryan female was entitled to in Germany. They were also open to concessions as far as the children were concerned, even though "bastards" could naturally not be treated as racially "pure." But these visits never really meant anything to me, because I was never for a moment tempted to abandon my husband or children. The callers with their satanic lures always had to leave empty-handed.

July finally came to an end. The agonizing waiting period would soon be over. August came and nothing happened. But on August 10, I got a call from the district police that I should immediately report to a Mr. Sieber in room 27. Exhilarated, I screamed into the phone: "Has my husband arrived?" Although the immediate answer was "No," the next words – "It's about his release" – elevated my spirits to the extreme. What a glorious morning!

Naturally I hurried straight to Mr. Sieber who asked me the familiar questions: where my husband was employed, whether I had children, who supported us, etc. The Gestapo already had in its possession at least two dozen sets of questionnaires in which all of these queries had been thoroughly answered. Repeating the answers to these monotonous questions left me completely disheartened. Finally I dared ask the most important question: "Has my husband still not returned?"

"Soon," the official replied. "This kind of inquiry usually precedes release."

I was again able to calm down. It was difficult if not impossible to tell if the functionaries were intent on tormenting me or if they would have liked to help but had not been able to skirt the merciless apparatus of the secret police and dared not try. In any case, I soon heard from my partners in affliction that they too had been summoned. One sadistic clerk even attempted to trick some of the wives with a cruel prank. They were given the train's number with which their husbands would arrive the next day at the Westbahnhof in Vienna. Numerous women were lured to the train station where, anticipating the arrival of their loved ones, they rushed from one exit to another, from midday into the night and on into the early hours of the next morning – all in vain. A quixotic, devilishly cruel Nazi joke. This was the type of gentleman who now held office!

The endless treadmill of my pilgrimages began once again. I sought out all of the same officials whom I had seen earlier and discovered new faces everywhere. Only later did experts explain to me that there was a system behind this rapid turnover of personnel. With absolute patience and tenacity, and despite all rejections, I tried again and again to arrange a meeting at the Gestapo's central office. At last I made it past the gate guard. My repeated request to speak with the director of the press office finally moved a clerk to issue me a permit. After a long search I found the right place. A new face once again! And initially a gruff rejection. But I had gradually learned how to deal with these types: my unflinching determination soon unnerved this powerful figure, and he began to respond to me. With the courage of true desperation, I spoke:

"Two months ago on this very spot I was given assurance that my husband would be released on July 26, since a disciplinary period of six months had been noted on his file."

"Who told you that?"

"It was councilor Weimann who was director of the press office at the time."

"He had no right to say that. I know the file. It's simply not possible that a journalist would get off with less than six months."

I saw and heard nothing more and staggered out of the room. I later realized that tears must have been running down my cheeks the entire time.

I could not keep this extremely bad news to myself. Every one of the women who came around could read it immediately in my eyes. Yet this begging for my husband was the thing that sustained me. I would not let it get me down. I drafted new petitions and sought out new avenues of approach to the bureaucracy. I called on former friends who I knew had "connections." Many stumbled over their words in spineless embarrassment. Some, very few, tried their best and dropped in on influential Nazi friends. But very soon they lost their appetite for this risky venture since, in most cases, they were curtly advised against meddling. Dachau was too dangerous.

I located a new department for filing petitions: the office of the senior public prosecutor Welsch. His office was in the building of the former Austrian Imperial Council, the Reichsrat. I was unsuccessful several times when I tried to enter this fortress but on September 14 I was able to gain entrance with a pass I had fought hard to obtain.

At this point I must tell about a letter that I had received fourteen days earlier from my brother-in-law in Java. Its content was more or less the following: "With the help of a friend employed by the Viennese Gestapo, I've been able to get the following answers to my repeated inquiries: 'Herr Reich was editor of a daily newspaper that has always agitated against National Socialism. We have proof that he has also taken part in this agitation. He will remain in Dachau until he understands that everything he wrote about National Socialism was a lie. The diet in Dachau is sufficient, although he may lose his paunch. He will, however, return home . . .'"

When I earnestly implored Welsch to approve my new petition, he simply replied that at the moment there was not the slightest chance that this would happen. That was the last straw. I could no longer contain myself and was overcome by anger and desperation. The people up and down the corridor must have heard my screaming: "This is supposed to be a nation under the rule of law? I'll prove to the world that my husband is innocent. Guiltless, as well, of the offenses that he's been accused of here. This has to be recognized abroad, wherever this pack of lies is sent." In my agitation I squeezed and crushed the letter from Java.

The magic word "abroad" did not go unheard. "What's that? Who wrote from abroad? To whom? About what?" Welsch's curiosity and interest had been aroused, and I instinctively knew that I had hit the mark."

"Here's the letter, sir!"

Welsch read it, and his face betrayed an ever more pensive expression. My agitation had reached a crisis stage. I felt a decisive point had been reached. There will either be a miracle or everything is lost. Finally Welsch asked me:

"May I keep the letter?"

I told him he could, and was cordially dismissed.

Eight days later I received the following telegram that had been sent from the main train station in Weimar:

"I'll be at the Westbahnhof at 6 in the morning on Sunday. Max."

My husband was free.

Shall I describe his arrival? How I was overcome with joy – and how I didn't recognize him with his head shaven bald? He got out of the train in tattered clothes that were not his own. Even though they had not been able to make him into a criminal, at least they had given him a criminal's appearance. I was ashamed for the children's sake. And my husband shared this feeling. They loved their father, but now in their eyes he looked like a "criminal." Shaven, no collar, his shirt was open, with his elbows protruding awkwardly from the sleeves. I first took the children outside and then finally welcomed my husband home. Finally, finally!

The worst was over. Or was it? The harassment began anew. My husband was required to report to the police on a daily basis.

Every day he ended up talking to a different official. I was constantly at his side since I was afraid to leave him alone. After a few days a policeman showed up at our home. He asked why my husband hadn't regularly reported in at the duty room. I tried to make it clear to him that we had, in fact, been there daily and that we had been told that everything was in order. These abominable sadists had, however, neither made any note of his reports nor were they prepared at this point to confirm his visits. It was simply part of the system to keep people anxious and fearful. Either it was regulation that persecution was done for its own sake or it was the officials amusing themselves. With great energy and zeal I prepared our departure. Nothing went smoothly in this regard as well. I had the confirmation of the American consulate that our papers were in order. My uncle had agreed that I should immediately come with the children. My husband, who had lived in Vienna for forty-five years, was unfortunately born in the small town of Wieselburg in Hungary and was placed on the Hungarian quota; therefore his opportunity to emigrate would be later. But it would never be our turn if we didn't get out soon, as soon as possible. We had to leave the children behind in order to save their father. My only thought was to leave quickly!

My husband was already keeping a low profile. The secret police came again and again to check on him. We kept the back window toward the garden open so that as soon as the bell rang, my husband was on the windowsill, ready to take flight. He had also laid out his old heavy sword. If he were taken by surprise, he was determined not to be taken without a heavy cost; above all, he was determined not to be dragged off again to a concentration camp. He had become frantic, and I couldn't convince him to abandon such desperate measures.

So it was that we lived under constant stress – if this can be called living. At night we dared not simply fall asleep. And when we had dropped off into a leaden slumber for a short while, we were startled awake – bathed in perspiration and trembling from head to toe – by the slightest noise.

And our rescue came, once again like a miracle. A cousin of my husband living in London sent us our authorization to emigrate.

We left.

Should I now explain how I left my children behind? Or how the poor wretches on the train were hassled and battered at the border crossing; how their last possessions were confiscated, how my husband was literally kicked over the border, and how he took it with a laugh as the end of his suffering? As an "Aryan" I was not harassed.

Do we now have reasons for complaint?

Certainly not. Yet the future before us looks so dismal. Delighted to have escaped a homeland that had fallen into the clutches of the devil, we were now aware of the reason that foreign countries were called "das *Ellend*" (misery) in Middle High German.

At an age when we might have hoped to enjoy the modest fruits of our thirty years of honest labor, we were leading the mendicant lives of refugees. The American visa doesn't arrive. I'm not allowed to travel there before my husband, and it may take years for him to get permission. But we are living in freedom in Great Britain, and we are treated as guests. For that we are truly grateful. But we want to work, have some kind of occupation. We no longer want to be dependent on the generosity of others, but rather help our children build their future. My husband was a journalist, but he has also done many months of forced labor and was often beaten into unconsciousness and tortured. If he only could do some lawn work, unload train cars – if only he could do something! All he's allowed to do is to stand in line for hours on end for the weekly handouts.

This is not a criticism of the public welfare committee that accomplishes wonderful things. These appease our distress, but the distress remains.

The children are growing up in the care of others. But finally, with the help of good-hearted, generous people, we have been able to bring them to England as well. They have been rescued. Have they been saved for our sake?

We don't have the tram fare even to see them at least every Sunday. A trivial adversity to be sure, but we're now over fifty and have been separated from them for a while; now we still remain separated.

Why are we living and what are we waiting for? For the American visa that refuses to show up. For the British work permit that is not granted.

Should we complain?

No, a thousand times no. We can count ourselves lucky and we often are. We're really not ungrateful, on the contrary: my husband regularly wakes up in terror at night when in his dreams he has once again been subjected to the horrors of the concentration camp. And I often see this hardened man crying in his sleep. Tears pour relentlessly from his closed eyes down the face I love so dearly. He weeps – or something in him seems to weep – for more than a quarter of an hour. When I wake him, he knows nothing of these dreams. He has no memory of them. It must have been something terrible, a dream vision almost as bad as the reality he has lived through. This is the reality he has survived but which brought martyrdom to many tens of thousands.

It remains our firmly held hope, however, that so much injustice and corruption may not be triumphant in the end, that Germany will finally be freed of its tormentors, and that the world will release the German people and all of mankind from this evil plague.

Editor's Notes

Even during his incarceration in Dachau, Maximilian Reich had decided that, if he survived the concentration camp and was liberated, he would bear witness to what happened there. He had resolved that he was morally obligated to make the world take note of the atrocities committed by the National Socialists and give support to their victims.

But the sports journalist had little experience writing a report of this kind. It's clear from the beginning of the handwritten notebooks that, on the one hand, he was uncertain how he could convey the crimes of the perpetrators, while on the other hand, protect the victims still living as well as friends or family untouched by the events. He had begun to write the manuscript in the first person, but soon abandoned this perspective.

Was he afraid that some of the figures in his report might be identified? After reading the report, it can easily be imagined what such identification might have meant for those of his comrades who had remained in concentration camp. Nor did he want to place family members in Vienna in danger. Or, did he soon realize that it was impossible for him to express what were, at times, very personal feelings so directly? In any case he decided to write the report in the third person and to use fictitious names.

It's difficult to grasp today that such artifice would be used in a document of this kind. In the second version – which exists as a copy of a typed transcript – my father has already come to the conclusion that it is essential to return to a first-person narrator.

Comparing both manuscripts, it's immediately evident that the handwritten notebooks are considerably more personally and emotionally tinged than the typed transcript that is comparatively more sober and objective. However, since the original notebooks contain numerous, sometimes shocking details that are omitted in the later version, I decided to integrate them, as well as to provide the correct names wherever possible. This proved possible since my father had made a list of some of the fictitious names and included the actual corresponding names in parentheses. He had, at times, also made a mistake while writing, identifying the person by his own name that he then crossed out. So I was able to recognize many of the people who turned up in his narrative.

The following system emerged: he always called Nazis by their real names, whether on the editorial staff, in the concentration camp, or in administrative positions. In contrast, he supplied relatives, friends, Nazi opponents, and of course those inmates still living in concentration camps with fictitious names.

I have attempted to reconstruct the chronological sequence. The numbering of the chapters in the manuscript was not helpful in doing this. Some headings are numbered, some are not. And whole chapters are missing.

Max Reich tried in vain to find a publisher in England for this book even before the war in 1939. There was no one who dared confront an English public with the truth about the concentration camps in Germany. I doubt that he looked for a publisher in Vienna for his book after his return in 1946, since scarcely anyone at the time was eager to take up this unpleasant topic of the recent past. He was not an assertive person who could have aggressively pushed through his own agenda.

Before I go into the details of each manuscript, I'd like to say a few words about my parents that seem important. My father was the son of a rabbi and descendant of generations of rabbis whose roots reach back to Spain of the 15th century. He married a Christian who was convinced that she stemmed from a purely "Aryan" family. I'll say something further about this at a later point.

My father was known far and wide for his humor. I believe that the most essential factor in his survival was his humor. He could tell jokes for hours on end. During an hour when there was nothing to laugh about, he said: "If you lose your sense of humor, you've lost everything." Even in the middle of the infernal life of the concentration camp he would always try to cheer up his comrades with his humor and save them from total despair. Among the inmates there were also several comedians and cabaret artists who had a similar strategy.

In this context I also must mention that my father's fame as a joke teller had curious consequences even until 1988. This commemorative year had brought a considerable number of things back to the surface. Just like after the war, people gloated about their Jewish friends and relatives. One example was a cousin of mine. I had been invited to her house for a snack together with one of her former office colleagues. Our conversation turned to my father and that he had been in a concentration camp. The other lady wanted to know why he was released. I answered truthfully: that I didn't really know and that he himself had never known. My cousin interrupted and declared: "But of course we know." I was stunned "What do you know?" "But it's quite evident. It must have been that he won the camp administration over and was released because of his talent for telling jokes."

So this was the way our "Aryan" relatives had worked it out. My cousin seems not to have understood the implication – namely, that my father had curried favor with the SS! She was naively oblivious to this implication and dismayed that she had "offended" me when I brought it to her attention.

To this day the puzzle surrounding his release has not been solved. My mother had moved heaven and earth in order to get his release; another possible intervention might have been that of Annemarie Heine. She was the niece of Rudolf Hess and a very talented concert pianist. In 1938 she was subletting a room in our relatives' home where I was also living. It could well be that my uncle or aunt had asked her to put in a good word with Hess. Today I find it incomprehensible that I never asked Annemarie, whom I often saw after the War. Was that also part of the all-encompassing silence?

p. 11: I find it incomprehensible that a journalist could still be so blind on March 11, 1938. There's no denying that my father was naïve and unsuspecting. He had already been warned in January that he should take steps to ensure his own safety as well as that of his family. He simply didn't want to believe that he was in any danger. Since he was unaware of any culpability, why should he take flight? And where should he go?

In 2003 I had the opportunity to contact Lizzie Lobstein, formerly a fashion journalist who had worked for the "*Vorwärts-Verlag*" (Progressive Publishing House) in the 1930s. She wrote to me that she had left Austria in 1936, because it was already clear to her then what direction the political winds were blowing. Evidently, there were people who were able to gauge these winds much earlier.

Pp. 19 and 28: There are repeated expressions in the manuscript of a faith in God. For example: "God will help me through this time as well" and "And then, only God can help us further." And in the concentration camp he often makes mention of praying. That my father, the only son of a rabbi, should not also have become a rabbi, but a sports journalist – and what's more, marry a Christian – must have been a terrible disappointment for his parents. He writes about the guilt he feels towards them in the concentration camp when he reflects on his martyrdom, and wonders if it might be a punishment ordained by God. In any case, even though he wasn't religious, he did believe in God. As far as I know, he didn't go to synagogue, and until 1938 I didn't even know he was Jewish. At the time my mother had to fill out a school questionnaire on which she had to state parental religious denominations. For my father she wrote "mosaic." I didn't know the word and probably asked about it, but the answer didn't seem to have cleared up things for me. The topic was never mentioned at home. I can vaguely remember one weekday that he spent at home and, when I asked about it, he told me it was a holiday. It must have been Yom Kippur. I believe he observed it as a day of penance and fasting. Did I ask any more questions? I don't think so.

p. 17: I had not been with my mother during the Schuschnigg speech but was sitting in my grandmother's room. My mother rushed in, agitated and white as a sheet, and told us about the speech. It made my grandmother so sick that she vomited. It was only then that I understood that something terrible must have happened. Only I had no idea what it was.

p. 31: Again and again the lack of exact dates and dating errors cause confusion. Reading the handwritten notebooks, which doubtless represent the most direct source of his memories, it seems that his arrest took place on March 13. Here he depicts the arrival of the Gestapo as if it had occurred in the afternoon. The first typed version, however, reads: "On the evening of the March 17 . . ." He also mentions in this manuscript that he saw me on the street and called out to me. And then something dawns on me that he doesn't mention – that my mother had quickly sent me to the store for bread when the detective arrived so that I wouldn't see my father's arrest. Did my father intentionally fail to mention dates or did he falsify them (like he did with names) to prevent a search for evidence.

As far as the arrest is concerned I've left the reports of my mother and father as written, although the details often appear to be contradictory (for example, who actually opened the door). People's memories of events just aren't always the same. And it was important to me to allow both parents to express their own versions.

p. 39: According to information at the Dachau Memorial, the prisoner Johann Stern (number 76) died during the trip. There were a total of 151 names on the list issued in Vienna on April 1, 1938; the number of those who arrived in Dachau was 150.

p. 43: The word "scoundrels" (*Lausejungen*) for the SS that is used several times sounds much too harmless for us today. The Austrian "snotty-nosed brats" (*Rotzbuben*) seems more appropriate to me.

p. 109: It's interesting that my Jewish father uses Christian allusions several times, such as "Christ" and "Golgotha."

p. 23: My teacher, Albine Mayer, was always very sweet to me. I know that I attended the elementary school on Schreibengasse until May 13, 1938 – I have an essay notebook in which the last essay bears this date. But apparently my mother took me out of this school before the end of the school year, since I have all my report cards except the one for the summer semester of 1938.

p. 178: Willy Kurtz was transferred to Ausschwitz on October 17, 1942 and in the course of the wave of exterminations, he was killed.

p. 180: I can remember that her relationship to this nephew who had so deeply offended her in 1938 became very intimate after our return, albeit only after my father's death. She even offered to take care of his three children while he and his wife went on vacation.

Comments on the Postscript to Buchenwald

Although Max Reich wrote the following chapters, it's clear that they were not based on his personal experience since he was no longer in Buchenwald at the time. I have in my possession, however, a carbon copy of a report by his friend and co-internee, Hans Mathias Eisenstädter, in which these episodes are depicted, and must assume that Eisenstädter was his informant. He was released in 1939 and first emigrated to England. And I know that he often met with my father in London. It's apparent that they spoke about my father's developing manuscript. At this point in time it seems that Eisenstädter had no intention of recording his own experiences. In February 1940 he travelled together with his family to the United States and wrote down his own account only much later[14] under his recently changed name, John Mathew Ellis – probably with no intention of publishing it. He did, however, send a carbon copy to my father, and this then came into my possession.

Comments on Emilie Reich's Manuscript

p. 202: My mother was in error with regard to her "purely Aryan" family tree. Her entire family was of the opinion that their

---

[14] A copy of the "Account of my detention in the concentration camps Dachau and Buchenwald" by John Mathew Ellis (13 pages) is on file at the *Dokumentationsarchiv des österreichischen Widerstandes* (Documentation Center of the Austrian Resistance) under the call number 29466.

ancestors had been "pure Aryan." But during the war it emerged that the great-grandmother on the mother's side had been a Jew. About 1987 my cousin Heidi did some research and discovered that the ancestors on this side of the family can be traced to Jerusalem as far back as 1702 and a certain Israel Frankl.

About two years ago, a relative in my mother's family had told me about a letter that describes the "disgrace into which the family had fallen." He had not known who had written the letter because only the first page was there, without a signature.

When I got my hands on this letter in 2004, I knew immediately who had written it. I knew this handwriting only all too well! It was my Aunt Heddi's, my dear Aunt Heddi, my mother's oldest sister. She wrote about "our grandmother's troubling roots," and that the "research was much worse than we could imagine." But that my dear Aunt Heddi wrote the following was truly upsetting:

"What would that mean for our whole family that up to now had been so proud of its Aryan lineage . . . The consequences are inconceivable . . . Maybe an appeal to the *Führer* for clemency. We simply can't believe that with this horrible discovery, an entire family that has always felt thoroughly Germanic and Aryan as well as having been considered and respected as such everywhere, that this family would be plunged overnight into misery and misfortune, stigmatized in the eyes of the entire world."

But when *my* family was plunged into misery and misfortune these relatives found that completely appropriate. I was not entirely able to suppress a feeling of satisfaction, however belated.

It had been an advantage for my mother, however, to believe that she was "Aryan" since she could approach the Gestapo and other authorities quite differently than her Jewish fellow sufferers.

p. 204: ". . . I am too old . . ." My mother was 51 in 1938.

p. 204: The "deus ex machina" Uncle Viktor is a strange figure. He was the brother of my grandmother on my mother's side who had emigrated to America when he was still young. During his visit to Vienna in 1938 he had raised hope in my mother's mind that he could send affidavits for the entire family without difficulty. Later he seems to have qualified that and wanted to vouch only for her and the children.

A short time ago I accidentally came upon his letter to my mother dated February 14, 1939. She had written him from London, asking him to honor his promise. My parents were then still counting on moving the family to the United States. We had even sent the few things that we had been able to bring with us directly to New York. These included, among other things, the remarkable hand tufted rug that my mother – just like Penelope – had crafted during those long nights of my father's incarceration.

In his answer to my mother, Uncle Viktor clearly retracted his promise and asked her to consider that he was already past 75 and that this might prove to be an obstacle.

p. 209: The telegram puzzles me. If my father was released from Buchenwald on October 12 and this 12th was a Wednesday, it is impossible that he can have been in transit to Vienna until the following Sunday – even if we make allowance for the eight-kilometer march by foot from Buchenwald to Weimar in his debilitated condition. Nor does that correspond to my recollection (hat purchase). Did my mother intentionally give an incorrect date, and if so, why? I can't believe that my mother had forgotten what day it was. Oddly enough, my father completely refrains from describing his arrival in Vienna. I think he found this too intimate, too personal, quite in line with his temperament. So he left it to my mother to describe the traumatic scene. My own memories also differ from hers. I know that we took the first streetcar to the Westbahnhof. I thought for years it had been the Ostbahnhof; i.e., housed within the structure of the Südbahnhof. My mother sensed that something had gone wrong and went into the train station by herself, leaving my sister and me standing outside. We had assumed that our cousin Fritz would also be there, and, to pass the time, we made up silly rhymes, for example: "Look, look, Fritz comes near, but alas he's drunk too much beer." It's strange that I can remember such details and my sister can't. My mother was gone for a long time. Finally she appeared, shaking, as pale as a sheet, and announced: "He hasn't arrived!" But she then decided to go in once again and finally returned, this time at his side. She hadn't recognized him! He also seemed alien to us, considering he had no hair on his head, no moustache, and was emaciated to the extreme – he had changed significantly. He must have asked her in his telegram to bring along a shirt and suit because she had brought a suitcase along. What particularly disturbed him, however, was that she had not brought along a hat – she must have forgotten it. I can still remember that we headed down Mariahilfer street in order to purchase a hat for him.

p. 210: Our day of departure, as best we can determine, was November 9, 1938. It surprised me that my father, in the original version of his report, had depicted the departure as if we, his daughters, had traveled with our parents. That's not correct. We left Vienna later on January 28, 1939 with a Quaker-sponsored transport of children. Why my father wrote it this way is not clear. We were already in England when he finished the manuscript. Strangely enough, my mother writes quite openly in her part about the fact that she was forced to leave us behind and leaves it to the imagination how painful that was for her.

p. 210: The mention of "a cousin of my husband" surprised me at first. But my father did have two cousins who lived abroad. One of them, Nathaniel Reich was a well-known Egyptologist in Philadelphia; the other one, Albert Reich, was in France at the time. When I read the manuscript for the first time, I knew nothing about a cousin in London. It was only in 2004 that I learned there was, in fact, such a cousin. I had always thought that, in the end, it had been the Quakers who had made my parents' emigration possible. In any case, shortly after their arrival in London in November 1938, both were invited to the country estate of the well-known Quaker family Cadbury where they were looked after with great warmth. Since they were hourly expecting news of the children's transport that would bring my sister and me to join them in England, they were able to enjoy this paradise only for a short time.

I must have lived with Aunt Marie probably since September 1938 and went to the fourth grade of elementary school in the Eslarngasse in the Third District. During the days right after the

Anschluss, things didn't go quite as smoothly as my Aunt Marie has described them. The teacher may well have been a friend of Aunt Marie and accepted me in her class for her sake, but the relationship between teacher and pupil was strained. This became evident in my grades. Although I had previously been an excellent student, my grades now fell abruptly. I failed an arithmetic quiz and was afraid to own up to it to my aunt since I knew that in this family such failings were punished with slaps. Although this didn't happen, I did have to spend hours doing practice exercises.

Once I was really punished, but I couldn't imagine why. The punishment – I recorded it in a little diary that I kept in those days and still have – was to memorize the chapter "The *Führer* at Technical School" from *Mein Kampf*!

During the few months I spent at this school I became friends with only one girl. Her name was Lina, and one day she asked me to come home with her because her mother wanted to meet me. I found her mother lying in bed, apparently in poor health. The visit developed into a genuine interrogation: why was I living with my aunt? Where were my parents? Why were they in England? Might they be Jewish? I immediately understood what danger I was in and lied. No, my parents weren't Jews, but one of my grandmothers had been Jewish. She grumpily took note of my replies, and I was finally allowed to leave. She forbade her daughter, however, from having anything more to do with me.

My family's emigration to England was a success, but my parents suffered terribly from homesickness. Even a song like "*Wer hat dich, du schöner Wald*" (Eichendorff, Mendelssohn-Bartholdi) could make my mother burst out in tears. This unappeasable homesickness was an essential factor in their unwavering decision to return to Austria, by hook or crook, at the first available opportunity. But for my father as a journalist, the problem of living in a foreign country whose language he never quite mastered, played an even more essential role.

After the outbreak of the war, the former concentration camp inmate was interned once again and spent months in a camp for "enemy aliens" on the Isle of Man. Today that seems completely insane, but at the beginning of the war, the English were apparently unable to determine who among the numerous refugees were for and who against Nazi Germany. When my father was later asked how he was able to cope with this additional internment, he always replied: "In comparison to the concentrations camps in Germany, the Isle of Man was virtually a paradise."

Even during the war years my father worked tirelessly to prepare his return to Austria; among other things, by contributing his services to the Austrian section of the BBC.

In 1946 he received a telegram from the news service of the Federal Chancellery with the invitation to return to Vienna and launch a newspaper. It was the *Wiener Montag* whose Chief Editor he remained until 1948. Among his documents I found the following, deeply upsetting letter, dated July 6, 1949:

. . . I have taken legal action against the "Wiener Montag" and won. I was the paper's founder and Chief Editor but left because of a change in its direction during my absence at the Olympic Games. At the moment I'm working only part time for the Weltpresse but have a range of offers – among them, the management of a large newspaper directed at young people. Have you heard anything from P.? All of a sudden he hasn't replied to any of my last letters which I regret, since he is such a decent man and there is a great lack of those here in Vienna. I don't associate with anyone here, my best friends are all gone. I bury myself in my work in order to calm myself when I see Nazi mugs appearing on the horizon. They get bolder every day and are already entrenched in all the administrative offices. Politically they are forming a fourth party and nominating their candidates for office. How did the painter Liebermann answer the question in 1936 about what it was like in Nazi Germany? "You can hardly eat enough to barf as much as you'd like!" And that's the way I see it now. But just don't think that because of that I've abandoned myself to the black melancholy of Weltschmerz. There's not a trace of that! I've simply limited my associations to two or three people whom I still trust.

When I found the letter, I was surprised that it was still extant. It was only later I realized that it bears the stamp of the Austrian censor. It had not been allowed through the censor's office and was returned to the sender.

Last of all I want to report on a joyous occasion. The

municipality of Vienna decided in 2007 to name streets after three of their most prominent sports journalists. The three are Edi Finger, Heribert Meisel, and one of the pioneers of sports journalism in general, Maximilian Reich. The honor comes to him fifty years after his death, an honor that he was owed during his lifetime.

Photographs and Documents

(All photos are from the archive of Henriette Mandl, unless otherwise noted)

Photo of Max Reich, early 1930s

Photo of Willy Kurtz, fourth from the left, at the Viennese Stadium in 1933, after the victory of Austria Vienna over Ambrosiana Milan in the Mitropacup final.

Preis 50 g

Preis 40 Pf.

DER BOX-RING

ZEITSCHRIFT FÜR BOXSPORT / GYMNASTIK / ATHLETIK UND ÄHNLICHE GEBIETE

3. JAHRG. — 22. SEPTEMBER — Nr. 15/16

Engl Sportkappen und Modehüte

Adolf Sachsel

Wien

Die Professionals vor die Front!

Photo of Willy Kurtz, in the middle at back. Title page of *Der Boxring*, tabloid for boxing, gymnastics, track and similar sports. Vol. 3, Nos. 15-16, September 22, (1930s)

Photo of Traudi and Etti Reich (front) and cousin Heidi as children.

Photo of Etti Reich (standing) behind the child star Waltraud Haas at the Viennese ice skating club.

Das Schwarze Korps

ZEITUNG DER SCHUTZSTAFFELN DER NSDAP

A page from the SS-tabloid, *Das Schwarze Korps*, dated April 6, 1938: featured is an inflammatory article aimed at Jewish journalists. With a photo (clipping) of Max Reich.

Text about Reich: "The Jew Maximilian Reich also pranced merrily in the dance of the other atrocity propagandists and badgering writers." [ÖNB Wien + Signaturen]

Staatliche Kriminalpolizei
Kriminalpolizeileitstelle W i e n
Inspektion I B

Transporte von Schutzhäftlingen Wien, am 1. April 1938.
nach dem Konzentrationslager "D a c h a u ".

I. Transport.

Am 1. April 1938 erfolgte der I. Transport von Schutzhäftlingen nach dem Konzentrationslager in " D a c h a u . "
Anzahl: 151 Mann.

Der grösste Teil der zum Abgange bestimmten Schutzhäftlinge bestand aus höheren Beamten des ehemaligen Bundeskanzleramtes, Minister, Bürgermeister von Wien, Beamte der Polizeidirektion und des Generalinspektorates, dès Heimatdienstes, der Vaterländischen Front, der Gendarmerie und Kaufleute aus der jüdischen Rasse stammend.

Die Zusammenstellung des Zuges hatte durch das Gefangenhaus zu erfolgen und erforderte - da keine Erfahrungen diesbezüglich vorhanden waren - einiges Kopfzerbrechen und Arbeit. Schwierigkeiten ergaben sich durch das Einbringen der in anderen Einsatzstellen untergebrachten Schutzhäftlinge. Durch Zusammenarbeit aller an dem Zuge interessierten Stellen gelang es jedoch alle Schutzhäftlinge rechtzeitig stellig zu machen. Auftragsgemäss mussten alle Schutzhäftlinge tags vorher Wagenweise und allein in eigenen Zellen untergebracht werden.

Der Abtransport erfolgte mit 9 Zellenwagen im Abstande von 5 - 6 Minuten, Er erfolgte anstandslos in der Zeit zwischen 19 und 21.00 Uhr.

Der Abtransport hinterliess bei allen S.H. einen gewissen psychischen Eindruck, hervorgerufen durch das Dabeisein der eigenen ehemaligen hohen und höchsten Vorgesetzten.

Die Abfertigung erfolgte durch Polizeimajor Herzog.

52) O s i o Dr.Alois
53) P a u l Dr.Josef
54) P a m m e r Dr.Maximilian
55) P e n z Rudolf
56) P o u k a r Raimund
57) P r e t t Adolf
58) P r o k s c h Adolf
59) P t a k Emil
60) P u l t a r Dr.Erich
61) P u l t a r Walter
62) R a u c h Leopold
63) R e i c h Maximilian
64) R e i t e r Josef
65) R o n g e Max

Excerpt from the Dachau transportation list. [Documentation Center of the Austrian Resistance.]

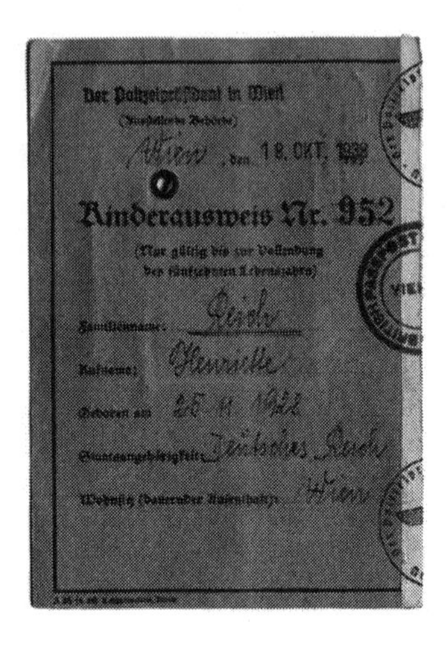

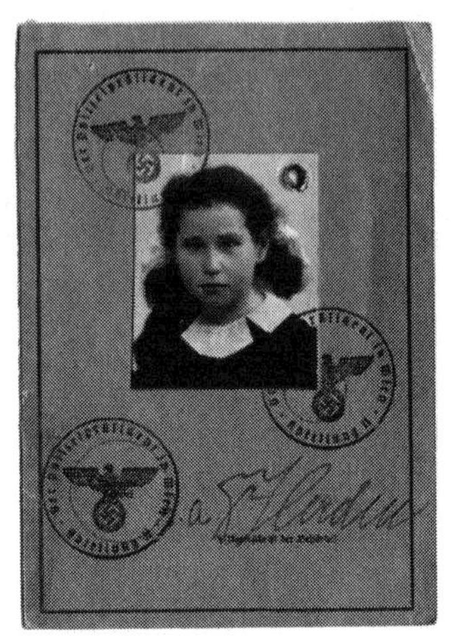

Etti Reich's ID as a child for the transport to England in January 1939.

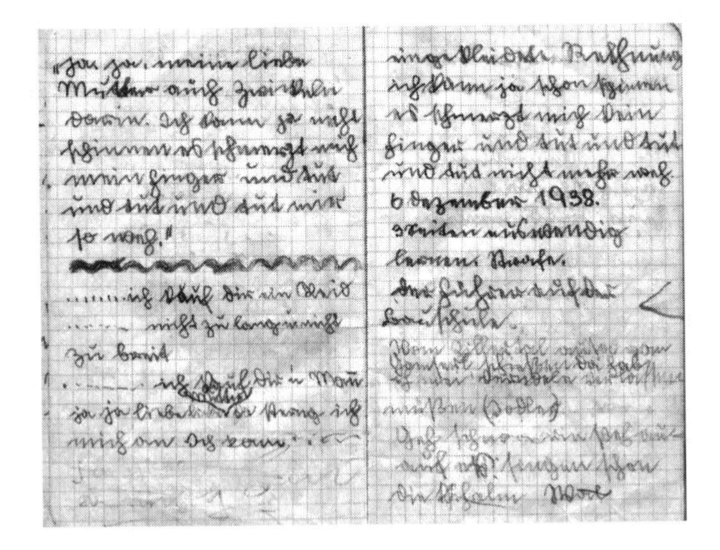

Pages from Henriette Reich's diary: "December 6, 1938. Memorize three pages. Punishment. The Führer at Technical School." (From: *Mein Kampf*)

VII. Kapitel 86

Vorläufig liegt noch Totenstille über den im Dunkel des Wagens ...

Wagen. Da schreit plötzlich einer mit Wahnsinnsstimme heraus: Nach Dachau ins Konzentrationslager!

Ein anderer kreischte, dass es einem durch Mark und Bein geht: „Lebewohl, Weib und Kind, wir sind verloren!"

... Hand in der meinen: „Fred, jetzt heißt es, Mann sein! Stark sein, um Größeres zu ertragen, stark sein für die Rache!"

Der Wagen hält mit kreischenden Bremsen. Die zwei Polizisten, die sie eskortiert hatten, flüsterten uns zu: „Brillen herunter, Augen schützen!"

Und nun beginnt ein Höllentanz mit grauenhaften Bildern, die kein [illegible] zu malen vermöchte....

Page 86 of Maximilian Reich's handwritten manuscript. Written in England after his emigration in November 1938. Chapter VII.

Photo of Max and Emilie Reich in England, 1943.

CABLE & WIRELESS LTD

ISSUING OFFICE

NO.

SENT OUT

BY

RECEIVED PARTICULARS

VIA IMPERIAL

The first line of this Telegram contains the following particulars in the order named: Prefix Letters and Number of Message, Office of Origin, Number of Words, Date, Time handed in and Official Instructions, if any.

CW 435 WIEN 32/27 16 1600 T19

MAXIMILIAN REICH LONDON SW 11
107 NORTHCOTE ROAD

RUECKKEHR ZUM WIEDERAUFBAU OESTERREICHISCHER
PRESSE DRINGEND ERFORDERLICH OESTERREICHISCHE
VERTRETUNG WEGEN EINREISEERMOEGLICHUNG BITTEN
BUNDESPRESSEDIENST WUENSCHT EHESTES EINTREFFEN
STOP MEZNIK BUNDESPRESSEDIENST

Reply VIA IMPERIAL

435 SW 11 107

Telegram from Meznik, July 16, 1946

Photo of Emilie, Max, and Henriette Reich in the Salzkammergut in the winter of 1946.

Vor- und Zuname: Reich
Ort und Tag der Geburt:
Staatsbürgerschaft: Österreich
Stand (ledig, verh., gesch., verw.): verh.
Beruf:
Wohnort:
Körpergröße:
Gesicht: oval
Farbe der Augen: blau
Farbe der Haare: grau
Besondere Kennzeichen: keine
Ort und Datum der Ausstellung
Unterschrift des ausfertigenden Beamten

Top photo: Max Reich's identity card in four languages. Issued in October 1946 in Vienna.

Lower photo: Max Reich (right) with colleagues and friends at the coffeehouse Parzifal after his return, probably 1950.

Max Reich in the early fifties.

Henriette Mandl at the exhibition of the Austrian Exile Library (Exilbibliothek), 2003.

WOLFGANG NEUGEBAUER

Historical Afterword

Maximilian Reich and the First Transport of Austrians to the Concentration Camp at Dachau in 1938

In 1938 the concentration camp at Dachau registered an influx of 18,695 prisoners. At least half of them were Austrians. The first arrival of 150 Austrian prisoners took place three weeks after the violent annexation of Austria by Hitler Germany on April 2, 1938. Based on the presence of many well-known politicians, among others, Leopold Figl and Alfons Gorbach – both destined to become Austrian Federal Chancellor in later years – the term "Transport of the Prominent" has come into common usage.[1] Among the 150 Austrians was the sports journalist Maximilian Reich who remained a prisoner in Dachau and Buchenwald until October. Soon after his release at the end of 1938 and the beginning of 1939 he put down his recollections on paper while in English exile. It was the first written report of an Austrian concentration camp prisoner which, unfortunately, at the time remained unpublished, and only now – almost 70 years later – is published here for the first time.

The National Socialist Terror in Austria in March and April of 1938 [2]

Although the precise timing of the annexation also came as a

---

[1] Wolfgang Neugebauer, "Der erste Österreichertransport in das KZ Dachau 1938," *Dachauer Hefte* 14, *Verfolgung als Gruppenschicksal*, n.d. (Dachau 1998) 17-30.

[2] For detailed accounts, see: Wolfgang Neugebauer, "Der NS-Terrorapparat," *The National Socialist Governance in Austria, 1938-1945*, eds. Emmerich Tálos et al. (Vienna 2000) 721-743; Wolfgang Neugebauer and Herbert Steiner, "Widerstand und Verfolgung in Österreich im Zeitraum vom 12. Februar bis zum 10. April 1938," *Anschluß 1938. Protokoll des Symposiums in Wien am 14. und 15. März 1978* (Vienna 1981) 86-108.

surprise to the National Socialist leadership – it was triggered by Chancellor Schuschnigg's sudden decision to hold a referendum – the organizational preparations for an expansion of its system of terror into Austria, a system tried and tested during five years of governance in Germany, had long been started. A memorandum had been generated in the main office of the Security Service that determined how the security apparatus in Austria was to be structured, in particular the offices of the Gestapo.[3] Formidable police and SS-forces accompanied the Wehrmacht to Austria and, to some degree, were there earlier. Heinrich Himmler, as chief of the SS as well as the German police of the Internal Affairs Ministry, was in charge of the campaign of terror in Austria. Together with a staff of select SS and Security Service people he arrived before dawn on March 12, 1938 at the Aspern airfield in Vienna where he immediately initiated the first courses of action, particularly with regard to personnel and organizational matters. For example, he appointed the chief of the Austrian SS, Ernst Kaltenbrünner, as State Secretary for Security.[4] A particularly auspicious event for opponents of National Socialism was the assignment of the Department of Security – stipulated in the Berchtesgaden Agreement of February 12, 1938 – to the National Socialist Seyß-Inquart whose political loyalty was still not a matter of public record. Consequently, all police documents, and above all those concerning the illegal Left, fell into the hands of the new rulers. Presumably, based on information and documents from Austrian National Socialist partisans in the security apparatus, lists of Austrians to be arrested had already been compiled in Berlin as was done later for other occupied countries as well.[5]

The German police authorities were, from the very beginning, able to rely on the Austrian National Socialists, who – on their own

---

[3] See: Alwin Ramme, *Der Sicherheitsdienst der SS* (Berlin 1969) 100.

[4] Heinrich Fraenkel and Roger Manvell, *Himmler. Kleinbürger und Massenmörder* (Frankfurt/M 1965) 71 ff.; Dieter Wagner and Gerhard Tomkowitz, "Ein Volk, ein Reich, ein Führer!" *Der Anschluß Österreichs 1938* (Munich 1968) 254 f.

[5] Such lists for Great Britain and the Soviet Union have been confirmed. Cf. Werner Röder: *Sonderfahndungsliste UdSSR* (Erlangen 1976).

initiative – had begun arresting known Nazi opponents already during the night of the "revolution" of March 11-12, 1938. The "spontaneous" terror of the local Nazis assumed at times such proportions and forms that the political leadership – interested in a controlled approach – was forced to restrain it. The Chief of Security Police Heydrich complained on March 17, 1938 to the Viennese district chief Bürckel that "in recent days, members of the Party had allowed themselves large-scale and completely undisciplined abuses"; there was absolutely no reason for such "unauthorized actions" since "with the invasion of the troops," the Gestapo had "immediately begun its operations." Heydrich gave notice of an intervention "against such criminal acts" to be carried out with the "harshest methods" and "unsparing severity."[6]

The victims of the first wave of arrests immediately after the occupation were representatives of the now expired "patriotic" regime: Communists, Socialists, anti-Nazis exposed by their work in cultural and media sectors, and Jews. The figures fluctuate between 50,000 and 76,000 arrests within the first six weeks.[7] Although this reflects an entirely plausible order of magnitude, an exact determination will probably never be possible since there are no records at all of the numerous local arrests made by Party, SA, SS, and HJ functionaries. Several thousand arrestees remained incarcerated for an extended period or were sent to a concentration camp – for the most part, to Dachau. Most were set free after a few days or weeks although many were then arrested again at a later date. According to the daily report of Vienna's Gestapo control center from December 10-12, 1938, "a total of 20,793 prisoners in protective custody had been processed" up to this point in time from this center alone.[8] As a rule, these mass incarcerations were accompanied by maltreatment, humiliation, theft, and other forms of per-

---

6 Dokumentationsarchiv des österreichischen Widerstandes [DÖW], *"Anschluß" 1938. Eine Dokumentation* (Vienna 1988) 440.

7 See: Karl Stadler, *Österreich 1938-1945 im Spiegel der SS-Akten* (Vienna 1966) 26f; Erwin A. Schmidl, Der "Anschluß" Österreichs. Der Deutsche Einmarsch im März 1938 (Bonn 1994) 232f.; Neugebauer and Steiner, *Widerstand und Verfolgung*, 92 ff.

8 National Archives Microcopy T 84 R 13, 39 752.

sonal assaults. In some cases politically unpopular prisoners were murdered, as for example, General Wilhelm Zehner,[9] the State Secretary of National Defense who had taken compulsory retirement. On the one hand, all of these measures were aimed at eliminating the leadership of political opposition to National Socialism. On the other hand, the aim was to create an atmosphere of terror that would discourage any resistance and oppositional impulses.

The "Transport of the Prominent"

In the Nazi system of terror, greater and greater significance was accorded the concentration camps, particularly as a type of pre-emptive prosecution, while the courts increasingly lost their relevance as the (traditional) instrument of political repression. Plans were prepared and debated to bring political representatives of the "corporate state" to trial – especially the Chancellor Kurt (von) Schuschnigg who had been arrested by the Gestapo in Vienna – but in the end were not carried out.[10] In contrast to the costly and protracted legal proceedings against prominent defendants – which also sparked international interest – it was simpler, attracted less attention, and was more quickly arranged to commit a detainee to a concentration camp following the Gestapo's protective custody order. For the masses of Austrian prisoners, some even held in preliminary detention in schools, Dachau was the nearest concentration camp. In the course of 1938 many were transferred to Buchenwald.

Vienna's Gestapo control center, established on Heinrich Himmler's orders just a few days before, was in charge of the make-up of the transport. Although no full Gestapo report exists,

---

[9] See: "Anchluß"1938, 435; More detail in: Daniela Angetter, "Gott schütze Österreich!" – Wilhelm Zehner (1883-1938): *Porträt eines österreichischen Soldaten* (Vienna 2006).

[10] See: Ernst von Weizsäcker's notes from July 5, 1938 as cited in: *"Anschluß" 1938*, 532f. State Councilor Eduard Ludwig, a Schuschnigg advisor, was the sole politician taken to court – on charges of abuse of authority – but he was acquitted. See: Gertrude Enderle-Barcel, *Mandatare im Ständestaat* (Vienna 1991) 149 f.

the allocation lists of the prisoners to the train's cars, drawn up by Unit II D, have been preserved.[11] According to allegations by the exiled Ludwig Soswinski, a certain Dr. Hackl – an illegal Viennese National Socialist who, prior to 1938, had already worked for the Gestapo in Berlin as a senior Chief of Detectives – was responsible for the lists.[12]

Based on a report, dated April 1, 1938, by Vienna's control center of criminal investigation (located on Elisabethpromenade in Vienna's 9th district – "Liesl" in prisoners' jargon), the transport was assembled and the prisoners brought by guarded rail car to the Westbahnhof on April 1. The "evacuation," as it was called in the report, "left a certain psychological impression on all security agents on guard, an impression evoked by the presence of all their own former senior and most senior superiors."[13]

The Composition of the Transport

The selection for the first transport of Austrians to a concentration camp corresponded largely to the political structure of the – nearly all male – prisoners: supporters of the Schuschnigg regime, Socialists, Communists, and Jews. The central thrust of the Nazi terror in March and April of 1938 was directed against Jews and representatives of the "corporate state" who were declared responsible for the persecution of the National Socialists from 1933 to 1938 and with whom the Austrian Nazis were anxious to settle personal accounts. The bulk of prisoners arrested for political reasons were politicians and functionaries of the Patriotic Front, ministry officials, law enforcement officers, Christian unionists, monarchists, and former leaders of the Home Guard. Since these measures, as well as the accompanying propaganda, also served to

---

[11] DÖW 532.

[12] Interview with Dr. Ludwig Soswinski on April 12, 1989, DÖW – Sammlung "Erzählte Geschichte," no. 192/2.

[13] The Viennese Gestapo's list of names can be found in the DÖW, archive number 532; this list corresponds with the register of the Arolsen international tracing service for the Dachau concentration camp in 1938 (Copy 12 800 in the DÖW).

influence the social-democratic labor force positively toward the regime, there were at the time only relatively few Social Democrats or Revolutionary Socialists – mostly Jews – arrested. Especially those politicians, or rather opponents of the regime, were chosen, who had spoken out in favor of a cooperative effort against the Nazi danger prior to March 1938.

An approximate classification of the 150 prisoners in the first transport to Dachau yields the following:[14] About one-third or 50 to 60 persons were Jewish;[15] a further third were supporters of the "corporate state," about half of whom were political functionaries, and half police and judiciary functionaries; in each case, about 10% were Socialists and Communists. Among the Jewish prisoners there was a particularly strong representation of politically engaged journalists, writers, and artists. The great majority of prisoners – with only 11 exceptions – came from Vienna. The Romany gypsies and other groups were taken into concentration camps in the course of later discriminatory campaigns.

Among the best known politicians of middle-class origins – besides the already mentioned Leopold Figl and Alfons Gorbach – were the secretary general of the Patriotic Front, Colonel Walter Adam, his chief of propaganda Fritz Bock who later served as commerce secretary and vice chancellor, the governor of Lower Austria Josef Reither, the mayor of Vienna Richard Schmitz, the earlier finance minister Ludwig Draxler, the president of the "corporate-state" union Johann Staud (who died in the Flossenbürg concentration camp in 1939), the state secretary Adolf Watzek, the chief of the news service of the state council Eduard Ludwig, Emperor Karl's former secretary and leader of the legitimists (Baron) Karl Werkmann. Among police and judicial

---

[14] The classification is the result of information garnered in oral and written recollections as well as numerous conversations with prisoners such as: Dr. Ludwig Soswinski, Erich Fein, Dr. Fritz Bock and Hermann Lackner. For additional evidence I am indebted to my colleagues in the DÖW, Prof. Hans Landauer and Prof. Dr. Jonny Moser.

[15] This number includes not only members of the religious community but all of those understood as "Jews" by the National Socialist regime as defined by the Nuremberg Laws.

officers there were: the commander of the detention camp in Wöllersdorf (Baron) Emanuel Stillfried, the deputy chief of the Austrian political paramilitary force Josef Kimmel, the Styrian security director Colonel Franz Zelburg, the General of law enforcement Rudolf Manda, the federal prosecutor and later minister of justice Josef Gerö, the counsel for the Oberland regional high court Dr. Alois Osio – whose brutal maltreatment is dramatically portrayed by Max Reich. That departmental head Robert Hecht became the first Austrian victim in Dachau – he committed suicide on May 30, 1938 – was no accident. He was of Jewish heritage and had advised Federal Chancellor Dollfuß in the establishment of the authoritarian direction and the "corporate state" in 1933/34. The first Austrian prisoners in Dachau were the sons (Max and Ernst [von] Hohenberg) of the archduke and heir to the throne, Franz Ferdinand, who had been assassinated in 1914. Both were resolute opponents of National Socialism, as was (archduke) Colonel General Josef Ferdinand (von) Habsburg who was imprisoned on either March 30 or 31.

Among the Social Democrats – in addition to Otto Bauer and Karl Seitz – the most important party representative was Robert Danneberg, party secretary, assemblyman, and fiscal councilor for Vienna. Danneberg and Major Alexander (von) Eifler, the leader of the Republican Protection League, were the best known. For the Nazis, Danneberg represented the epitome of the "Jewish-Marxist labor agitator;" in the course of "purging" of Jews from German concentration camps in October 1942, he was taken to Ausschwitz where he was murdered in December. Eifler died in Dachau in January 1945. There were as well a few other Social Democrats of Jewish extraction: the attorney Emil Maurer, for example, who became President of the Jewish Religious Community after 1945. Franz Olah (1910-2009) was the last survivor of this small group of Socialists among the prisoners in the "Transport of the Prominent." After the war he became President of the Federation of Trade Unions and Minister of the Interior.

Striking is the fact that in the first transport to Dachau there were no functionaries of the Austrian Communist Party, although the Communists later constituted the largest political grouping among concentration camp inmates. According to a report of the

Vienna state police control center "concerning the increase of Communist and Marxist propaganda activity, the refusals to work, etc.," it was not until September 27, 1938 that security chief Heydrich ordered the state police stations in Austria "to pay very particular attention to the pre-emptive battle against Communism and Marxism." Moreover, "pending further notice, all leading functionaries of the German Communist and Socialist Parties [are] to be taken into protective custody."[16] The best-known functionary of Austria's Communist Party in the first transport for highly placed officials was Ludwig Soswinski, a councilman in Vienna after 1945 as well as chair for many years of the *KZ-Verband* [The Federal Association of Members of the Austrian Resistance and Victims of Fascism] and vice president of the DÖW [Documentation Center of the Austrian Resistance]. Viktor Matejka, to whom we are grateful for numerous reports about Dachau, was sent there because of his work as a Christian functionary of the Austrian Chamber of Labor. In 1945 he became Communist Party councilor for cultural affairs in Vienna.

The farmer Paul Hutfleß from the Austrian Burgenland was the only National Socialist in the first transport. He had delivered informers' reports for the Patriotic Front.

As leading representatives of the Austrian Jews, Desider Friedmann, Jakob Ehrlich, and Robert Stricker were sent to Dachau. None of the three survived the camp imprisonment. The *Völkische Beobachter* referred to them, to the merchant families Burstyn and Schiffman as well as other Jewish prisoners on August 3, 1938 in its report about the opening of the malicious exhibit in Vienna, "The Eternal Jew." At the exhibit, "the visitor can see for himself that important and familiar Jewish figures are getting to know real work for the first time in their twisted lives."[17] The most noted artists in the transport were the writers Raoul Auernheimer and Fritz Beda-Löhner. The latter was a librettist for Franz Lehar – who refrained, however, from making a special plea for him – and

---

[16] DÖW 1576. Apparently, Heydrich meant Austrian Communists and Socialists when he said the "German Communist and Socialist Parties" (*KPD* and *SPD*).

[17] *Völkischer Beobachter*, Vienna edition, 3. 8. 1938.

died in Auschwitz in 1942.[18]

It can be assumed that Jewish journalists in particular, who were made responsible for the pro-government and anti-Nazi stance of their papers, were especially hated by the new rulers. This was no doubt the reason that Maximilian Reich and many other journalists were arrested. A malicious photograph appeared in the SS-periodical *Das Schwarze Korps* in April 1938 with the following text: "The Jew Maximilian Reich also pranced merrily in the dance of the other atrocity propagandists and badgering writers."[19] Reich got a glimpse of this dangerously incendiary article by chance a few months later in Dachau. His wife in Vienna reacted with horror as well to this journalistic attack.

Why Maximilian Reich, sports editor of the once Social Democratic – then Nazified – daily *Das Kleine Blatt*, was singled out from the large number of Jewish journalists for inclusion in the "Transport of the Prominent" cannot be adequately explained. This is particularly true since there were better known and politically more exposed journalists. Reich himself points out in his account that he had not given a thought about the possibility of arrest because at the time he had "never been politically active" and his "area of work and interests were basically sports." Like many other endangered individuals, he underestimated the brutality and the implications of National Socialism. The often-used term "rascals" [*Lausejungen*] for National Socialists in his autobiographical manuscript reflects this miscalculation. Emilie Reich believed it was an error because her husband "had never written a political article." She confidently continued her efforts for his release with the Gestapo and other Nazi agencies. Maximilian Reich, who was also a member of the Austrian Olympic Committee, may perhaps have expressed criticism of German sports (or German athletes) in his sports reporting, perhaps in conjunction with the Berlin Olympic Games in 1936. In any case, his journalistic work may have attracted the attention of an important Nazi functionary and

---

[18] See: Viktor Matejka, *Widerstand ist alles. Notizen eines Unorthodoxen* (Vienna 1984) 87 f.; Matejka, "Der erste Transport," *Österreichisches Tagebuch* 10. 5. 1947.

[19] *Das Schwarze Korps*, 6 April 1938, 12.

triggered his internment.

The Treatment of Prisoners

According to all available reports, it is evident that even during the transport the prisoners were constantly humiliated and abused by the accompanying SS-personnel. In SS-jargon the Austrians were "lazy coffeehouse rabble contaminated by Jews and priests." The journalist and author Mark Siegelberg – Dr. Max Siglberg according to the transport list – published probably the earliest firsthand report about the Austrian transport from Shanghai in 1940.[20] He believed that Austrian *Gemütlichkeit* had already come to an end at Vienna's Westbahnhof and that events proceeded "with a breathtakingly Prussian precision, intensity, and rapidity." Erich Bielka, on the other hand – an Austrian consulate official in Munich who was taken directly to Dachau on April 11, 1938 – saw Bavarians at work: "The Bavarians, as cordial as they are, can also be equally as brutal. I got to know Bavarians quite well enough in Dachau . . ."[21] The assaults began, as Maximilian Reich also reports, during the loading of the prisoners into the train at the Westbahnhof. Fritz Bock has written about the scene: "'Get out, you dogs!' And it began: the gauntlet we had to run that ended years later for many in death. A bunch of SS-thugs flailing at us with the butt of their weapons ordered us to run to the train cars . . . At the end of this 'jaunt' many of us had such battered mugs that they no longer resembled human faces."[22]

The assaults continued during the trip to Dachau and reached a first peak at the arrival in the concentration camp.[23] The prisoner

---

[20] Mark Siegelberg, *Schutzhaftjude NR.13 877* (Shanghai 1940), esp. 25 ff.

[21] Interview with Federal Minister Dr. Erich Bielka, Feb. 9, 1988, DÖW-Sammlung: "Erzählte Geschichte," no. 399.

[22] Fritz Bock, "Vierzig Jahre nachher," *Wien 1938* (Vienna 1978), 11-17, here 13. *Forschungen und Beiträge zur Wiener Stadtgeschichte*, Vol. 2.

[23] There are several reports by prisoners available in addition to the ones already cited by Viktor Matejka, Stefan Billes, Hermann Lackner, Mark Siegelberg and Ludwig Soswinski. Among others: Josef Nischelwitzer in

Rudolf Kalmar wrote: "When we arrived in Dachau, we were dragged from the train into the camp and beaten into a corner, where a group of so-called officers began a kind of interrogation. Each one of us was called forward and taunted. Every dirty joke caused animated approval. Every brazen comment was acknowledged with a nasty laugh."[24] Several of the prisoners' reports – including that of Max Reich – depict the spectacle of mustering the Austrian prisoners on the parade grounds in a corresponding fashion.[25] As a special kind of harassment, the SS-troops attempted to provoke Communists and Socialists into mistreating or humiliating the "patriotic" functionaries, that is, their former oppressors. This stirred up a precarious situation for all involved.[26] The prisoners' reports, including Max Reich's, also paint a consistent picture of the capos whose actions extended the terror of the camp SS-troops. Capos, who functioned as room and block elders or had charge of work details, were for the most part political detainees, but some had been incarcerated for criminal activities as well. They – who themselves were browbeaten by the SS – tormented, humiliated and mistreated their camp mates at will and worsened their plight still further.

Several weeks after the arrival of the Austrian prisoners in Dachau, SS-Reichsführer Himmler visited the concentration camp, had the Austrians summoned and tried to taunt and put them down. He told Stillfried, the former commandant of the Wöllersdorf political detention camp: "So now you see how it is!" Stillfried answered: "Herr Reichsführer, I would hope that we are treated here like your people in Wöllersdorf were treated!" Everyone,

---

Max Muchitsch, Die Rote Stafette (Vienna 1985), 135-138; Fritz Bock, DÖW 12 858; Bruno Heilig, *Men Crucified* (London 1941), 8-13.

[24] Rudolf Kalmar, *Zeit ohne Gnade* (Vienna 1946), 46.

[25] Beyond the sources cited above, see also: Matejka, *Widerstand ist alles* 80ff.; Stefan Billes, "Im ersten Transport nach Dachau," *Der sozialdemokratische Kämpfer* (The Socialdemocrat Militant), nos. 1-2 (1998), 5; Siegelberg, *Schutzhaftjude NR.13 877*, 35f.

[26] Billes, "Im ersten Transport nach Dachau" - Interview with Dr. Ludwig Soswinski, DÖW- Sammlung: "Erzählte Geschichte," no. 192/1, 69.

including Franz Olah – to whom we owe this depiction[27] – expected reprisals, but nothing happened and Stillfried survived. Hermann Lackner reported that the Jewish prisoner Emil Maurer, after admitting to Himmler that he was a Social Democrat, escaped retaliation. Another Jewish internee by the name of Korff, however, after he declared that he did not know why he was in the camp, was sent to the brig.[28] Max Reich graphically describes this incident in complete unanimity with the other witnesses. Reich goes into detail about the differences between the camp at Wöllersdorf and Dachau. Set up by the *Ständestaat*, the political detention camp Wöllersdorf – where Social Democrats, Communists and National Socialists were imprisoned – treated the detainees as political prisoners. They received proper nourishment, were not tormented or forced to do arduous labor and were able to receive visitors. Yet this did not deter the Dachau SS-troops from "taking revenge for Wöllersdorf." Reich devotes an entire chapter to the "camp punishments" in Dachau, as well as to the "suicides" provoked by the conditions of detention and to the inadequate "medical treatment."

The Austrian inmates, some of whom had shortly before belonged to the upper levels of the socio-political establishment, were forced to adjust quickly to the conditions in a German concentration camp if they wanted to survive. Fritz Bock wrote: "We Austrians were the main attraction of the Dachau camp. We were assigned the most difficult tasks and worked twelve hours every day to the point of physical collapse. We starved and froze . . . It is no wonder that suicides were a daily occurrence."[29]

Maximilian Reich examines the relationship between "Aryans" and Jews in a separate chapter. He reports that the "Aryan" and Jewish inmates were segregated right at the start in Vienna and in Dachau were accommodated in their own "blocks" or barracks. The Jewish prisoners were discriminated against by the SS or the capos, particularly in the work schedule, something that was a life-

---

[27] Franz Olah, *Die Erinnerungen* (Vienna 1995), 95.

[28] Interview with Hermann Lackner, DÖW- Sammlung: "Erzählte Geschichte," no. 129.

[29] Bock, "Vierzig Jahre nachher," 14.

or-death matter in the camp. Reich also mentions, however, that a few of the prominent Austrian "Aryans" – for example, the Viennese mayor Dr. Schmitz, the commandant of Wöllersdorf Baron Stillfried, the judge Dr. Osio and both sons of the Archduke Franz Ferdinand – had no less a burden to bear than the Jews. With one anti-Semitic exception, he describes the relationship between Jews and non-Jews as one of "camaraderie" and "no worse than the internal relationships within each group"(58). In spite of the SS prohibition banning Jews from visiting the "Aryan barracks," intimate contacts developed that included conversations and – very cautiously – political discussions. "There was no separation of Jew and Aryan" (67). Although this may be characteristic for Dachau in 1938, the overall situation of the Jews a few years later – in comparison to the non-Jewish German (and Austrian) prisoners and in other concentration camps – was dramatically worse.

Cultural and Political Aspects

A cultural life developed in Dachau even under these terrible conditions, a cultural life in which the Austrians played an essential part.[30] Rudolf Kalmar describes the performance of a drama about a chivalric tournament he had written, "The Night of Blood on Schreckenstein." It was staged by Viktor Matejka and performed by established actors. The SS-guards missed the satire of Hitler in the play.[31] Fritz Grünbaum remained a cabaret artist until his horrible end, as his friend in camp, Ernst Federn, wrote to his widow in 1945: "I still remember very well that in Dachau I believed I would never in my life be able to laugh again. But Fritz Grünbaum retaught me when he put on a cabaret performance for the first time in a German concentration camp."[32] Maximilian Reich also points to those "performances" on Sunday afternoons in which "Austria's best known cabaret artists" – Fritz Grünbaum, Paul Morgan, and

[30] See: Nico Rost, *Goethe in Dachau. Literatur und Wirklichkeit* (Munich n.d.). The Dutch literary critic Rost has also chronicled conversations with Austrian figures involved in culture and the arts in his Dachau diary.

[31] Rudolf Kalmar, *Zeit ohne Gnade*, 183ff.

[32] *Aufbau*, 17 August 1945.

Herman Leopoldi – appeared, performances which, in reality, were not permitted, but which were not expressly forbidden. "Just like in the better days," the performers moved from one inn to the next, that is, from barracks to barracks. Jura Soyfer, then just 26 years old – one of the greatest talents of Austrian literature – composed his "Dachau Song" ("Barbed wire loaded with death . . . ") during the few weeks of his camp detention. His friend, Max Hoffenberg, also a detainee, wrote the following:

> Unlike Buchenwald, Sunday afternoons free of work details were characteristic of the life at the Dachau camp. One would encounter almost no SS-guards at the barracks during this time. Something akin to a cultural life unfolded on this afternoon. Together with the noted Viennese composer Hermann Leopoldi and the cabaret artist Fritz Grünbaum, Jura often enough generated a bit of edification for us, although it was strictly forbidden; for example, by challenging us with impromptu games. One Sunday afternoon he read the "Dachau Song" which he had written in secret – I have no idea when since we were together twenty-four hours a day. It made a huge impression on us.[33]

Cultural accomplishments did not increase anyone's chances of survival. Jura Soyfer died in Buchenwald on February 16, 1939; Fritz Grünbaum in Dachau in January 1940; only Hermann Leopoldi survived. He was co-author of the "Buchenwald Song" together with Fritz Beda-Löhner – who died in Auschwitz. The Austrian exile Jean Améry wrote the following about the frailty of the intellectuals in the concentration camp: "Life in the camp demanded above all else physical agility as well as a physical courage that necessarily bordered on brutality. Academics and scholars were rarely blessed with these traits."[34]

Although political discussions were strictly forbidden in camp,

---

[33] Fritz Hermann, *Jura Soyfer, Die Anfänge eines volksverbundenen österreichischen Dichters* , phil. Diss. (Vienna 1949), 181 f.

[34] Jean Améry, *Jenseits von Schuld und Sühne* 2nd ed. (Munich 1966), 14.

they soon started among the incarcerated Austrians. The main themes were the causes of Austria's demise and the future shape of political relationships. The detainee and later President of the "Austrian Resistance Movement," Franz Sobek recalls: "During every spare minute in the concentration camp we were thinking politically, constructing the future, assigning portfolios, as well as working on an understanding between the Reds and Blacks . . ."[35] The shared misery, the indispensable solidarity, but also insight into mistakes made in the past and the realization that National Socialism was the common enemy – now and in the future – all this brought the Austrians closer together, on a political as well as a human level. Stefan Billes wrote: "On Dachau's main road, former adversaries discussed the unhappy past of our homeland. And even if we stuck by our convictions, one thought was common to us all: when we achieve liberation, we will construct a democracy and do everything possible to prevent the recurrence of a fratricidal struggle."[36] Particularly for those in the middle class caught up in authoritarian ways of thinking, the democratic learning process was taking place. Franz Olah has shared Emanuel Stillfried's statement: "I have become a democrat here in Dachau! We always learned that we had to obey the government. Now I realize that there must be an opposition."[37]

It emerges in almost all of the prisoners' reports that the Austrians understood themselves as Austrians and most of them looked ahead to an independent Austria. As a Jew brought to Dachau "in protective custody," Maximilian Reich thought of himself as an Austrian. Even in the camp he proudly pointed out to the SS his service as an Austrian officer in the First World War. In this context, the question posed by the SS-guards – "What are you?" – could get awkward. Ludwig Soswinski reported that the answer "German" was not a possibility, that "Austrian" was perilous, so

---

[35] Ernst Trost, *Figl von Österreich* (Vienna 1972), 122 f.

[36] Billes, "Im ersten Transport nach Dachau," 5.

[37] Olah, *Erinnerungen*, 79. See also: Hans Becker, *Österreichs Freiheitskampf* (Vienna 1946).

you answered "Viennese."[38] Underlying the conversations and discussions about the future shape of Austria was a patriotic and democratic optimism that could not be missed. Fritz Bock wrote: "In spite of the historical events of these weeks and months, we never for a minute believed that Austria had disappeared from the map forever. And even in the summer of 1938 on Dachau's main street, after we had to some extent adjusted to camp life, whenever we could, we talked about nothing else than what we would do when Austria was once again free. Although none of us knew . . . whether we would survive the next day, we never gave up the hope and belief that there would again be an Austria."[39]

One development began in Dachau that had a formative significance for the history of the Second Republic. The cooperation between the Social Democrats and the middle class – archenemies to the point of civil war at one time – had partial roots in Dachau's "main street spirit" and later in other concentration camps as well. A central impulse for overcoming Pan-German conceptions and for the growth of an Austrian National consciousness emerged from the suffering in Hitler-Germany concentration camps.[40] Admittedly, however, the perception of the "main street spirit" and of the unconditional solidarity among the prisoners is not without controversy. The conversations and discussions cited here took place mainly within the group of political inmates. Those persecuted for racial and other reasons – Jews, Romany gypsies, those labeled "anti-social," homosexuals, etc. – were often excluded simply due to their separate living areas. The cohesion of camp inmates, in so far as it ever existed, later fell apart in the course of the Cold War. The discussion of the alleged "prisoner community" in concentration camps is, however, beyond the scope of this essay, all the more since Maximilian Reich – because of his relatively short imprisonment in Dachau and Buchenwald – was not much

---

[38] Interview with Dr. Ludwig Soswinski, DÖW-Sammlung:"Erzählte Geschichte," no. 192/1, 71.

[39] Interview with Dr. Fritz Bock on March 24, 1983, DÖW-Sammlung: "Erzählte Geschichte," no. 409.

[40] See: Felix Kreissler, *Der Österreicher und seine Nation* (Vienna 1984), esp. 223 ff.

confronted by this dilemma.[41]

Releases

The mass arrests and confinements of Austrians in concentration camps in March and April 1938 also had implications for foreign affairs. Ernst Weizsäcker, the State Secretary in the Department of Foreign Affairs wrote in his notes for May 16, 1938, that "the general public around the world, above all in England's political circles, is extremely concerned about events in Austria. And the English have exploited various arrests to spread fabrications about atrocities."[42] The German Embassy in London reported to the Department of Foreign Affairs about a visit by Lord Halifax. He had inquired about the fate of several political figures – all members of the former government – as well as academics who had been detained. At the same time he pointed out that this question "was of considerable importance for the shape of German-English relationships."[43] This diplomatic pressure led to a dialogue between Weizsäcker and Chief of Security Police Heydrich on July 5, 1938, during which the individual detainee categories were discussed. This discussion, as well as the possible releases being considered, extended only to higher-ranking Schuschnigg supporters, legitimists and internationally known academics. Heydrich concurred in principle to the "need in foreign affairs," not to let the "Austrian arrests turn into a long-term burden." According to Heydrich, those 3,900 Austrians still detained were to be released with the exception of those to be put on trial – more precisely,

---

[41] See esp.: Wolfgang Sofsky, *Die Ordnung des Terrors. Das Konzentrationslager*, 2nd ed. (Frankfurt/M. 1993); Robert Streibl and Hans Schafranek, eds., *Strategie des Überlebens. Häftlingsgesellschaften in KZ und Gulag* (Vienna 1996). The following article presents a remarkable analysis of an early report on a concentration camp: Christian Fleck and Albert Müller, "Bruno Bettelheim and the Concentration Camps," *Journal of the History of the Behaviour Sciences*, vol. 33 (I), Winter 1997, 1-37.

[42] Cited in: *"Anschluß" 1938*, 529.

[43] Airmail-Telegram of the German Embassy in London to the Department of Foreign Affairs in Berlin on June 28, 1938, *"Anschluß" 1938*, 529 f.

"those elements," around which "politically dangerous groups could form."[44]

Apparently on the basis of this consideration of foreign affairs, most of the Austrian prisoners of middle-class, Catholic, conservative origins were released from the concentration camp before the war broke out in 1939. They were confronted, however, with multiple restrictions – such as, for example, compulsory registration with the police. A few, like Leopold Figl, were arrested again later for activities in the resistance and brought back to a concentration camp. Jewish prisoners were let go in 1938-39 if they committed themselves to leave Germany and were able to show entry clearances for their country of destination. A few Socialists were released as well. Communist detainees, provided they were unable to "emigrate" as Jews, remained in general in concentration camp confinement until the end of Nazi rule.

It is against this backdrop that the release of Maximilian Reich on October 12, 1938 from the Buchenwald concentration camp must be seen. As her report reflects, Emilie Reich persevered with all her might and courage to come to the aid of her husband. Both personally and in writing, she inundated countless NS authorities, above all the Gestapo, and petitioned acquaintances for interventions in getting him released. These efforts had little or no chance of success. Not a single one of those imprisoned at the time was released as a result of actions by family members. On the other hand, the efforts to create the possibility of an exodus abroad were significant, since a release from camp became a possibility only in that case. Many sources exist confirming the fact that such papers were obtainable only with the greatest difficulties, primarily due to the entry limits of many nations. Following the failed efforts to obtain an American visa with the help of an uncle, the departure for England – with the help of a cousin abroad – took place in November 1938. Worries about the two children left behind who were able to join their parents in January 1939 are reflected in Emilie Reich's manuscript, a document written before the reunion. Clearance for entry was in fact a matter of life or death: while Max Reich and his family survived the Holocaust, his friend and

---

[44] Ernst von Weizsäcker's notes on July 5, 1938, *"Anschluß" 1938*, 531 f.

companion in camp, Willy Kurtz, was taken from Buchenwald to Auschwitz in 1942 and murdered.[45]

The "Transport of the Prominent" was only the prelude to repression, deportation, and mass murder on a scale never before seen in history. Further shipments to Dachau of human cargo from Austria followed: on April 11, 1938 a succession of prisoners from Salzburg was brought in. On May 24 a consignment of 170 persons consisting of Jews, "patriots," and leftists arrived. Among these were the governors of Upper Austria and Burgenland Heinrich Gleißner and Hans Sylvester, the future president of the National Council Felix Hurdes, the social democratic attorney Heinrich Steinitz, and the Viennese Communist Party functionaries Fritz and Joseph Lauscher. On May 31, 46 prisoners from Tyrol and Vorarlberg, mostly police officials, arrived in camp. Then came two shipments, one on May 31 and one on June 3, each with 600 Jewish prisoners from Vienna. The admittance of detainees from Austria to concentration camps reached its first high point during *Reichskristallnacht* in November 1938 when 3,700 of 6,547 apprehended Jews were transferred to the Dachau facility.[46] Finally, the mass deportations from Vienna began in October 1939 (the Buchenwald and Nisko transports) and after February 1941 that eventually led to the murder of the better part of Austrian Jewry.[47]

---

[45] According to documents in the DÖW (the compilation of names of Austrian victims of the Holocaust), Willy Kurtz died on December 9, 1942. Their close ties are also underlined by the fact that they were Registered almost one after the other in Dachau: Reich had the Dachau camp number 13875, Kurtz 13872.

[46] All information stems from the Dachau admissions book for 1938, DÖW 12 800. With regard to the pogrom in November, see also: "Tagesrapport der Gestapo Wien vom 17. – 18. 11. 1938," National Archives, T84 R13, 39 814.

[47] *Deportation der österreichischen Juden und Jüdinnen*, Dokumentationsarchiv des österreichischen Widerstandes, *Katalog zur permanenten Ausstellung*, 76-85.

SHORT BIOGRAPHIES

MAXIMILIAN REICH was born in 1882 in the western part of Hungary in Wieselburg (Moson, today's Mosonmagyaróvár) as the son of a rabbi. The family moved to Vienna around 1892. School leaving examination, one-year volunteer. Member of a first selection of superior Viennese soccer players. An editor since 1913 with the *Fremden-Blatt*, primarily as a sports journalist. From 1914-18 an officer in the reserves, in the end as first lieutenant. After that a career in journalism, among other positions, at the *Kleines Blatt* that appeared in the Vorwärts-Verlag. Temporarily dismissed after February 1934; hired back in April 1934; Editor at the *Kleines Blatt* and the weekly *Das Frauenblatt* on staff of the *Arbeiter-Sonntag.*

Arrested by the Gestapo on March 17, 1938; taken with the first transport to Dachau on April 1, 1938; to Buchenwald in September 1938. Released in October 1938; emigration to England in November 1938. Internment on the Isle of Man 1940-41. With the German Service of the BBC from about 1942. Invitation to launch *Wiener Montag* at the end of 1946, became Chief Editor; while he was temporarily away, the paper changed publishers and he resigned because of a basic change in the newspaper's philosophy. Following employment at the *Weltpresse.* Died in Vienna in 1952.

EMILIE (MAUTZI) REICH (1887 Vienna – 1959 Vienna), daughter of a Catholic family. Following training as teacher she taught at a secondary school. Married 1914. Children: Heinz (1918-1927); Gertraude (b. 1920), married Portisch; Henriette (b. 1928), married Mandl. Went into exile with husband. Despite initially deficient English skills, she taught elementary school classes in reading, writing and arithmetic for board and lodging at the "School of the Holy Child" (an Anglican Benedictine convent with boarding school outside London). She gave piano lessons and learned to play the organ in order to accompany the mass. After his release from internment, Maximilian Reich also worked there as a gardener. 1945 moved to London into the home of a physician and family friend. Sewed gloves at home. 1946 return to Austria. 1947 to Vienna. This return was not easy for her. She supported many students in the neighborhood with private lessons.

Her only writing was the appendix to her husband's manuscript.

HENRIETTE MANDL was born in 1928 in Vienna. Evacuation to England with the children's transport in January 1939. School in Laleham ("School of the Holy Child"); school leaving exam in the summer of 1945. 1947 return to Vienna. 1947 – 1951 academic studies in English and art history at the University of Vienna, completing her Ph.D. Taught in the USA 1962 – 63 and 1969 – 70 as an Associate Professor. 1967 Lecture tour in the USA. Books: *Wiener Altstadt-Spaziergänge* (Vienna 2006, First published in 1987); *Vienna Downtown Walking Tours* (Vienna 1987); *Cabaret und Courage – Stella Kadmon* (Vienna 1993); *In Search of Vienna* (Vienna 1995).

WOLFGANG NEUGEBAUER, Ph.D., historian, until 2004 Honorary Professor for contemporary history, Academic Director of the Documentation Center of the Austrian Resistance. Last publication in 2005: "*Der Wille zum aufrechten Gang,*" together with Peter Schwarz.

FRANCIS MICHAEL SHARP is Professor emeritus of German at the University of the Pacific in Stockton, California. Professor Sharp earned his MA and PhD in German literature at the University of California in Berkeley and taught at Princeton University for 6 years before returning to California in 1979. His publications on Austrian writers and poets include a book on Georg Trakl as well as articles on Trakl, Bernhard, Frischmuth, and Handke. His translations include the Israeli-Austrian Doron Rabinovici's first novel *Suche nach M: Roman in zwölf Episoden* (*The Search for M*, Ariadne, 1997).